INDIA AND THE WEST

HARVARD UNIVERSITY CENTER FOR THE STUDY OF WORLD RELIGIONS

Studies in World Religions

edited by
M. David Eckel

Studies in World Religions publishes monographs, translations, and collections of essays on the comparative study of religion, on religious traditions, and on methodological issues in the study of the world's religions, as well as proceedings of conferences and colloquia sponsored by Harvard's Center for the Study of World Religions.

Number 4 ⎯⎯⎯⎯⎯⎯⎯⎯⎯⎯⎯⎯⎯⎯⎯⎯⎯⎯⎯⎯⎯⎯⎯⎯

INDIA AND THE WEST
The Problem of Understanding
Selected Essays of J. L. Mehta

INDIA AND THE WEST
The Problem of Understanding

Selected Essays of J. L. Mehta

Scholars Press
Chico, California

INDIA AND THE WEST
The Problem of Understanding

Selected Essays of J. L. Mehta
With an Introduction
by Wilfred Cantwell Smith

Library of Congress in Publication Data

Mehta, J. L. (Jaswant Lal), 1931-
India and the West, the problem of understanding.

   (Studies in world religions ; 4)
   1. Philosophy—Addresses, essays, lectures.
1. Title. II. Series.
B29.M453   1985   85-2050
ISBN 0-89130-826-1
ISBN 0-89130-827-X (pbk.)

Printed in the United States of America
on acid-free paper

To

John Braisted Carman

in friendship and gratitude

CONTENTS

FOREWORD

In a lecture that marked his last semester as visiting professor in the Center for the Study of World Religions, Professor Mehta remarked:

> I suppose it is this sense of a mysterious unity in all otherness as concretely experienced and enabling us to want to listen to the alien voice, that constitutes the Western preoccupation with the other, as it does the non-western openness to winds blowing from the West.

In his own graceful way, Professor Mehta was commenting on the complex currents that ran through his own scholarly career and enriched the experience of all who worked with him as students or as colleagues in his years at Harvard. For many he seemed to embody the spirit of cross-cultural philosophical and religious studies. Trained in India in western psychology and philosophy, Professor Mehta was able to stand in a creative sense on the margins of two traditions. He not only could speak with authority from both the western and Indian perspectives, but he could reflect on the act of speaking itself, in a way that continually sparked new insights for those of us who were fortunate enough to work with him.

The essays in this volume were chosen by Professor Mehta and the editorial staff of *Studies in World Religions* to show both the range of his scholarly interests and the way in which those interests developed during the major portion of his career. The reader will find that the essays are arranged in rough chronological order. The first essay, "The Concept of the Subjective," was presented at the All-India Seminar at the Centre of Advanced Study in Philosophy, Visva-Bharati University, in 1965,

the year in which Professor Mehta became Professor of
Philosophy at Banaras Hindu University. The last seven
essays in this volume first appeared between 1968 and
1978, the period in which Professor Mehta's attention was
shifting to problems posed by the American academic
environment. In 1968 he began the series of visiting
appointments at Harvard that culminated in his full-time
presence on the Harvard faculty from 1973 to 1978. The
essays "Problems of Inter-cultural Understanding in
University Studies of Religion" and "Heidegger and
Vedanta: Reflections on a Questionable Theme" show the
interest in cross-cultural questions that came to play
such an important role in his thinking during his years at
Harvard. Both these essays were written during his years
as a visiting professor in this Center.

As editor of the *Series* I have the pleasant responsibility to acknowledge the help of many colleagues and
friends who have contributed to the production of this
volume. First, there is Professor Jane Smith, my pre-
decessor as editor, who presided over this project in its
early stages and whose editorial wisdom is evident in many
ways throughout the book. Professor Smith was ably assisted
by William Darrow, whose editorial and production skills
are so amply demonstrated in earlier volumes in this
series. More recently the jobs of editorial and production assistants have fallen to Mary McGee and Helen Schultz,
and with them the responsibility of overseeing the myriad
of steps necessary to bring a manuscript to completion.
To these four and to all others who have had a hand in the
production of this volume, I am deeply grateful.

Finally, I would like to express my gratitude to
Professor Wilfred Cantwell Smith, who agreed in the last
few months before his retirement from Harvard to add an
introduction to this volume. In his final lecture at the
Center, Professor Mehta spoke of Professor Smith's conception of human history as essentially religious history as

a concept that helped lead the discipline of the study of religion out of its infancy and into maturity, a maturity in which it could find "an integrative conceptual center and a comprehensive, unifying perspective." Those words describe the vision that Professor Mehta was seeking in his own essays. It is appropriate that Professor Smith should add his own voice to this volume, and for that we are very grateful.

Harvard University   M. David Eckel
January 1985

INTRODUCTION

To any thinker pondering the intellectual problems of
the modern world, the reward will surely be great from
studying these uniquely illuminating pieces. They are
the work of an acute intelligence, philosophically expert.
That is obviously an important point; yet equally significant, and underlying the adverb "uniquely" just used, is
that the author furnishes us with the insights of a highly
qualified and sensitive participant observer. Only as we
learn to observe that in which we participate do we move
towards enhanced understanding.

Religious pluralism is beginning to be taken seriously
by religious thinkers; cultural pluralism by thinkers
about our own as well as others' cultures; philosophic (or
"worldview") pluralism has been less attentively developed
as yet, but is surely coming. A first step in each case
in one's becoming carefully aware of other positions,
vision, views, accurately delineated by outsiders; a
second, increasingly recognized, is becoming aware of them
as they appear to those within. I have pled that a third
step, now possible and requisite, is a becoming construc-
tively aware of how one's own appears to outsiders.

Not that the author of these chapters is an outsider.
He helps us all with the desired fourth step: becoming
consciously self-critical of our own orientation, and
critically self-conscious of the pluralism that subsumes
our separateness and today characterizes our being.
Professor Mehta has appropriated modern Western Philos-
ophy--especially, of course, Heidegger, on whom he is
recognized in the West as an authority--more deeply and
with more acuity than have most Westerners. He is a

salient and admirable example of the present-day univer-
salism of "modernity" in its meaning of the Western-
generated modern outlook. Yet he comes to it not from the
West but from India; and modernity cannot be fully understood unless recognized as Western-derived but global-
become, and unless understood as, once global, therein
more complex than before. The outlook serves those--
Westerners--for whom it is continuous with, however
aberrant from, their past; and also now those--for
instance, Indians--for whom it is discontinuous, however
inescapable, or however even preferred. We cannot, any of
us, understand that in which we participate unless we
understand the other co-participants.

Even our own criticism of modernity is firmer if we
discern more sensitively how it appeals to, and how it is
seen by, our fellows around the world.

Yet even apart from the pluralism issue itself, we are
helped much more fully to understand our thinking by the
assistance offered in the penetrating work of a close
participant observer.

Readers will find in these pages illumination on many
matters in which they are already engaged. Let me mention
a few that I personally have found of moment. To comparativists, striving to understand cultures other than their
own, there is reward in, for instance, the paper "Understanding and Tradition" proffered here. It was given
originally as the presidential address to the Metaphysics
and Epistemology section of the Indian Philosophical
Congress; and it therefore shows an Indian expounding to
fellow Indians current European analyses of the concept of
"understanding" (chiefly Dilthey, Husserl, Gadamer,
Heidegger), and their relevance to modern (modernized,
Westernized) Hindu intellectuals' apprehension of the
centuries-long Indian tradition to which they are in some
ways heir and from which in some ways distanced. For the
Western student of India--especially the English-speaking

Western student, whose familiarity with recent Continental thought may not be firm; yet for any Western student--the paper's significance lies not only in the substantive contribution to the problem of a modern understanding of India's past, a problem in which a Westerner is also engaged, but further, in its illuminating of a major aspect of India's present-day transitions.

Comparable is the piece on the Western idea of progress and on the important recent Western criticisms of that idea. This may be taken both as substantively interesting in itself, and as an outsider's comment, addressed in the first instance by an Indian to Indians.

Another matter that I myself, as a religionist, found illuminating is the author's changing attitude to religion, an attitude whose development can be traced here by a careful chronological reading. Mehta is a philosopher, by profession and by temperament. At one point he explicitly affirms, of course, that the philosophy/religion duality rests on a specifically Western view of things, and has to be left behind if the Indian tradition is to be seriously appreciated. Once again he was here speaking originally to Indians, while the observation is of course relevant to Western attempts to understand that tradition. To use these categories, and particularly the distinction between them, in interpreting what has been going on there, is to impose, and inevitably to distort. Various of us who are comparative historians of religion have come through our historical studies to the same conclusion, of course, and have written about it. Yet it is one thing to see this, however sharply, and another--given our modern condition, and our modern language and our modern thought-patterns and our social realities--to be able to speak or to think or to work or to live in terms of discernment.

Mehta himself, with his fundamental philosophic interests, and in his highly modern, highly Westernized, spirit and awareness and education, for long paid no attention to

religion, explicitly. He grew up in India, but in its
modern phase, feeling like many intellectuals there in our
day quite negative about religion, he has said; and he
remarks in a recent paper not here published that for him
the first lecture on religion "that made sense" he heard
in his fifties (from a Western academic). Nevertheless in
the latter part of his life, and this is slightly evident
in the later papers gathered here, he seems gradually to
have become a little less distant from Western religious
thought, at least to the point of taking serious note of
recent developments, and seeming to sense that a
philosophic analysis should take such note.

Is this perhaps related to the fact that comparative
religionists have of late taken primary interest in Indian
thought, even its "philosophic" thought (and even in him
as a humane thinker)? (One of the world's leading Chinese
scholars of Chinese thought, himself a contemporary
thinker of substance and originality, mentioned to me
recently that he had had occasion to remark to his fellow
philosophers in a recent [Western] philosophic congress
that Western academic thinkers in philosophy, supposedly
universal, are in fact strikingly less, and in religion,
reputedly narrow, in fact strikingly more, hospitable to
and interested in Chinese thought.

However that may be, there is reward in observing how
a mind like Mehta's has been attracted by the philosophic
thought of continental Europe in this century more than by
the Anglo-Saxon; and especially, by the thought of
Heidegger. Has the affinity for Heidegger something to do
with that thinker's profound critique of the rest of the
Western philosophic tradition? Indeed, one might find
oneself speculating as to whether Heidegger's inherent
significance, in turn, may have something to do with the
point that the received distinction between philosophic
and religious is idiosyncratic and not finally valid.
Yet if one is to think in terms of that distinction,

Continental philosophy in the twentieth century, not least
Heidegger, has been on the whole rather closer to what is
meant by religious than has Anglo-Saxon. No doubt it is
an over-simplification, but perhaps not in the end a
misleading one, that Mehta's choice of Continental
thinkers for close study may have that sort of
significance for the comparative religionist.

It is perhaps unfair to raise this issue about a
writer who has himself made only a little of it. The
short piece "Beyond Believing and Knowing" here is,
however, germane; and in a paper published elsewhere Mehta
has written that "For an Asiatic, the fascinating thing
afoot in Heidegger's work is the appropriation of the
religious" into philosophy. (Admittedly, that sentence is
but one among a hundred, and is not developed.) I venture
to raise the matter only to illustrate my contention that
readers will indeed find stimulus in Professor Mehta's
writings for many a question in which they are interested,
as well as illumination of the topics directly addressed.

Perhaps I may close by noting, as illustrative of the
riches here, that in one footnote to one paper (n. 24 of
the final essay here) is propounded in passing a precious
new idea potentially richly productive: a number of doc-
toral dissertations are suggested in this one provocative
insight. I may also add that I find myself shedding a
tear that the author and the editors have, no doubt for
compelling reasons, had to omit from the collection
certain other essays of this enormously intelligent writer
that I personally have found helpful.

Harvard University   Wilfred Cantwell Smith
June 1984

THE CONCEPT OF THE SUBJECTIVE

   Speaking of the rise of modern philosophy, Hegel
remarks in his *Lectures on the History of Philosophy*, "Now
we come for the first time properly speaking to the
philosophy of the new world and begin with Descartes....
Here we can say that we are at home, and, as sailors after
a long voyage upon stormy seas, we can cry 'land.'"
Hegel's reference here is to Descartes' discovery of the
realm of the subjective, the solid ground on which
philosophy treads henceforth, triumphantly marching to its
consummation in Hegel's own theory of the Absolute Spirit.
From the perspective of developments in recent European
philosophy, such as Phenomenology and Existential
Philosophy, it may indeed be said that the entire history
of modern philosophy since Descartes is in a sense the
history of the explication and development of a theory of
subjectivity. The conception of the subjective has varied
according to the metaphysical, epistemological or ethical
preoccupations of the philosophers from Descartes to Hegel
and according to their rationalistic or empiricistic
preconceptions. Whether the subject is conceived as the
ego cogito of Descartes, as the Leibnizian monad, as the
Transcendental Ego of Kant, as Fichte's Infinite Ego, as
the Absolute Spirit of Hegel, or as Freedom, with
Schelling, whether we follow the line of thinkers who
pursue the Cartesian *cogito* or of those who followed
Locke's "way of ideas", in each case, the realm
which is being directly or indirectly explored is the
field of human subjectivity.

Originally published in *Visva-Bharati Journal of
Philosophy* 2 (1966): 40-57.

The subjective, as opposed to the objective, may be understood in the sense of the "merely subjective", the false or the irrational. It may mean, secondly, the merely private and solipsistic as against the inter-subjectively, universally valid. This is the contrast which Heraclitus brings out in Fragment 92: "So we must follow the common, yet though my word is common, the many live as if they had a wisdom of their own," and again in Fragment 9: "The waking have one common world, but the sleeping turn aside each into a world of his own." The subjective may be understood, thirdly, in the sense of the psychological, following the Cartesian metaphysics of the dual realms of *res extensa* and *res cogitans* and his conception of the latter as a kind of container swarming with ghostly *cogitans*. This is the sense of the subjective in which it has been subjected to detailed scrutiny and scathing criticism by the later Wittgenstein, by Ryle and by Sartre. But, again since Descartes, the subjective has also been understood in the sense of the transcendental, as the ground and source of all objective validity and of the intelligibility of all that is objectively given. Far from constituting the realm of the false, of what merely seems, of that which encapsulates me within my own self and of the psychological, subjectivity in this sense refers to that transcendental sphere in man which alone can provide an absolute foundation to our experience and in which is grounded the "objectivity," i.e., the truth, of all that is. Subjectivity in this sense is the *subjectivum veritatis*, the *hypokeimenon*, the ground and fundament of all truth and of all that is. And it is in this sense of the term that modern philosophy may be regarded as consisting of a series of contributions towards a theory of the subjective.

Wherein lies the subjectivity of the human subject? What is its constitution? How is it related to the objective sphere? The traditional textbook account of the doctrines of the modern philosophers is largely dominated by the perspectives of the theory of knowledge, whereas the attempt to answer these questions in recent philosophy, in particular by Husserl and Heidegger, goes beyond the merely epistemological conception of the subjective and seeks to reopen the question on the ontological level. The theory of subjectivity, in other words, is an onto-logical inquiry into the nature of the subjective, in the sense in which, according to Kant, the question, "What is man?" is already implied in the three central questions of metaphysics: "What can I know? What shall I do? What may I hope for?" The main purpose of this paper is to present this new perspective on the problem of subjectivity that has been opened up in recent Continental philosophy. Not more than passing reference will be made here to the doctrines of Descartes, Kant, or Hegel, much less an attempt to re-interpret their views from the perspective of present-day developments. A great deal of the thought of Husserl, Sartre and Merleau-Ponty constitutes a cri-ticism and re-interpretation of the Cartesian *cogito* and Hegel's dialectical theory of consciousness, with its central doctrine of negativity, undergoes an existential-istic re-interpretation in the philosophies of the last two. Heidegger offers a re-interpretation of Kant's Transcendental Analytic in studied opposition to both the Hegelian and Neo-Kantian schools and yet incorporates Kantian and Hegelian themes, annulled and sublated, into his own critical inquiries into the subjectivity of man from the perspective of the question of the sense of Being. The task of tracing these developments and trans-formations, however fascinating, cannot be attempted here. Husserl's Phenomenology, with its claim to set aside all metaphysical and epistemological presuppositions, provides the starting-point and the setting for contemporary inquiries into the nature of the subjective, but here too we can do no more than use it as such, leaving it to others to explore this primeval forest and expound the Husserlian theory of the subjective in detail. Nor is it

possible to enter here into the details of Sartre's theory
of consciousness and explain how the for-itself, or existence conceived as a creative void, as freedom and as a
perpetual transcending of the given, ceaselessly liberates
itself from the empirical self, the other and the in-
itself, and how it is engaged in the interminable labour
of an active transformation of both the self and the
objective world regarded as the product of man's work. In
Kant's and Hegel's theory of the subjective, in Schelling
and in Kierkegaard and above all in Sartre, freedom is
conceived as the very being of the subject. For Heidegger
also the subjectivity of the subject lies in freedom and
the little that he has written on this topic marks a
significant advance over the thought of his predecessors.
This, too, would require a paper by itself to develop and
will not therefore be further touched upon here.

Modern philosophy has been widely characterized as a
philosophy of subjectivity but in recent times it has
become more and more apparent that the deeper we dig into
the subjectivity of man, the further are we carried beyond
a conception of the subject in the sense of the traditional subject-object dichotomy. Husserl's quest of
transcendental subjectivity eventually took him into a
region which can hardly be called subjectivity in the
traditional sense, as Ludwig Landgrebe has pointed out.
Sartre's absolute consciousness has, as he himself
remarks, no longer anything of the subject in it. But it
is above all in the thinking of Heidegger that we see how
the most sustained effort to lay hold of the essence of
subjectivity eventually leads to the annulment of the
concept of the subjective and to its most radical
criticism in the history of philosophy. For this reason,
this paper will concentrate on an exposition of
Heidegger's views and criticism of the subjective, dealing
with other thinkers only as they lead up to it or are
relevant in this context.

For Husserl, the wonder of all wonders is the pure ego and pure subjectivity or consciousness. Like Descartes, Husserl is primarily concerned with "a complete reforming of philosophy into a science grounded on an absolute foundation, with a radical re-building that satisfies the idea of philosophy as the all-inclusive unity of the sciences, within the unity of such an absolutely rational grounding." For, as he remarks, "With the Cartesian discovery of the transcendental ego, a new idea of the grounding of knowledge also becomes disclosed: the idea of it as transcendental grounding." As with Kant, his concern is with apodicticity and objective validity in the sciences, and his philosophizing a quest for absolute foundations. Like both he discovers these foundations in transcendental subjectivity. For Kant, transcendental consciousness constitutes the structure of pure reason, not itself experienced but inferred, not given in direct, lived experience but deduced. Unlike Kant, however, Husserl seeks, with Descartes, for the ground in the "fundamental fact" of the experienced "I am". But, unlike Descartes, Husserl is not content merely with the bare identity of the "I am" as the only thing given as indubitable in transcendental self-experience. Nor does he attempt, like Descartes, "to use the *ego cogito* as an apodictically evident premise for arguments supposedly implying a transcendent subjectivity." The phenomenological epoche (the bracketing of the world as directly experienced in the natural attitude), "lays open an infinite realm of being of a new kind, as the sphere of a new kind of experience: transcendental experience." Husserl plunges into the task of a laying open of this infinite field of transcendental experience and through his method of successive reductions, aims at bringing into existence "a science of concrete transcendental subjectivity, as given in actual and possible transcendental experience, a science that forms the extremist contrast to sciences in the hitherto accepted sense."

The phenomenological reduction is a reversal of the
naive, natural attitude of an unquestioning acceptance of
the world, the sum of all that is given to me in experience, and brings me to an awareness of the activity of my
own consciousness as the source and ground, along with
other consciousnesses, of all such givenness. The sphere
of immanence or subjectivity in which these activities of
world-constitution occur, however, cannot itself be any
given entity or part of the world. It cannot be anything
but is a pure, transcendental subject, beyond the world,
itself not a thing and yet the ground of the givenness of
all things. In classical Idealism, transcendental reflexion led from the world to a sphere of pure validity and
ideality, to a sphere of pure *Principles*. In phenomenology, on the other hand, the reduction leads to a sphere
of *experience*, equally pure, transcendental and grounding
in character and yet a sphere of pure subjectivity of
which it cannot be said that it is in the same sense in
which all that is given to us is in the world. Husserl's
attempt to ground the truth of the experienced in "the
fundamental fact of the experienced 'I am'" and not in the
sphere of pure principles thus immediately raises the
question of the ontological status of pure subjectivity.
This was pointed out by Heidegger in his letter to Husserl
concerning the latter's draft of the article on Phenomenology for the *Encyclopedia Britannica*:

> There is agreement between us on the point that
> what is, in the sense of what you call "world",
> cannot be explained in respect of its transcen-
> dental constitution through a going back to an
> entity having the same kind of being. But this
> is not to say that what makes up the locus of the
> transcendental is not at all something that is.
> It raises rather the *problem*: which is the mode
> of being of the entity in which "world" is
> constituted?....It needs to be shown that the
> mode of being of a human being is totally
> different from that of all other entities and
> that precisely because it is such a mode of being
> that it contains hidden within itself the
> possibility of transcendental constitution.
> [This] is a central possibility of the factually

existing self....The constituting subject is not
nothing, hence it is something and has being--
although not in the sense of something given.
The inquiry into the mode of being of the
constituting source is not to be evaded.

Such an inquiry, Heidegger adds, is precisely the task of
Being and Time. To be accessible even in pure experience,
this constituting source must *be*, but what is is part of
the world. The only alternative left for Husserl--since
for him to be was to be objectively given--was to think of
it as the sphere of absolute being as against the
conditioned being of the world. And this is no answer to
the question raised by Heidegger.

Reading the Cartesian starting-point from an experienced *cogito*, Sartre took the logical way out of this
difficulty by eliminating the transcendental ego and conceiving of pure, impersonal consciousness as a nothingness, a nihilating field of the for-itself forever constituting the "I" as well as the world and forever liberating
itself from them. Transcendental consciousness is for
Sartre "a fact which is absolute," "a first condition and
an absolute source of existence," whereas the Cartesian
cogito is a fully reflexive, positional or thetic
consciousness in which it becomes its own object; Sartre's
transcendental consciousness is non-thetic, immediate and
pre-reflexive consciousness of itself. Such unreflected
consciousness or consciousness in the first degree constitutes the transcendental sphere, the sphere of *absolute*
existence, i.e., a sphere of pure spontaneities which are
never objects and which determine their own existence.
Sartre is enabled thus to attain to a transcendental
grounding sphere without introducing into it anything of
the world.

Heidegger chooses another way out of the difficulty.
In Sartre, the series of phenomenological reductions is
transformed into a single act of pure consciousness
tearing itself away from the world, from the whole sphere
of objects, through a movement of nihilation rather than

reflection. Heidegger, on the other hand, completely
by-passes the whole notion of reduction in his conception
of the phenomenological method. How then does he go back
from the world as given to the transcendental sphere in
which its ground is to be disclosed? He does this by
reopening the entire problem on the ontological level and
unfolding it from the perspective of the question of
Being. He makes an explicit and radical distinction
between beings and their being, between the ontic and the
ontological, where what is, the ontic, is the grounded,
and the being of what is, the ontological, is the ground.
He holds fast to the insight that the ground of what is
cannot be found in anything that itself is a being and
that the being of what is cannot itself be a being.
Heidegger also realised that any inquiry into Being, any
ontological inquiry into the ground of beings, must be
rooted in an investigation of the being of man in whom
alone the sense of Being manifests itself. This investigation of man's being or of subjectivity is therefore
designated as fundamental ontology by him. In inquiring
into man's being, Heidegger looks for something more basic
than the transcendental ego or consciousness, for an
ontological level deeper than the level of consciousness,
in terms of which one can understand what it means to be
consciousness itself. The subjectivity of the human
subject lies solely, according to Heidegger, in the
transcendence which is inherent in him. As he puts it
(WGIS): "Transcendence denotes the very essence of the
subject; it is the fundamental structure of subjectivity....To be a subject is to be a being in and as
transcendence." Consciousness, the transcendental ego
self-hood, the subject-object-relation are all secondary
concepts and pre-suppose the basic fact of transcendence,
in terms of which they can all be defined. "It is only
through an elucidation of transcendence," Heidegger
declares, "that we can seize the possibility of a
determination of what 'subject' and 'subjective' mean.

Transcendence can be disclosed and grasped not by a flight into the objective (as in Platonism) but solely through a continuously renewed ontological intepretation of the subjectivity of the subject, an interpretation charac- terised as much by its opposition to 'subjectivism' as by its refusal to subserve 'objectivism' of any kind." The term *Dasein*, which Heidegger uses in place of conscious- ness, the transcendental ego or subject, is meant to convey this reference to man in terms of the transcendence inherent in him. What precisely is the *Dasein*, or as he alternatively puts it, the *Dasein* in man? Literally, it means the being or happening (*Sein*) of the "there" (*Da*), of overtness or opening up and it aptly describes the being of man, for he is a being who *is* as having to be his own overtness, clearing or illumination. Man is this there-ness of himself, of the world and of other beings, some like himself, others unlike. The name *Dasein* was chosen for the ontological sphere in which man stands as man, Heidegger explains, in order to seize in one word the relation of Being to the essential nature of man as also the essential relation of man to the openness of Being as such. In using this term "being there", he does not merely substitute a traditional term by a new one. As he has said, "It is not merely the word *Dasein* that takes the place of the word 'consciousness' and neither is it the fact designated as 'being there' that takes the place of what we call by the name of 'consciousness'. 'Being there' names rather that which should first of all enter into our ken and then appropriately be thought about, as the place, namely of the location of the truth of Being." In *Being and Time*, the essence of being-there is said to lie in its existence and this term too is meant to designate man's unique mode of being, i.e., his openness to Being or rather the fact of his being this openness itself. "The existential nature of man is the reason why he can represent being as such and why he can be conscious of them. All consciousness presupposes the ecstatically

understood existence as the *essentia* of man, where
essentia means that which enables man to be man. But
consciousness does not itself create the openness of
beings, nor is it consciousness that makes it possible for
man to stand open for beings." Consciousness is not an
entity itself but the mode of being of the entity called
man or, alternatively, in Quentin Lauer's words, "the mode
of being which things have when we are conscious of them."
For these reasons, the inquiry into the structure of
transcendence in man is called by Heidegger the Analytic
of *Dasein* or existential analytic rather than a theory
of consciousness.

Central to Husserl's theory of consciousness is the
conception of its intentionality, the view namely, that
"all consciousness is consciousness of something and that
as a *cogito* it bears within itself its own *cogitatum*."
The "of" is inseparable from consciousness. It is not a
merely static relation connecting two entities, however,
for consciousness is here conceived as activity and
orientedness towards. Consciousness as intrinsically
intentional does not merely objectivate its data, refer
them to poles of identity and synthesize them but also
constitutes the object through its own "achievements." We
may describe it as a dynamic field generating meaningfulness in things, "constituting" them as also itself as a
stream of acts through its innermost time-building depths,
characterized by Husserl as "absolute subjectivity."
Consciousness is not an entity or region of inwardness
standing by itself, not a container and not a mirror; it
neither causes the world of objects to come into being nor
is it made up of representations of these objects. The
conception of consciousness "as intentionality" implies
the rejection of the notions of an object in itself, of a
consciousness closed in on itself and producing the world
out of itself, out of the subject-object dualism of
traditional ontology. The merit of intentionality, it has
been remarked, is to explode idealism by projecting

consciousness towards the world by placing it in the
world. The world is tied to consciousness as ever already
giving itself to it and consciousness is tied to the world
as always having to give sense to it. By emptying
absolute consciousness of all content and transforming it
into a nothingness to which the world (i.e., everything,
including the "I") is wholly external, Sartre has given a
more radical sense to intentionality. Consciousness is
now itself defined by intentionality, by the movement
towards the object by virtue of which it transcends
itself. As he says, "Consciousness is purely and simply
consciousness of being consciousness of that object. This
is the law of its existence." Far from being a disinterested spectator, however, consciousness is engaged in a
ceaseless struggle with the brute-in-itself, with all
those "things" which can be objects for it, constituting a
meaningful world out of them, becoming ensnared in the
world because it is itself a lack, tearing itself away
from it by virtue of its absolute freedom, an emptiness,
in the massive fulness of being. Sartre has even charged
Husserl with misunderstanding the essential character of
intentionality. Pure subjectivity is not something that
can be given prior to the act by which it goes out of
itself to posit the given. As he says, "For consciousness
there is no being outside of that precise obligation to be
a revealing intuition of something, i.e., of a transcendent being." In other words, to say that consciousness is
consciousness of something is to say that it must produce
itself as a revealed-revelation of a being which is not it
and which gives itself as already existing when consciousness reveals it. Consciousness has no other being than
that of being a nihilating presence both to itself and to
things. Intentionality thus implies on the one hand that
consciousness in its very mode of being is embedded in a
world, that in Heidegger's words, it is a being-in-the-
world, or in Merleau-Ponty's, that we are subjects "wedded
to a world." On the other hand, the intentionality of

consciousness implies that its essence lies in transcending itself, going out of itself on existence or just
openness. It is precisely to refer to this openness
characteristic of man that Heidegger uses the term being-
there (Da-sein) and declares that the essence of Dasein
lies in its existence. As in the case of consciousness,
Heidegger finds intentionality itself rooted in something
more basic, namely, the transcendence inherent in Dasein.
As he remarks, "If all relating oneself to beings is
characterized as intentional, then intentionality is only
possible on the basis of transcendence; it cannot be
regarded as being identical with transcendence, far from
being itself the condition that renders transcendence
possible." (WGI5) It is thus that the theory of subjectivity, which Husserl developed in terms of consciousness,
the transcendental ego, intentionality and reduction, is
at the same time taken up and radically transformed in
Heidegger's philosophy in which these concepts find no
place. Sartre and Merleau-Ponty retain the traditional
term consciousness to designate human subjectivity, though
not without radical alteration in their ways of conceiving
its essence and structure. Consequently they retain also
the notion of intentionality, whereas in Heidegger this
basic directedness of man's being-there towards the world
is transformed into care, which is itself to be understood
in terms of temporality, and which represents man's
specific way of being open to Being.

The inquiries into the nature of subjectivity
conducted by Husserl, Heidegger, Sartre and Merleau-Ponty
are phenomenological rather than speculative and their
concern is with analysis of the structure and foundations
of experience rather than with metaphysical construction.
It will therefore be useful if a brief mention is made
here of some of the consequences for the phenomenological-
existential theory of subjectivity which follow from this
approach. We have already seen that according to the view
heralded by Husserl, consciousness is not a worldless

entity, unrelated to the world to begin with and in its
essence. Its very being lies, as Heidegger was to say
later, in being-in-the-world and it is the structure of
this concrete subjectivity with which, following
Heidegger's systematic attempt in *Being and Time*, Sartre
and Merleau-Ponty are concerned. In its basic intention,
therefore, this view seeks a radical overcoming of the
classical alternative of Realism and Idealism and of the
subject-object dichotomy; it may in fact be considered as
an attempt to carry reflection about subjectivity to a
deeper level than was accessible to traditional
"epistemology." The transcendental ego or pure consciousness of Husserl is neither a disembodied *res cogitans* nor
a detached "I think" but is inserted and involved in the
world; it is an engaged consciousness and its life is
"life-experiencing-the-world."

In the second place, subjectivity in this view is not
conceived as "*Bewusstsein überhaupt*," consciousness in
general, but as a particular, individual locus of awareness and spontaneity, not as an abstract principle but as
a concrete structure. The transcendental ego in Husserl
is a particular ego, "my own transcendental ego," a
solipsistically reduced ego. It is for this reason that
the constitution of the alter ego in me, i.e., the problem
of intersubjectivity assumes cardinal importance in his
theory of consciousness. In the fifth of the Cartesian
Meditations, he even speaks of "the total nexus of that
actual and potential intentionality in which the ego
constitutes within itself a peculiar ownness." Heidegger
makes this notion of ownness even more basic and
incorporates into it the Kierkegaardian conception of the
single, existing individual, responsible and free,
infinitely concerned about his own being and anxiously
taking upon himself the either-or of his own being. The
Analytic of *Dasein* in *Being and Time* opens with a
statement of this principle of Ipseity (*Jemeinigkeit*,
each-his-ownness, in-each-case-mineness), where Heidegger

pointedly remarks that the entity to be analysed is not
just an indifferent, anonymous being-there or man in
general but we ourselves. The being of this entity is *in
each case mine.* In its very being it is related to its
own being, is delivered over to its own being, as something it has to be and as that which is "at stake" for it.
"The being which is at stake for this entity in its very
being is in each case mine." Similarly, consciousness for
Sartre constitutes "a synthetic and individual totality
entirely isolated from other totalities of the same type."
It is an individuated spontaneity, even though impersonal
in the sense that there is no transcendental ego to own or
inhabit it. And yet, inasmuch as consciousness exists as
a presence to itself, a certain selfness or ipseity
characterizes all consciousness; as a privation or nihilation also each for-itself is defined as this particular
consciousness by being a particular privation or nihilation of a particular in-itself and not of being in
general. The plurality of consciousness, realized in the
form of a double reciprocal relation of exclusion, is for
Sartre a "primary fact," "a scandal which no logical or
epistemological optimism can cover" and which even
ontology can only seek to describe without being able to
overcome it.

A third feature of the subjective as developed in
existential thought is the conception of its facticity and
finitude. Husserl, it will be recalled, takes as his
starting-point the *fact* of the experienced "I am", though
it was not until the closing phase of his career that he
was led to reflect on the implications of this factuality,
basically different from the factuality of all other types
of entity in the ontological sense. This he calls the
faciticity of man's being and it lies in the sheer "that"
of his being thrown into existence, in being delivered
over to the "that it is and has to be" of his *Dasein.*
Man's existence is qualified by his thrownness, by his
finding himself already there in the world and left to

himself to be what and how he can in the midst of
entities, upon which he is dependent. The projects of
understanding with which man, as already existing in and
as the openness of Being, seeks to grasp the world, are
always thrown projects just as he himself in his being is
a thrown possibility, already conditioned by a past. They
are determined by all the factual particularities of the
situation in which such projects are made, not excluding
the historical. All knowledge or disclosure of truth is
thus factitious and hence imperfect, coloured and shot
through with concealment. Man has no other "essence"
except his existence, by virtue of which he ceaselessly
runs ahead of himself and projects himself upon the
future. Existence is conditioned by its facticity and
thrownness and is thus determined by the past, the
has-been. Another character of man's way of being is
termed fallenness or forfeiture by Heidegger. This is the
tendency to exist as abandoned to and taken up with the
world, as scattered among the things of the world, as not
being himself and disowned, as caught up in the present
and so faced with the task of disengaging himself from it
and winning his selfhood. Existentiality, facticity and
forfeiture together constitute the full structure of man's
being. This Heidegger defines as care, to be understood
not in the sense of a psychological process or fact but in
the ontological sense of being the condition of the
possibility of all such processes and indeed of all
experience. And care itself, i.e., the being of man, his
subjectivity, is intelligible only in terms of temporality
as its ultimate ground.

Hegel's conception of the subject as Absolute Spirit,
which can assimilate everything to itself through the
exercise of total reflexion and to which nothing can in
principle remain alien or opaque, was the culmination of
the Platonic striving to bring all that is factual under
the transparency of essence. Against this reduction of
the subject to pure and absolute thought, against this

supremacy of the concept, Kierkegaard, Marx, Feuerbach, Dilthey and others brought forward cogent criticisms which all tended, despite the diversity of their approaches and interests, to affirm the finitude of the human subject, its irreducibility to pure reason and its concreteness and historicity. The later Schelling in particular, showed that spirit or reason in its ceaseless self-meditation experiences the sheer "that" of its own activity as a "that" which resists the transparency of reason and so cannot be conceived as a pure "what". In contemporary existential thought, this critical reaction against Idealism has developed into a phenomenology of the concrete subject and in Heidegger this takes the form of an ontology of man and so also in Sartre. The human subject, instead of being conceived as a detached spectator engaged in universal reflection, is shown to be rooted in the irreducible "that" of existence. The subjectivity of this subject is not to be found in a timeless essence but in the finitude of man's factual existence in a particular historical situation. It is true that man's subjectivity lies in freedom and transcendence, but this freedom and transcendence are finite and conditioned by the sheer contingency of man's givenness to himself as a possibility to be realized, his being given over to himself, as well by his dependence upon entities other than himself. The givenness of entities and the occurrence of himself as such transcendence does not lie in the power of man; as transcendence, man exists as grounding in character, but he himself is powerless over both the sheer "that" of being a ground and of that which he grounds through his creative projects.

Heidegger is at great pains to show that the being of man cannot be determined on the basis of traditional epistemology which regards man as essentially the subject of knowledge and conceives the latter as a relation between subject and object. Knowing is itself a derivative mode of *Dasein*'s being-in-the-world and is grounded

in a prior being-already-with-the-world which is
essentially constitutive of *Dasein*'s being. As a way of
being, knowing represents a modification of the primordial
being-in of *Dasein* and of the disclosure of a world that
goes with it. "Knowing does not in the first instance
produce a *commercium* of the subject with a world, nor does
it arise from an action of the world upon a subject.
Knowing is a mode of *Dasein* founded upon being-in-the-
world." Man's being or subjectivity therefore cannot be
identified with a cognitive subjective in the narrow
sense. Similarly, when subjective is understood in the
sense of the *a priori*, the subject means not an entity
which at first is unrelated to a world but subject in the
"ontologically properly understood" sense of *Dasein* as
constituted by its being-in-the-world. Apriority has in
fact nothing to do with inherence in an ideal, worldless
subject, as Scheler and Hartmann had demonstrated even
before Heidegger, nor is it confined to knowledge as such
and to the categorical structure of the known. Apriority
extends to the ontological and existential sphere of the
whole of experience and refers primarily to the factual
subject, *Dasein*, and to its being-in-the-world. One of
the basic aims of Heidegger in *Being and Time* is to
demonstrate that the conception of Being implicitly taken
for granted in all ontology up till now has been that of
an entity simply there, present at hand, objectively given
or *vorhanden* and that in consequence the being of man also
has so far been understood in the light of that conception. Man's unique mode of being, however, is radically
different and therefore inaccessible to the traditional
ontology of the *Vorhanden*. It cannot be determined in
terms of the categories which are applicable only to
substantially given, *vorhanden* entities. Unlike all other
entities, man exists, i.e., he *is* as transcendence, as
being-in-the-world, as comprehending being, as concerned
with his own being, as sheer possibility, thrown into
being and yet always ahead of himself towards his own

future, in short, as care. The true character of human
subjectivity is describable only in terms of existentialities, not categories, and these are to be thought of
not as properties qualifying it but as ways of being of
the factual *Dasein*.

The traditional ontology, the "I" or the self is
regarded as the true *subjectum*, the underlying ground, as
that which remains the same through the multiplicity of
its experiences. But in this way one still conceives the
"I" or self as something *vorhanden*, present-at-hand and
substantially given, whereas the "substance" of man lies,
not in any ideally constructed or inferred entity that is
presumably unchanging and abiding but in his existence, in
the factual way of his being-in-the-world as *Dasein*. If
the "I" and selfhood are essential determinations of
Dasein, they must be given an existential meaning, for it
is as existing that we can gain or lose our selfhood, can
realize ourselves or fail to do so. In our average,
everyday mode of being, we go out into and are merged in
the world of our preoccupations, including our being-with-
others, and are thus not "ourselves". The "who" of this
everyday being-with-others is the anonymous "they", the
everyman, where each man is the other and nobody his own
self, where the self of *Dasein*, or that of the other, has
not yet found (or lost) itself, being dissipated in the
"they" and the world of its practical concerns. Disen-
gagement from this mode of being and disclosure of selfhood always occurs first as a sweeping away of all that
veils and darkens it, as a pulling down of the fence of
dissimulation which man raises up against his own self.
Thus "the self-sameness of an authentically existing self
is divided by a wide gulf from the identity of an 'I' that
remains the same in the midst of a diversity of experiences." The ontological concept of the subject
characterizes the sameness and permanence of something
that is all the time substantially present and not the
selfhood of the "I" *qua* self and hence to determine the

"I" ontologically as subject in this sense is to regard it
as a *vorhanden* entity. The self as ontologically constituted, in other words, cannot be derived either from an
"I" substantially conceived or from a subject and neither
is it the permanently *vorhanden* ground of care as the
being of man. It must rather be understood existentially
in terms of man's authentic potentiality of being himself,
i.e., in terms of the authenticity of *Dasein* as care. The
permanence of the self lies, in this view, not in the
persistence of an abiding subject but in the constancy and
steadfastness of the *Dasein* that has achieved authentic
existence. And since, according to Heidegger, the being
of *Dasein* (i.e., care) is itself grounded in temporality,
the subject in the ontological sense of the existing
Dasein is temporal through and through. Neither timeless
nor worldless, human subjectivity is yet not something
"in" time or "in" the world. Such a mode of being belongs
to substantial, objectively given entities alone, whereas
Dasein, the non-substantial factual subject, is in its
very ontological constitution worldly and timeish. With
care as its being, it is itself rooted in a primordial
temporality, of which time as an unending succession of
"nows" is a derivative and degenerate manifestation and
which is the ultimate condition of the possibility of the
being-there of man as being-in-the-world. This is also
the reason why historicity is an intrinsic constituent of
the subjectivity of man and of world as an existentiality
of *Dasein*.

"Everything that is," Heidegger has remarked, "*is*,
independently of the experience, the cognition and the
comprehending through which it is revealed, discovered,
and determined. But its being "is" only in the understanding of that entity to whose being there belongs such
a thing as an understanding of Being." Idealism is right
in emphasizing that Being and Reality are only "in
consciousness," i.e., that they manifest themselves only
within man's understanding and that Being, ever

transcending the entity of which it is the being, cannot
be explained in terms of beings. But does this mean that
man is the ultimate subject or ground of all that is?
Man's true subjectivity lies, as explained above, in the
Dasein in man, but does this mean that *Dasein* constitutes
a subject in relation to the being of all beings or to
Being as such? *Subjectum* is the Latin translation of the
Greek *hypokeimenon* and means literally what underlies,
what lies at the bottom and constitutes the basis, that
which already by itself lies before and presents itself.
Before the modern period in philosophy was ushered in by
Descartes, not merely man but every entity, in so far as
it has being, was conceived as *subjectum*, both in the
ontological sense of anything that is as well as in the
logical sense of the subject of all predication. It is
only since Descartes that man, the human ego, has come to
mean in a predominant manner the "subject" as that which
lies at the ground of everything that is taken as being.
Torn from the Medieval security of faith in the salvation
of the individual immortal soul, man has since then been
thrown back upon himself, to seek within himself the certainty and assurance of what he can know, aim at and have
in his grip. It is Heidegger's merit to have shown how
the history of modern Western philosophy since Descartes
constitutes the story of the unfoldment and rapid
acceleration of a subjectivism in which not only does man
become the ground and measure of everything but in which
there is a complete transformation of what it means to be
measure and ground, of what it means to be true and of
what it means to *be*. The modern quest of objectivity, in
science and in philosophy, is itself a manifestation of
this subjectivism, for here everything that is is
conceived as being an object for a subject and as being
grounded in a subject. As he says,

> At the beginning of modern philosophy stands the
> sentence of Descartes: "I think, hence I am."
> All consciousness of things and of the totality
> of what is is traced back to the self-

consciousness of the human subject as the
unshakable ground of certainty. The reality of
the real is determined henceforth as objectivity,
as something that is conceived as projected and
held over-against and confronting it, *by* a
subject and *for* it. The reality of the real
means representedness *by* the representing subject
and *for* it.

The objectification of all that is is accomplished through
the activity of re-presentation which aims at so bringing
entities before itself that man can count on them,
ascertain and certify them, hold them fast and catch and
possess them in his grasp through his conceptualizing
thought. When man is regarded as subject, his being thus
emerges as of the nature of pure willing and his relationship to what is an assault on his being.

In defining man as *Dasein* and his substance as existence, Heidegger sought to overcome this conception of man
as subject, though at the stage of writing *Being and Time*
he was still enmeshed in the idiom of the subjectivistic
tradition. The core of human subjectivity lies in its
openness to Being, not merely in his standing out of
himself, i.e., his ek-sistence, but in his insistence, in
his standing within the light of Being. In this sense man
is no "subject", neither within Reason nor as Spirit, but
himself subject to the happening of that primordial
un-hiddenness which carries him, needs and uses him and
which Heidegger calls the Truth of Being itself and not
merely the truth of beings with which metaphysics has so
far concerned itself. Man's relationship to others, to
things and to himself rests, as indicated earlier, on his
openness to Being and on the projective and interpretative
understanding of Being inherent in him. In this sense and
to this extent only man is grounding and a subject. But
once it is realized that man's relationship to these is
itself rooted in the way Being reveals itself in man and
in the way it at the same time conceals itself from him,
that neither the being of beings nor the Truth of Being
itself is a construct of man and his understanding and

that the relationship of man and Being is entirely
governed from the side of Being, everything turns round,
as it were, and it becomes necessary to determine man's
nature in the light of Being rather than in terms of an
eternal essence intrinsic to man as such alone. Man is
seen now as no longer a subject, the self-grounding ground
of all that is, for his own nature is found to be grounded
in the Truth of Being as such. He is neither a subject as
conceived substantially and categorically, as a *vorhanden*
entity, in the metaphysical tradition nor, in the ultimate
instance, a subject in the existentialistic sense dwelt
upon earlier in this paper. The existentialities of man,
his being-in-the-world as existence, his facticity and
forfeiture, care itself as the being of man, have now to
be understood as being grounded in the Truth of Being in
which man has his dwelling. For man, as Heidegger puts it
in the non-conceptual language of a thinking that is no
longer representational, is not the lord of what is; man
is the shepherd of Being.

> Man is rather "thrown" by Being itself in the
> Truth of Being so that, ek-sisting in this
> manner, he may keep watch over and tend the Truth
> of Being, in order that in this light of Being,
> what is may manifest itself as it is. Whether
> and how it manifests itself, whether and how God
> and the gods, history and nature enter into the
> clearing or luminosity of Being, present or
> absent themselves, does not stand under the
> decision of man. The arrival of what is depends
> on the destiny of Being. For man, the question
> that remains is whether he can find that
> appropriate and adequate function of his own
> nature which is in correspondence with this
> destiny; for it is in conformity with this that
> man, as one who ek-sists, has to guard the Truth
> of Being. Man is the shepherd of Being.

The understanding of Being, both the being of things
and his own, is inherent in man as his very essence and
specific virtue. But how he understands it and in what
terms he conceives it does not depend so much upon man's
will to conceive as on the way Being reveals itself to and
conceals itself from him. "The understanding of Being,"

Heidegger says, "does not mean at all that man as subject possesses a subjective representation of Being and that Being is a mere representation....Understanding of Being means that man by nature stands in the openness of the project of Being and endures the understanding as thus meant. When the understanding of Being is conceived in this way, the representation of man as subject is, to speak with Hegel, brushed aside." The conception of man as subject is a consequence of man's erroneous way of *being* in relation to Being and of understanding this relationship accordingly. But this "error" is a fateful one not only in the sense that it determines henceforth all his dealing with himself, with others and with all that is, but in the sense that it is not so much man's doing as something fated and brought to pass by Being itself. In the second place, the conception of man's being as subject is itself rendered possible on the basis of an *a priori* conception of the being of what is as itself the *hypokeimenon*, the underlying ground, prevailing throughout in the entire metaphysical tradition of the West. The subjectivity of man is only the modern form, and a consequential modification of what Heidegger calls the subjectivity of Being in this tradition. How the concepts of subject, ground and enduring presence, in terms of which Being has been conceived since Plato, are utterly inadequate to the truth of Being itself cannot be dealt with on the present occasion.

THE PHILOSOPHICAL NECESSITY OF EXISTENTIALISM

Existentialism as a movement of thought is not limited
to the academic field of philosophical scholarship but
embraces the wider sphere of cultural activity: literature, political writing and popular philosophy and
religious thought. It has been widely assailed by critics
as the effervescence of a passing mood, as a phenomenon of
decadence or as symptomatic of the spiritual malaise which
has overtaken the world today. As a philosophy it has
been decried as a merely transitory outbreak of irratio-
nalism, romanticism and as a futile gesture of despairing
revolt against the time-honoured classical tradition of
western metaphysics. And yet it would be a mistake, as I
shall try to show in this article, to treat it as one of
the "isms" that blossom for a while in the intellectual
field, spend their force and wither away. Like its counterpart in the Anglo-American world, Logical positivism,
it has few adherents today. It has already become part of
the history of philosophy and contemporary European
thought is moving into fields which cannot be designated
with the title of Existentialism. Of the living philosophers who fathered this movement few are agreeable to
being called existentialists. Even Jean-Paul Sartre, who
was, is now more concerned with assigning limits to this
type of thought than claiming for it a place comparable to
the great philosophies of the past. We must not, however,

Two lectures given at the University of Delhi in 1966,
originally published under the title "Existential
Philosophy" in *Proceedings of the All-India Seminar* (2),
Centre of Advanced Study in Philosophy, Banaras Hindu
University, 1967, pp. 85-107.

on this account lose sight of the seriousness of intellectual purpose behind the strictly philosophical core of the
movement nor neglect to take stock of the abiding contribution to philosophy that this movement has made. In the
course of this essay I shall try to give an idea of the
historical background and philosophical necessity of
existentialism, say something about the general features
of existentialist thought as represented by Jaspers,
Heidegger and Sartre, and conclude with remarks aimed at
assessing the enduring philosophical worth of this new way
of thinking.

Existentialism, in the first place, is the expression
of a peculiar historical situation in the spiritual condition of the man of today. If, as Hegel said, philosophy
is its time grasped in thought, then existentialism is the
characteristic manifestation of the spiritual climate of
the present age. It is a philosophy of crisis, giving
voice to a situation in which established certainties have
broken down, values and forms of bygone order no longer
experienced as binding. Such situations of homelessness
and spiritual insecurity are a recurring feature of man's
historical life on earth. Classical expression of such
moods can be found in the Old Testament as well as the
New, in Greek tragedy, in Socrates, the Stoics, Saint
Augustine, Pascal, Jacobi and Hamann. In modern times, it
is above all the Danish theologian Soren Kierkegaard,
generally called the father of this movement, who has
contributed massively to the breakdown of inauthentic and
false securities and who has laid down the basic pattern
of a new mode of philosophical reflection. He has laid
bare the implications of spiritual crisis and insecurity
and opened up a new area of philosophical exploration, the
field of concrete, individual subjectivity. But even
Kierkegaard dwelt in the security of faith and as a true
Christian had an eternal God standing unshaken in tne
midst of a world gone to rack and ruin. Since Friedrich
Nietzsche, who gave for our era the definitive expression

to the final breakdown of past values and of the Platonic-Christian framework within which western man lived till then, even this last refuge of religious certainty has gone. The secularized faith in Reason and Progress which marked the buoyant optimism with which the present century opened was finally uprooted by the two world wars and the time was ripe for poet and philosopher to lament, to herald and to depict the desolate landscape of a world-wide wasteland and look for a hidden seed or gem from which a new spiritual life could blossom or a new ray of light could go forth into the future. If existentialism is a philosophy of crisis, it is one which has arisen in response to the deepest extremity of man's intellectual condition in the course of his historical existence. And to the extent to which human spiritual life has an aspect of perennial crisis, the insights of existentialism constitute an essential supplement to the classical *philosophia perennis*.

But existentialism, far from being a passing fad, vogue or malady, supplements traditional metaphysics even in a more far reaching sense than the one mentioned above. The central characteristic of the founders of western philosophy and science, the Greeks, was their attitude of pure, detached contemplation, their pursuit of reality as objectively given, their quest of an unchanging conceptual order which would correspond to it and enable us to grasp it. This attitude and approach to reality, beyond the opposition of rationalism and empiricism, is responsible for the development of metaphysics as a scientific discipline along with that of logic as its principal instrument. But this pursuit of objective, rationally ascertained knowledge left out of account the concrete reality of the thinker himself, with his hopes and fears, his aspirations and cravings, his concern with his own self and its relation to the world. The realm of the subjective and of the soul's destiny, of all that matters

in life, of life itself, one may say, was left to literature, art and religion. It is only with the discovery of
man as an individual since the Renaissance and of the
realm of the subjective since Descartes that the way has
been paved for the appropriation of this realm by
philosophy. Cartesian subjectivism, however, was itself
linked up with its inseparable counterpart, rationalistic
objectivism, and it was not until recently that philosophers have been able to reach beyond the subject-object
dichotomy to a deeper conception of human subjectivity.
All existentialist thinkers are united in their rejection
of objectifying thought, following Kierkegaard's declara-
tion that subjectivity is truth. Says Kierkegaard,

> when the question of truth is raised in an objec-
> tive manner, reflection is directed objectively
> to the truth, as an object to which the knower is
> related (as another objectively given entity).
> Reflection is not focussed upon the relationship,
> however, but upon the question of whether it is
> the truth to which the knower is related....When
> the question of truth is raised subjectively,
> reflection is directed subjectively to the nature
> of the individual's relationship; if only the
> mode of this relationship is in truth, the
> individual is in the truth even if he should
> happen to be thus related to what is not true.
> [Further,] the only reality to which an existing
> individual may have a relation that is more than
> cognitive, is his own reality, the fact that he
> exists; this reality constitutes his absolute
> interest. Abstract thought requires him to
> become disinterested in order to acquire know-
> ledge; the ethical demand is to become infinitely
> interested in existing....The real subject is not
> the cognitive subject...but the ethically
> existing subject....The ethical lays hold of each
> individual and demands that he refrain from all
> contemplation, especially of humanity and the
> world; for the ethical, as being the internal,
> cannot be observed by an outsider.

Kierkegaard took recourse to paradox, irony and devious
modes of indirect communication. Jaspers warns constantly
and explicitly against taking the basic terms of his
philosophy as referring to objectively cognizable entities

and wishes his philosophizing to be understood as appeal rather than as a series of statements, from one existing individual to another. Heidegger has struck the hardest blow against the traditional ontology of objective presence and regards genuine thought as a response to the call of Being, an evocative gesture of thanksgiving and surrender. Sartre's concern is with the *cogito* but not in the Cartesian form of thought confronting an object. The starting-point of philosophy for him is the pre-reflexive *cogito*, prior to the emergence of the subject-object dichotomy and its immediate aim is not detached contemplation of a pre-given reality but thinking in the perspective of a possible change, change towards greater freedom, inner as well as outer. Marcel distinguishes sharply between problem and mystery, the former calling for a universally valid answer, the latter eluding all objectification because here the subject is involved in what it is trying to understand and therefore cannot stand over against it. In Marcel's words,

> My effort can be best described as an attempt to establish (an ontology) which precludes all equation of being with *Ding*....My aim [is] to discover how a subject....is related to a reality which cannot in this context be regarded as objective, yet which is persistently required and recognized as real....The undertaking [has] to be pursued within reality itself, to which the philosopher can never stand in the relationship of an onlooker to a picture.

It is in this sense that existentialism must be regarded as a completion, a corrective and necessary supplement to traditional metaphysics. Unlike the latter, it does not aim at laying down universally valid and necessary propositions about what is the case but develops a new mode of reflection more adequate to that dynamic unobjectifiable reality in which the thinking subject is inextricably involved and which is of the utmost moment and concern for it.

What then is existentialism and what, if we consider
only the central philosophical core of its doctrines, are
the philosophically relevant and serious influences that
have gone into its making and the issues and disciplines
that have emerged from it? It has often been remarked
that existentialism cannot be defined in one sentence,
that it is not a single, well-defined movement within
philosophy possessing a common set of ideas, that it is
not a philosophy but a mood embracing a number of
disparate philosophies, the differences among them being
more basic than the temper which unites them. There is
consensus among textbooks as to the principal representatives of this philosophy: Nietzsche and Kierkegaard are
commonly included as forerunners but an important
anthology also includes selections from Heraclitus, the
Old and the New Testaments and Meister Eckhart, from
Nicolas Berdyaev, Jacob Boehme and Pascal, from Hasidism,
from Schelling, Feuerback and Karl Marx, from Hermann
Melville and Dostoevsky. Among contemporary thinkers,
Karl Jaspers, Martin Heidegger, Jean-Paul Sartre and
Gabriel Marcel are generally included, but also sometimes
the Spanish thinker, Ortega y Gasset, Maurice Merleau-
Ponty, Jacques Maritain, Martin Buber, Albert Camus,
Rainer Maria Rilke, Franz Kafka, Paul Tillich, Franz
Rosenzweig and Edmund Husserl. To this list may be added,
among forerunners, the psychoanalyst Sigmund Freud, and
Henri Bergson and Wilhelm Dilthey as representatives of
Lebensphilosophie; amongst contemporaries, Protestant
theologians like Karl Barth, Brunner, Bultmann, Gogarten
etc., and Catholics such as Guardini, Przywara, Hacker and
Peter Wurst. Among psychiatrists, we may also include
Binswanger, Boss, Strauss, May, Fraenkel, Moreno, Rogers,
Laing and Cooper. What is common to all of these is their
concern with man in the depths of his being, either in
relation to a transcendental reality, or in relation to
other men, or in his own Promethean self. These writings

may be regarded, from their different perspectives, presuppositions, points of departure and approach, as contributions to the discipline of philosophical anthropology,
which must be sharply distinguished from psychology and
all other empirical sciences of man. As Jaspers has said,
"Existence-philosophy is the way of thought by means of
which man seeks to become himself; it makes use of expert
knowledge while at the same time going beyond it. This
way of thought does not cognise objects, but elucidates
and makes actual the being of the thinker." It is a way
of thought, not a set of doctrines; what it says is
neither made up of definitions nor of factual assertions
but is meant to persuade, awaken, appeal and alter. Its
subject is man, but man as he may become, man in his
height and depth, man as necessarily involved in a
non-empirical reality. In intention at least, it is an
attempt to answer the question, "What is life?" without
metaphysical or theological presuppositions. It
investigates man not as a thing or an objectifiable
reality but as *existence*.

What does this term mean in the usage of the principal
existential thinkers? The term "existence" refers, not to
everything that is, but to the mode of being peculiar and
proper to man, to which he may fully attain or from which
he may fall away. For Kierkegaard, existence refers to
that inwardness of subjective life in which the man of
faith goes out towards God and by thus becoming a pure
Christian realizes his own self. This is an inwardness
which can never be made the object of knowledge; in
Sartre's words, "This subjectivity rediscovered beyond
language as the personal adventure of each man in the face
of others and of God--this is what Kierkegaard called
existence." It is a state of being, moral and religious,
rather than one of knowing, and so involves choice and
commitment. Jaspers takes over this Kierkegaardian
concept but de-theologizes it. For him existence is

> that which can never become an object, the source
> from which my thoughts and actions spring....
> Existence is that which is in relation to itself
> and thus to its transcendence. Man is more than
> his empirical being, more than consciousness in
> general, more than reason and spirit. As the
> condition and enlivening source of all these,
> man's existence is the dark ground of his
> becoming a self, the hiddenness from which I
> encounter myself as emerging and for which alone
> transcendence becomes actual.

Man is potential existence and takes his life from a
primal source that lies beyond mind. He fulfills this
potentiality of existence in relation to transcendence and
in communication with others. In Marcel also the concept
of existence includes the notion of becoming oneself,
through relation to transcendence. In *Being and Time*,
Heidegger has explained, with greater precision and
clarity, what he means by existence and has also made a
number of valuable distinctions which have been ignored by
other existentialist thinkers. Unlike other beings, which
merely are there as objects or things, man exists, i.e.
his mode of being is such that it cannot be stated through
the categories of objective being. Further, to say that
man exists means that he *is* in such a way that he
understands himself in his being, is concerned with this
being, that for each man his own being is at stake. In
the next place, each man understands himself not only in
what he *is* but in terms of what he *can be*, he understands
himself in terms of his possibilities, in terms of his
ability to be and of a future towards which he is
anticipatively oriented. Man's being, he asserts, is
care. To go out beyond himself to the possibilities of
his being and be aware of himself in relation to them is
the unique way of being which Heidegger calls existence.
Man's essence, Heidegger remarks, lies in his existence as
thus described. Heidegger has repeatedly insisted that
his use of this term is meant in a radically different
sense than that in the Existence Philosophy of Jaspers or

the Existentialism of Sartre. The interests of
Kierkegaard and Jaspers are largely focussed on the
existentiell, i.e., on the description of factual
experience, whereas Heidegger seeks to inquire into the
conditions of the possibility of such experience and
therefore concerns himself exclusively with the analytic
of existence in the manner of Kant--his inquiry is
existential. For Heidegger, man's supreme feature lies in
his ontological awareness.

> Without the comprehension of Being inherent in
> man, man would never be the entity that he is,
> even if he were to be equipped with the most
> wonderful faculties. Man is a being who is in
> the midst of other entities in such a way that,
> in this being, the entity that he is not, and the
> entity that he is, have become simultaneously
> manifest. This mode of being of man we call
> existence. Only by virtue of the understanding
> of being is existence possible.

In order to indicate his distance from the Kierkegaardian
concept of existence--which is also in essentials that of
Jaspers-- and from that of Sartre in particular, which is
derived from the Medieval contrast between *essentia* and
existentia, Heidegger later spells it as ek-sistenz, and
characterizes it as the ecstatic standing within the
illumination of Being. Man stands out of himself and
stands within the light of the truth of Being--he ek-
sists, and it is this that makes him a man and not any
sort of actualization of an essence or possibility. The
basic tenet of existentialism as formulated by Sartre
says, existence precedes essence. In doing so he takes
existentia and *essentia* in the sense of traditional
metaphysics which since Plato says: *essentia* precedes
existentia. Sartre only converts the sentence. But the
converse of a metaphysical statement still remains
metaphysical. As such a statement, it remains oblivious,
like all metaphysics, of the truth of Being.

Heidegger's criticism of Sartre implied in the above, however, is not quite fair and shows some lack of understanding. It is strange that Sartre, with whose name the existentialist movement is more closely associated than with anyone else, does not use the term "existentialism" in his properly philosophical books and articles up to and including *Being and Nothingness*. It was only later, in his polemical writings, that he unwillingly took up the label. As a competent critic points out, existence in Sartre does not have its classical meaning, i.e., the actualization of a being, the reality of a being, as opposed to its simple logical possibility, the fact of existing. It is no longer the "complement" of essence but appears as the transcendental condition of the possibility of essence. Nor does it have the "existential" meaning of lived existence (as we find in his literary works) or the Kierkegaardian meaning of separation, of interiority or relation to transcendence. It designates solely consciousness, in all its simple purity, translucency, negativity, spontaneity and freedom. As Sartre explicitly states in his biographical work, *Saint Genêt*, "This authentic subjectivity which he touches beyond and within being, within and beyond the possible, is *existence*." Again, "And this particularity which is no longer an object for any one, not even for himself, which is not, which is in the making, is situated beyond being and language...this creative consciousness is: existence...a faceless freedom...beyond the empirical self." About the philosophical background and details of Sartre's concept of existence, however, I shall enlarge in a subsequent essay devoted entirely to this thinker.

As the above examination of the concept of existence has made clear, existential philosophers differ from one another in a far-reaching sense in their views. This arises from the fact that neither Kierkegaard nor Heidegger and Sartre, neither Jaspers nor Marcel, is a

mere existentialist in the ordinary sense. Each is
concerned with something more than man's peculiar mode of
being, each has a different starting-point, each a
different philosophical end in view. Kierkegaard, from
whom almost all basic existentialist concepts derive, was
inspired by a primarily theological or religious passion.
Heidegger's main problem is the question of Being and his
systematic working out of the structure of existence in
Being and Time is only incidental to that. Sartre's
concern is with human freedom, inner as well as outer and
social, and like Heidegger he derives from the school of
Husserl's Phenomenology. So does Maurice Merleau-Ponty.
Jaspers is in the line of the classical thinkers of the
perennial philosophy and has striven to build up a system
in which the new and revolutionary insights of Kierkegaard
and Nietzsche have been used to supplement, synthesize and
re-write the contributions of the great classical
philosophers in a Kantian and broadly religious framework.
Marcel is a Catholic engaged in analysing the relations
between man and man in terms of the Christian concepts of
faith, hope and charity, and of fidelity, transcendence
and the all-enveloping mystery of Being. We may aptly
conclude, therefore, with the words in which O.F. Bollnow
characterizes the significance of this type of philosophy:

> Existentialism, viewed historically, is the
> beginning of a philosophy which places man, with
> his real tasks and problems, finally and uncondi-
> tionally, in the centre of philosophical thought.
> Systematically considered, existentialism is an
> enduring limb of philosophy, which keeps its
> entire body in a state of perpetual unrest by
> virtue of its polar relation with the whole. But
> existentialism can never become itself the whole
> of philosophy. There is no such thing as a pure
> existential philosophy.

It remains, therefore, to see how existential thinking
joins hands with, and itself exists in the medium of, an
intellectual concern that is deeper and more comprehensive.

Existentialism is something more, it must be repeated,
than a merely popular philosophy and deserves serious
attention, even though only as a part of a comprehensive
and constructive philosophical endeavour. In the writings
of Martin Heidegger, Jean-Paul Sartre and Merleau-Ponty,
it has been developed on the firm basis of a sober philosophical discipline like Phenomenology. In the process,
Phenomenology itself is being creatively developed in
directions hardly envisaged by its founder, Edmund
Husserl. At the hands of men like John Wild in the United
States and Paul Ricoeur in France, not to speak of a host
of less known thinkers, a new branch of this discipline is
emerging under the name of Existential Phenomenology. It
is impossible for any student of Existentialism to make
headway in the study of existential classics such as *Being
and Time, Being and Nothingness* and Merleau-Ponty's
Phenomenology of Perception without a sympathetic understanding of the aims, method and terminology of Phenomenology. It is hardly possible to give, within the short
space at my disposal, even a rough idea of what Phenomenology is and how it has developed since it was launched
as a new, serious philosophical discipline with the publication of Husserl's *Logical Investigations* in 1900-1901.
Suffice it to say that, like analytical philosophy in the
English speaking countries, Phenomenology has provided on
the Continent during the past few decades not merely a
school or trend in philosophy but also the language, the
medium, in which philosophizing has been carried on there
and is now radiating to other parts of the world. Terms
and phrases like intentionality, intuition of essences,
consciousness, phenomenon; the eidetic, phenomenological
and transcendental reductions; the epoche, the bracketing
or suspension of belief common to the natural attitude,
transcendental field and transcendental experience;
constitution, subjectivity, the transcendental ego, the
Lebenswelt--all these constitute the everyday jargon of

the philosopher schooled in Phenomenology. And they are
used, it must be remembered, not in the service of
developing a system of speculative metaphysics in the
traditional manner but in the interests of what Husserl
called an as yet non-existent discipline which is both a
first philosophy and a radical empiricism. The approach
is descriptive and concrete, seeking to avoid presuppositions deriving from metaphysics or from scientific
knowledge and yet striving to get to the bed-rock of
experience. Its subject-matter is the Cartesian *cogito*,
but the *cogito* freed of its metaphysical accompaniments,
re-enforced by Kantian transcendentalism and avoiding the
pitfalls of both realism and idealism in the traditional
sense. Instead of enlarging further, however, I refer the
student of existential philosophy who wishes to inform
himself about Phenomenology to the excellent introductions
provided e.g. by Pierre Thevenaz in *What is Phenomenology?*
and by John Wild in his recent writings. The early works
of Sartre on Imagination and on the Emotions, his
Transcendence of the Ego, all directly in the line of
Phenomenological writings, can acquaint the reader with
this type of thought and prepare him for the study of his
magnum opus, *Being and Nothingness*, which bears the sub-
title "An Essay on Phenomenological Ontology". Heidegger's
Being and Time contains an introductory explanation of
Phenomenology as he himself interprets it, and the
"Preface" in Merleau-Ponty's *Phenomenology of Perception*
is devoted entirely to giving, in a few compressed pages,
an answer to the question, what is Phenomenology? The
serious student will be well-advised to grapple with the
texts themselves rather than spend his time reading
popular expositions, either of Phenomenology or of Existentialism. I may add here a word on the use of the term
"ontology" in Phenomenology and by existentialists
influenced by it. For the Phenomenologist, the phenomenon, that which appears or manifests itself, is all that

is, without a noumenon hidden behind it, of which it is the appearance, illusory or otherwise. The study of phenomena is, therefore, for him the study of what is, of Being and the time-hallowed Aristotelian name for such a study is Ontology. Husserl employs the term freely, though his concern is not so much with what he calls the "formal ontology" of traditional metaphysics but with the material or regional ontology of the different realms of being. Sartre only follows him in this, though in an original fashion. Heidegger even identifies all philosophy with ontology and remarks in this connexion that "ontology and phenomenology are not two distinct philosophical disciplines among others. These terms characterize philosophy itself with regard to its object and its way of treating that object." The whole of *Being and Time* is devoted to what Heidegger calls "fundamental ontology", i.e., to an investigation of the structure of man's being, as preparatory to the inquiry into the nature of Being itself. We see already how Existentialism, seriously studied, leads to Phenomenology and that in turn into the central realm of philosophy, from the Greeks down to the present day.

Another point to which I may refer briefly here is the religious or theological background of Existentialism. In the case of Kierkegaard we have already seen that his concern was primarily the religious one of defending the possibility and the necessity of Christian faith in a world which had suffered the breakdown of the Christian doctrine of Creation. His immediate impact was first felt in the field of contemporary dialectical theology, on Karl Barth and his school and only later on philosophers such as Karl Jaspers and Martin Heidegger. From the latter then Rudolph Bultmann derived the conceptual tools for carrying into effect his programme of demythologizing in New Testament interpretation. The fact that the Christian certainty of faith has become more and more problematic

since the first Copernican shock, and as proclaimed, e.g.
dramatically in Nietzsche's words about the death of god,
has been at the bottom of the recent crisis both in
theology and philosophy and must be regarded as one of the
roots of Existentialism. It represents, from this point
of view, the twentieth-century philosopher's response to
the crisis of faith and the loss of revealed certainties.
In the west, it was left to Biblical religion to answer
the basic questions about the nature and destiny of man
and about his status in the universe; it was in terms of
the Christian revelation that he was provided with the
understanding that he had of himself. As a result of the
gradual secularization that has been going on since the
Renaissance, philosophy, as founded by the Pre-Christian
Greeks, has come to occupy itself more and more with
matters which formerly fell within the scope of revealed
religion. The discerning student can observe this
happening from Descartes down to Hegel; Existentialism
represents only the final stage in the attempt to reappro-
priate philosophically, i.e., in secularized form and
without needing the warrant and the guarantee of religious
faith, insights into human nature which religious faith
had sustained so far. These insights it now seeks to
derive immanently, from within the depths of man's
subjectivity alone and from this perspective one can speak
of all existential thinking as being in its basic motiva-
tion religious, irrespective of whether the philosopher
concerned subscribes to any creed, whether he is theistic
or atheistic. In Gabriel Marcel, a professed Catholic,
the preoccupation with religious problems is, of course,
obvious. But even in his case most of this original
analysis of the human condition owes nothing to revealed
religion. As he himself admits, the revelation of Divine
Grace is something that philosophy "cannot demand or
presuppose or enhance nor, to say it outright,.can it even
comprehend it." At the most philosophy can prepare for

its acceptance and in turn its prior awareness may prepare
philosophy to unfold in a dimension which otherwise would
have remained closed to it.

Sartre's case may seem to contradict our thesis, for
he is an avowed atheist. His position is, and is meant to
be, utterly unacceptable to a theist of any complexion,
Christian or otherwise. But why is it then equally
unacceptable to the orthodox Marxist, as his controversies
with Marxist thinkers show? In the second place, Sartre's
consuming passion for human freedom is not merely the
contemplative passion of the philosopher for depicting
reality as he finds it. He writes, first and foremost,
"in the perspective of a possible change," and in this he
is a true follower of Marx, who was not content with
describing the world but thought that the time had come
when philosophers should take upon themselves the task of
changing it. Sartre wants primarily to change, through
his writings, philosophical and literary, man's conception
of himself as well as of the world in which he lives.
This makes him uncompromising and adopt extreme positions
and express thoughts calculated to shock and hurt, in
particular, the respectable upholders of the established
order. But his driving passion is nonetheless religious,
no less than Nietzsche's. He is neither a metaphysician
nor a theologian but he cannot be denied the title of a
man of good and great faith. No longer living in a world
for which the God of revelation has reality, nor having
any use for the constructed God of the philosopher, he yet
finds in man the profound need to achieve this fullness of
Being which he projects in the idea of God. As he remarks,

> God is dead, but man has not for all that become
> atheistic. Silence of the transcendent joined to
> the permanence of the need for religion in modern
> man--that is still the major thing, today as
> yesterday....God is silent and that I cannot
> deny.--Everything in myself calls for God and
> that I cannot forget....As a matter of fact, this
> experience can be found in one form or another in
> most contemporary authors: it is the torment in

> Jaspers, death in Malraux, destitution in
> Heidegger, the reprieved being in Kafka, the
> insane and futile labour of Sisyphus in Camus.

Sartre has renounced God and sets out from the postulate,
God does not exist. The only Absolute he recognizes is
Consciousness and all his piety is laid up in man's
ability to liberate himself by work, by the work which
consciousness performs upon itself and by the productive
work which changes the world, material and social.
Writing about Andre Gide, Sartre says,

> He *lived* his ideas, and one, above all--the death
> of God....The problem of God is a human problem
> which concerns the rapport between men. It is a
> total problem to which each man brings a solution
> by his entire life, and the solution which one
> brings to it reflects the attitude one has chosen
> towards other men and towards oneself. What Gide
> gives us that is most precious is his decision to
> live to the finish the agony and death of God.
> He could well have done what others did and
> gamble on his concepts, decide for faith or
> atheism at the age of twenty and hold to this for
> his entire life. Instead, he wanted to put his
> relationship with religion to the test and the
> living dialectic which led him to his final
> atheism is a journey which can be repeated after
> him, but not settled by concepts and notions....
> He allows us to avoid the traps into which he has
> fallen or to climb out of them as he did. Every
> truth, says Hegel, has become so....Gide is an
> irreplacable example because he chose to *become
> his truth*. Chosen in the abstract, at twenty,
> his atheism would have been false. Slowly
> earned, crowning the quest of half a century,
> this atheism becomes his concrete truth and our
> own. Starting from there, men of today are
> capable of becoming new truth.

All Sartre's writings, and his life, constitute a massive
thought-experiment, very much in the manner of Nietzsche,
to draw out the implications for man of the lived
postulate that God does not exist. Perhaps it still
remains to be realized how all the riches of the
religious consciousness can be drawn without loss into the
new image of man that Sartre, as much a pilgrim of the
Absolute as any one, is helping to fashion, into the new
truth that man can yet become.

Let us next take Jaspers and see how the religious
question stands in the background of his philosophizing
and even explicitly forms the content of much of his
thought. Jaspers, it was suggested earlier, is a
philosopher with a backward glance, summing up, like
Hegel, all that he finds worthwhile in the philosophy of
the past and seeking to develop a thought-structure in
which the insights of past thought, Western and Eastern,
find a place. The thinking of Kierkegaard and Nietzsche
are for him events which require a reformulation of the
philosophia perennis, a rewriting of the history of
philosophy in the world and a re-assessment of the
Christian claim to lay down the archetypal pattern of
religious thinking. He seeks in short to develop a
philosophy, in terms of what has already been thought,
which is synthetic and comprehensive, which incorporates
within itself *all* wisdom, religious, metaphysical or
critical, Greek, Medieval or Modern, Eastern or Western.
But what is very much more interesting, in the second
place, is the process of secularization, the transformation of religious and theological notions into
philosophical, to which reference was made earlier. This
amounts, in fact, to a transformation of philosophy itself
in such fashion that it takes up within itself matters of
ultimate concern which so far have been the preserve of
warring religions. We can find the same process at work
in the thinking of Heidegger, and in reverse in the
theological work of a Tillich or a Bonhoeffer. We may
describe this alternatively as the quest of a unity of
religions on the philosophical level, but a level on which
philosophy itself is transformed in its nature, no longer
remaining merely contemplative but becoming a challenge
and an invitation, an instrument of self-knowledge and
self-realization. Jaspers expresses this hope for
philosophy in these words:

> By the side of traditional church religions and
> in polar relation to them, philosophy will
> become, as in (pre-Christian) antiquity, a form
> in which men will discover their unconditioned
> earnestness, in stillness and without noise. In
> many countries of Europe today, a kind of
> thinking about a common conduct of life is
> developing under the name of existence philos-
> ophy, differing from each other even to the
> extent of mutual foreignness but perhaps
> springing up out of a related impulse. This
> philosophizing has been growing here since the
> later Schelling, decisively set in motion by
> Kierkegaard, stimulated by pragmatic thought,
> tested in time's exigency. It recognizes itself
> mirrored in the older philosophizing, which was
> ever existence philosophy, but which today knows
> itself as determined by destiny through the
> extremity of the utter breakdown of earlier laws
> and validities....Is existence philosophy mere
> dreaming and wild fancy? If this is dreaming, I
> dare to answer, then it is one of those dreams
> from which is born, from time immemorial, all
> that is human and which makes life worth living.

For Jaspers, philosophy itself is capable of taking over
the place of religion, not as mere theory but as inner
action and realization, for Transcendence speaks directly
to individual men in the shape of truth and of the freedom
which enables him to become himself. Not only does
Jaspers conceive philosophical thinking as a form of
praxis which, as he says, springs up from that depth of
life where eternity meets time. He also seeks to overcome
the traditional alternative of revealed faith or nihilism
by conceiving philosophy as something one can live by.
Faith is no longer restricted to religion but becomes an
integral part of philosophy itself. To the elucidation of
his conception of philosophical faith Jaspers has devoted
an entire book and another, more recently, in which he has
examined such faith in relation to revelation. Philosophical faith, for Jaspers, however, never hardens into a
creed or dogma, for it is not grounded in anything objective and finite in the world. Such faith is life out of
the Comprehensive, that being which is neither subject

alone nor only object but encompasses both; it is guidance
and fulfillment through the Comprehensive. It has its
source in the non-objectifiable Comprehensive and because
it is not tied to any finite thing that has been made into
an absolute, it is free. The religious problem thus not
only forms the background of Jaspers' Existentialism but
constitutes the very core of its subject matter.

In the case of Heidegger, too, the preoccupation with
the religious question and with theology cannot be
neglected if we wish to understand his thought in its true
import. Unfortunately, however, Heidegger has not himself
explicitly discussed in his writings the precise details
of the role which religious and theological thought has
played in shaping and motivating his philosophy, barring a
few hints. This has led to grave misunderstandings in
various quarters, which are being only gradually removed.
The question is complex and I can only offer here a few
comments suggesting the necessity of keeping this aspect
of his philosophy in view. It is well-known that
Heidegger received his earlier education at a Jesuit
seminary where he acquired a thorough knowledge of the
Catholic doctrine. It was during these years in the
gymnasium that he got to know Franz Brentano's work, *On
the Multiple Meanings of Being in Aristotle*. Referring to
this early theological education, Heidegger has remarked
that without this theological origin he would never have
arrived on the way to thinking, adding that it is our
origins that determine what we become in the future. It
is also well-known that in Thomistic theology, the
Aristotelian doctrine of Being is developed within a
Christian framework. Later, during the years Heidegger
spent at Marburg, he came into intimate contact with, and
stimulation through, Protestant theology. His *Being and
Time*, in fact, grew out of this fruitful contact, a
contact which was not without conflicts and tensions of
the most intense type. It has even been asserted that

Being and Time grew out of a lecture delivered at a
gathering of Marburg theologians. It is not so well-known
that during his pre-*Being and Time* years Heidegger gave
lectures and held seminars on religious subjects. Among
these may be mentioned a lecture course on "The philosophical foundations of Medieval mysticism," another
entitled, "Introduction to the phenomenology of religion,"
one on "Augustine and Neoplatonism," a colloquium on "The
theological foundations of Kant," a seminar on Scholasticism, not to speak of the Addresses and Seminars he has
held with theologians in recent years. Some of his older
pupils have written works on Plotinus and Meister Eckhart
and his own extensive preoccupation with Kierkegaard, with
Hoelderlin and with Nietzsche amounted largely to a
wrestling with religious issues. Evidence of all these
influences lies scattered not only in *Being and Time* but
also in his other writings. From Kierkegaard he took over
directly many of the topics discussed in *Being and Time*,
such as existence, anxiety, situation, resoluteness and
choice, death, authenticity, repetition, possibility,
anonymity, the "moment". Even the definition of
philosophy given there has reference to a concept derived
from theology. As Heidegger defines it, both at the
commencement of the inquiry and at the end, philosophy is
universal phenomenological ontology, taking its starting-
point from the hermeneutic of *Dasein* which, as an analytic
of existence, has made fast the guiding-line for all
philosophical inquiry at the point where it *arises* and to
which it *returns*. The term "hermeneutic" used here comes
originally from the theological field and refers to the
art of interpreting and explicating the meaning of the
Holy Book. Its scope was expanded by the theologian
Schleiermacher to include the theory and methodology of
interpretation in general and applied by Wilhelm Dilthey
in the field of the humane and historical studies.
Heidegger uses it in a still wider sense in *Being and Time*

to interpret and explicate the being of *Dasein*, i.e., to
man in the aspect of his openness to Being. Because of
the historicity inherent in *Dasein* and because of its
facticity, such intepretation, even though ontological,
takes on the character of hermeneutic. The sheer "that"
of man as *Dasein* finding himself in the midst of the
world, along with others, in the particularity of his
situation, constitutes man's facticity, his thrownness,
which affects and determines all his projects of understanding. The explication of the being of man or of his
existence requires, therefore, not mere conceptual
analysis but an analysis which is interpretive in character, as in the case of a historical or literary document.
As has been shown by Heidegger scholars recently, this
basic conception of the historicity and facticity of
Dasein was derived from Heidegger's study of the structure
of religious experience in early Christianity. Many other
concepts of *Being and Time* can be traced back to Biblical
or theological sources. About the central notion of
"care", for example, Heidegger explicitly admits, "The way
in which 'care' is viewed in the foregoing existential
analytic of *Dasein* is one which has grown upon the author
in connexion with his attempts to interpret the
Augustinian (i,e., Hellenic Christian) anthropology,
having regard to the basic principles reached in the
ontology of Aristotle." Even his most original conception, that of historicity and temporality, can be traced
back to the eschatological *kairos* of Christian life-
experience as expressed in the New Testament.

Instead of multiplying examples, let us for a moment
try to understand what Heidegger is seeking to accomplish
with his analysis of existence, and indeed in all his
philosophical work, and why religious experience and
theology have been of so much significance to it. *Being
and Time* is devoted to an analysis of human existence. It
is not an empirical or *existentiell* analysis but

existential or ontological, for it seeks to arrive at the
most general and formal structure of man's being which
would constitute the condition of the possibility of any
concrete, actual experience whatever--whether scientific
(to which Kant restricted his analysis in the First
Critique), historical or religious, whether cognitive or
affective. Such an analysis of the ultimate ground-
structure of human experience may in fact be said to be
the aim of all his writings. To the extent to which it
has succeeded, it should be possible to derive from it any
and every form of concrete, particular experience as its
specification and especially those aspects of human
experience which have been dealt with by the various
religions. It would thus be in a position to provide the
most basic, the most neutral and the most comprehensive
language in terms of which the life-experience embodied in
these religions can be expressed, in terms of which the
nature and destiny of man, his place in the world, his
ultimate hopes and aspirations can be described. This, of
course, opens out the prospect of a "unified language of
the religions," to use an expression common amongst
logical positivists. But it also opens out the prospect
of an eventual "secularization" of religion in the sense
of enabling the translation of every religious concept
into a philosophical one, without absorbing, like Hegel,
the facticity of religious experience completely into the
concept. This is no loss to religion in so far as it is
an integral part of human experience, an ineluctable
dimension of man's being and the source from which his
existence derives its ultimate meaningfulness. And it is
a distinct gain to philosophy, to any philosophy which is
careful to guard the purity of experience and which,
instead of willfully imposing its categories upon
experience and thus falsifying it, remains loyal to its
humble task of seeking the adequate and disciplined word
which can depict and chart out, unveil and evoke the truth

of experience, without giving up its prerogative of ceaseless questioning and its basic stance of openness and
inquiry. The piety of thought lies in questioning,
Heidegger says; such asking may be folly in the eyes of
faith but it is in this folly that the essence of
philosophy lies. For it is only thus that philosophy,
like poetry in a different way, enlarges the area of the
communicable and brings men of diverse persuasions nearer
together. That in this process, philosophy transforms its
own nature, as suggested earlier, and itself takes on
something of the sacredness of the religious quest is no
mean gain for it.

I should like, in what follows, to say a few words
more about existentialism in general and how each of the
above mentioned existential philosophers is more than a
mere existentialist. This will also give an idea of the
kind and extent of philosophical knowledge presupposed in
the serious study of any of these. Phenomenology and
Christian religious doctrines have already been mentioned.
For the study of Sartre, a knowledge of Hegel is an
inescapable additional presupposition, for it is on
Hegel's *Phenomenology of Mind* and his *Logic* that Sartre's
dialectical theory of consciousness and his ontology are
based, as also his theory of interpersonal relations.
Marx is there always in the background and in the later
Sartre very much in the forefront. As the author of a
Critique of Dialectical Reason, not to mention the
contribution to thought made in his strictly literary
writing, Sartre is more than just an existentialist. For
Jaspers and Heidegger, close familiarity with the entire
range of European philosophy is essential, in particular
with Kant. The general framework of Jaspers' thinking is
Kantian and the grand synthesis of the thought of the
great philosophers of the past that he attempts is
effected within this framework. His delimitation of
knowledge, objective and universally valid, to the field

of science, his conception of Transcendence and his
condemnation of absolutizing and objectifying what we
learn in other fields are well-known Kantian themes. For
him Kant is *the* philosopher, a very prototype of this
calling. Kierkegaard and Nietzsche contribute powerfully
to his thought and provide the immediate challenge to his
work of synthesis, in which, of course, all the great
figures come in one by one. For Jaspers, author of a
three-volume work, *Philosophy*, of an enormous volume on
Philosophical Logic entitled *On Truth*, and of an equally
bulky first volume of a history of world philosophy, not
to speak of numerous monographs on individual philosophers, existence philosophy is identical with philosophy
or metaphysics itself. In addition, there is his work on
Psychopathology, with which he made his intellectual
start, and his *Psychology of World Views* in which his own
philosophy germinated. And during recent years he has
written extensively on matters which are of topical
urgency, like Bertrand Russell, and applied his wisdom to
matters which are relatively of the moment. This is true,
in even greater measure, of Sartre.

In the case of Heidegger, it is even more emphatically
true that he is more than an existentialist philosopher.
His *Being and Time*, which alone is concerned with
existence, is only a propaedeutic to the only question
that moves Heidegger: the question of Being. It does not
even aim at providing a comprehensive ontology of man and
analysis of existence but only so much as is essential for
the pursuit of the question of Being. In his other
writings it is not only ignored but explicitly disavowed
as the sole or proper task of the philosopher. In
reopening the question of the sense of Being, Heidegger is
led to a searching examination of the whole body of
Western metaphysics, emphasis being mainly laid on the
Greek founders, from the Pre-Socratics to Aristotle, on
the heralds of the modern age, Descartes, Leibniz, Kant

and Hegel and on Nietzsche, standing at the end of one whole era and proclaiming that end, in agony and joy, as the result of life-long wrestling with the attempt to comprehend the inner metaphysical foundation and destiny of the western intellectual tradition. No one without a thorough and imaginative grasp of this history can even begin to understand "the more than existentialist" in Heidegger.

In a sense these existentialist thinkers are antimetaphysical, but in another sense they provide us with a profounder glimpse into the realm of the invisible, opening new perspectives and dimensions of experience and bringing them within the scope of philosophical reflection. Each of them carries us in his own unique way, beyond the preoccupation with man, into realms largely untrodden hitherto and in ways of thinking which are novel yet undisciplined and on which we may safely wander, in delight and unexpected gain--Sartre to a comprehensive philosophy of freedom, Jaspers to Periechontology, Heidegger to a new conception of Being. If this is found of some relevance to the task of constructive philosophizing in this country and in building on the traditions which are inescapably ours, the serious study of this type of thought will have served its proper purpose in the context of the present state of philosophy here.

THE EXISTENTIALISM OF JEAN-PAUL SARTRE

As a philosopher and man of letters, Jean-Paul Sartre is "with those who want to change both man's social condition and the conception which he has of himself." Even though he takes as his point of departure the Phenomenology of Edmund Husserl and is deeply indebted to the analyses of existence in Heidegger's *Being and Time*, he is very far from viewing it as the task of philosophy merely to disclose, intuit and contemplate what is as such already given in an implicit manner. The driving power behind all his work, philosophical no less than literary, is freedom, and action born of freedom and in the service of freedom. His writings are stations on the way to this sole quest and if his reader is not to miss the continuity and unity of his thought, he must not overlook the itinerary for the destination, as Sartre warns.

Sartre's earliest philosophical works exhibit a marked preoccupation with the method and doctrines of Phenomenology. In them Sartre seeks not only to apply the phenomenological method to an investigation of such mental functions as Imagination[1] and Emotion,[2] as ways in which man relates himself to his world, but also subjects Husserl's phenomenology to searching criticism.[3] In doing so he at the same time foreshadows some of his later concerns, thus giving indications of the process by which

---

Lecture given at the University of Delhi in 1966, published under the title "Existential Philosophy: Jean-Paul Sartre" in *Proceedings of the All-India Seminar* (3), Centre of Advanced Study in Philosophy, Banaras Hindu University, 1967, pp. 119-133.

Phenomenology became transformed, in his major work[4], into a phenomenological Ontology of human existence. The descriptive phenomenology of the work on imagination, the imaginary and the emotions is not merely of psychological interest but is of considerable relevance to the basic philosophical issues about the nature of consciousness, its nihilating power, its freedom, its possible surrender to the "magic" of the emotions and its capacity to refuse being enmeshed in the world of causality. It is, however, in *The Transcendence of the Ego* that we find Sartre putting forward, in critical modification of a central doctrine of Husserl's, his own remarkable theory of consciousness, a theory which he later uses as the foundation of his own philosophical system in *Being and Nothingness*. This essay may indeed be characterized as pivotal in the making of Sartre's whole philosophy, for it is here that he achieves, through a radicalization of the Husserlian "reduction" and of the Cartesian *cogito*, what he calls "the liberation of the transcendental field and at the same time its purification." The second stage in Sartre's philosophical development is represented by *Being and Nothingness*, which goes on to exhibit, at great length, the structure of man's involvement in the world and the complex dialectic of the relationship between his own free subjectivity and all forms of objective being, including the empirical ego as well as other people and things. In these philosophical works and in his novels, plays, biographical and literary essays, Sartre has attempted to explore human subjectivity to its limit, depicting man's consciousness as free and yet captive in the world, endangered by the world of meanings it builds up and yet capable of winning its liberation in the midst of it. His latest philosophical work,[5] voluminous and as yet incomplete, seeks to explore the objective aspect of human reality to its limit in the hope of an ultimate synthesis of the two sides. Here Sartre investigates

man's social, collective and historical existence with a
view to building up an historical, philosophical
anthropology which can incorporate into itself both the
insights of existentialism into human subjectivity as well
as the objective, historical approach of a reformed
Marxist philosophy.

In *The Transcendence of the Ego*, Sartre wholeheartedly
accepts Husserl's notion of the intentionality of consciousness but proposes a more radical phenomenological
reduction than Husserl carried through. In Husserl, only
the psychological Ego fell before the *epoche*, while a
transcendental I was retained within consciousness as a
principle of unification, constitution and meaning.
Sartre points out that since in phenomenology consciousness is defined by its intentionality, it can by itself do
everything for which Husserl requires a transcendental
ego. The role of such an I within consciousness is not
only superfluous but is actually incompatible with the
phenomenological conception of consciousness as intentional. In addition, Sartre claims, such an *I* is even
"harmful", a "hindrance" to the pure lucidity of consciousness, an opaque blade within consciousness which
would divide and destroy it. "The transcendental *I* is the
death of consciousness." Even such an *I* is an object *for*
consciousness and must, therefore, fall before the stroke
of phenomenological reduction and go over to the side of
the world. With the rejection of this last vestige of
"opacity" from consciousness, the latter becomes completely pure, emptied of all content, sheer translucency.
Consciousness, though always consciousness *of* an object
transcendent to it, is at the same time immediate
consciousness of itself and requires no act of reflection
to be aware of itself. Its very existence is hence
absolute. Unreflective self-awareness is the very mode of
being of consciousness and it is such non-positional,
non-thetic consciousness or the prereflexive *cogito*, as

Sartre later called it, that renders possible the positional or reflexive consciousness in which consciousness
becomes an object to itself. Pure unreflected consciousness is for Sartre a non-substantial absolute, a "phenomenon" in the special sense in which "to be" and "to
appear" are one. It is, further, an impersonal spontaneity which "determines its existence at each moment"
and is thus pure freedom. Pure consciousness is existence
and prior to essence since all essences are "intentions"
or projects of consciousness. The Cartesian *cogito* is
reflective consciousness and it is on this reflective
level that the Ego really appears. The subject and the
object, the *me* and the world are both "objects for absolute, impersonal consciousness, and it is by virtue of
this consciousness that they are connected." Why then
does the ego arise at all? Its essential function, Sartre
suggests, is not so much theoretical as practical:
"Perhaps the essential role of the ego is to mask from
consciousness its very spontaneity...as if consciousness
hypnotized itself before this ego which it has constituted, absorbing itself in the ego as if to make the ego
its guardian and its law."

In the course of developing his conception of transcendental consciousness as impersonal spontaneity, Sartre
points out that this "monstrous" freedom is something more
fundamental than the freedom of the will, for the will
itself "is an object which constitutes itself for and by
this spontaneity" and presupposes it as its ground. What
Sartre calls "existence" is identical with this transcendental consciousness, is itself nothing else than pure
spontaneity, pure freedom, the utterly lucid principle of
subjectivity which confronts and goes out towards all that
is objective, "thingly" in character, "constitutes" it and
gives it meaning. Because this pure spontaneity or
freedom lies deeper than the *I*, it can happen that it
suddenly manifests itself on the reflective, empirical

level and overwhelms the ego. Then consciousness is overtaken by its own vertiginous freedom, and becomes anguished. According to Sartre, this fear of itself is constitutive of pure consciousness; it is an anxiety, he says, "which is imposed on us and which we cannot avoid: it is both pure event of transcendental origin and an ever possible accident of our daily life." This view of consciousness as anguished before its own freedom explains why we ever come to move away from what Husserl calls "the natural attitude" and perform the phenomenological reduction, thus rising up to the transcendental level of reflection. In the phenomenology of Husserl, Sartre says, the *epoche* appears as a miracle. But if the "natural attitude" is itself understood as the consequence of "an effort made by consciousness to escape from itself by projecting itself into the *me* and becoming absorbed there and if this effort is never completely rewarded, and if a simple act of reflection suffices in order for conscious spontaneity to tear itself abruptly away from the *I* and be given as independent, then the *epoche* is no longer a miracle, an intellectual method, an erudite procedure. Unfortunately, Sartre has not developed these ideas further nor clarified the deeper philosophical issues involved here. May it not be that this second, mediated movement away from projection and absorption into the *me* and the world occurs, as it must, in the full lucidity of consciousness, the latter is experienced as the pure freedom that it is but no longer as essentially anguished. For a consciousness that comes home to itself and its freedom, fear of itself cannot be constitutive.

It should be borne in mind that in this essay and in *Being and Nothingness*, Sartre writes from a point of view which is phenomenological rather than metaphysical. The consciousness of which he speaks is not consciousness in general but this or that particular consciousness, a spontaneity which is impersonal and yet *individuated*, and

which as pure intention is always in the midst of the
world. Sartre liberates and purifies the "Transcendental
Field" by emptying it of everything that can be an object
to it (the ego, "all physical, psychophysical, and psychic
objects, all truths, all values") and shows this absolute
consciousness to be "quite simply a first condition and an
absolute source of existence." But he does this in order
to pass on to his main task, viz., the return to the
world, to "the level of humanity" at which the *I* has
already appeared and man "plunged back" into the world.
It is on this level that *Being and Nothingness* deals with
the human reality, analyses man's concrete experience as
moulded by the dialectic of his relations with himself,
with others, and with things. Transcendental
phenomenology is now transformed into a phenomenology of
human existence.

In *Being and Nothingness*, Sartre goes on to develop a
"phenomenological ontology" on the basis of the theory of
impersonal, non-substantial and prereflective consciousness given in the earlier essay. Since every thing is
exterior to pure consciousness, consciousness itself is in
a sense *nothing*, as Sartre said there. In the later work,
this conception of consciousness as something negative and
negating, barely hinted at in earlier writings, emerges
fully developed and plays the central role in Sartre's
dialectic of experience. Consciousness is pure transparency, spontaneity and intentionality; but it is also
pure negativity, not only itself a nothing but an essentially nihilating presence. This is the first of the two
regions or modes of being in Sartre's ontology and is
designated as "being-for-itself." The second is the
region of "being-in-itself," the sphere of pure
positivity, sheer thinghood, opaque and self-identical,
encompassing the entire realm of the mental, the bodily
and the physical, with which consciousness ever stands
confronted and in dialectical relation with which it

ceaselessly wrestles. Like Heidegger, Sartre also
criticizes Husserl for not inquiring into the mode of
being of consciousness: his own answer to this question
is, as mentioned above, that consciousness *is* as
transparency, spontaneity, negativity, as for-itself. But
in *Being and Nothingness*, the nihilating character of
consciousness looms so large that Sartre identifies
consciousness (i.e., existence) with Nothingness, as
opposed to the in-itself which is then simply designated
as Being. Sartre rejects both realism and idealism. Consciousness, the for-itself, and what it is consciousness
of, the in-itself, together constitute a structure in
which neither of the two can be reduced to the other.
They are bound together by the internal relation of
negation: "the for-itself constitutes itself outside the
in-itself as negation of the latter."

Being-in-itself is the intentional object of
consciousness and is transcendent to it. It is sheer
objectivity, opaque and massive. The principles of
Identity and Noncontradiction apply to it. "Being is,
being is in itself, being is what it is," as Sartre puts
it. It has no becoming, is untouched by otherness, is
non-temporal. It has neither possibility nor necessity
but simply *is* and thus utterly contingent. It is that
which consciousness itself is not but of which
consciousness is a revealing intuition as the other than
itself. Being-for-itself is the very opposite of all
this. For Sartre the basic "Ontological Difference" is
not the difference between Being and beings, as with
Heidegger, but the difference between consciousness and
being (i.e., the in-itself), between existence, as the
pure spontaneity of consciousness, and essence, which,
though projected by existence, threatens to enslave it and
congeal it into a thing. Echoing Heidegger, Sartre says
that consciousness is a being which in its being questions
its own being and it does so, he adds, because that being

implies a being other than itself, i.e., the object *of* which there is consciousness. Such questioning presupposes negativity, an implicit comprehension of non-being and itself a manifestation of the nihilating character of consciousness. Non-being, the "other" to the positivity of being thus lies like a worm coiled in the heart of being, like a hole or fissure in being, a haunting presence in us and outside of us, in Sartre's picturesque language. It is because consciousness is essentially nihilating, a "decompressing" of the in-itself, and able to "secrete a non-being which isolates it," that it can disengage itself from the in-itself and manifest itself as freedom.

Consciousness is self-nihilating, perpetually escaping the causality of the past and spontaneously going out towards and intending a world. It is wholly "project" of the *world*, however, and its freedom is always "situated", i.e., freedom relative to a situation and *in* a situation. The freedom of consciousness, further, is a project of freeing, an unending task for consciousness, not something that *is* already there, once and for all. This abyss of freedom, anchored to nothing, is revealed in moments of anguish in relation to our past or future possibilities, in moments when we are forced to assume responsibility for choosing one way or the other. Unable to bear this anguish and this freedom of which it is an index, we take recourse to various strategies of escape: flight into the "spirit of seriousness" (i.e., seeking reasons for action in the nature of things or in the values supposedly "attached" to them), belief in psychological determinism, projecting the freedom of consciousness on the ego, conceived as the agent of actions, and, finally, "bad faith," a kind of self-deception by which we dissociate ourselves from our own mental states. We live mostly in bad faith, trying not to be what we are. Sartre goes even so far as to assert that to realize absolute sincerity

towards oneself, to be what one is, is an impossible task,
for this would be to abrogate the negativity of the
for-itself and to convert consciousness into an in-itself.

Consciousness is not what it is and it is what it is
not, as Sartre paradoxically formulates the inherent negativity of Consciousness, in contrast with the in-itself,
which is what it is, which wholly *is*. Consciousness, as a
pure spontaneity, can never be turned into an in-itself,
into a self-identical block of being. It is always ahead
of itself, escaping itself; positing its own unity, it
constantly evades identity. Consciousness is merely
present to itself as not being itself. The law of being
of the for-itself, Sartre says, is to be itself in the
form of presence to itself. Such presence implies not
being itself and "supposes that an impalpable fissure has
slipped into being," but it is a fissure which is wholly
negative, for consciousness as presence to itself is
separated by itself, *by no thing*. The principles of
Identity and Non-contradiction do not obviously apply to
the peculiar mode of being of the for-itself. But
consciousness has also in "something of which it is not
the foundation--its presence in the world" and to the
sheer contingency of the in-itself. Free to give meaning
to its situation, consciousness cannot create it and
cannot, therefore, give a foundation to itself. In
addition, since it is always possible that a particular
for-itself as such could also not be, it shares all the
contingency of the in-itself. This is what Sartre calls
the facticity of consciousness; consciousness is both
consciousness of its own nihilating freedom as well as of
its facticity and "complete gratuity." Because of his
practical concern with the destiny of "the human reality"
in the world of things, Sartre philosophizes on what we
may call the level of the Sāmkhya, a level on which the
plurality of consciousness and their several possibilities
of being enslaved and liberated are all real. Sartre is

not interested in the analysis of concepts nor is he
concerned primarily with the question of ultimate reality.
Hence it may be confusing and perhaps not quite legitimate
if criteria belonging to the level of the Vedānta are
applied to his thought.

The for-itself posits itself as not being the
in-itself and thus there arises its internal relation with
the in-itself which the for-itself experiences as a lack.
Being-for-itself is awareness of a lack of being, of the
concrete plenitude of the in-itself; consciousness hence
is a perpetual striving to make good this lack by
achieving a totality of being-for-itself-in-itself. The
attainment of such an ideal value is clearly impossible
and yet this ideal haunts human consciousness in the form
of the concept of God. In straining after this mode of
being, in appropriating into itself the positivity of the
in-itself, consciousness projects values, through his acts
of choice, and pursues them as his goals. Such pursuit of
values, according to Sartre, is both a necessity for man
and yet a task impossible of achievement. Consciousness,
further, is always projected toward its particular
possibilities, transcends itself toward them, and is hence
necessarily involved in the structure of temporality. In
this structure, the past, as *my* past, is not sheer nothing
but stands to my present in the relation of an in-itself
to which I may go on giving fresh meaning but which I am
powerless to change. The present is the presence of
consciousness to the in-itself and, as perpetually
vanishing, it is a perpetual flight before the in-itself.
The future is that towards which consciousness, as not
being what it is, projects itself in a vain effort to
complete its own lack. "The future is the ideal point
where the sudden infinite compassion of facticity (past),
of the for-itself (present), and of its possible (a
particular future) will at last cause the *Self* to arise as
the existence in-itself of the for-itself." This is an

impossibility and the for-itself keeps pressing on towards
the future as pure project; what is realized slips back
into the past as an in-itself and consciousness moves on
as something always *to be*. Inasmuch as consciousness
assumes its past as *its* past, is present as a lack to an
in-itself and is of the nature of a project, always ahead
of itself, temporality constitutes, in the unity of its
structure, the very mode of being of consciousness: its
perpetual escape from being sucked in by the in-itself as
well as its ceaseless striving to incorporate the in-
itself within itself as for-itself. The in-itself simply
is and has neither a past, nor a future, nor a present.

Sartre, as mentioned earlier, philosophizes on the
level of concrete experience. On this level there is not
only a plurality of consciousness but each consciousness
is at the same time a being for-itself as well as for-
others and is aware of itself in the constant dialectical
interplay of the I and the other. Sartre gives credit to
Hegel and to Husserl for the importance they attached to
the phenomenon of subjectivity but criticizes them both
for treating the relation between two consciousnesses as
one of knowing rather than of being. We have "knowledge"
of objects, of the in-itself, not of our own subjectivity
which is immediately and pre-reflexively apprehended. The
other as proved or known can only be another object.
Heidegger saw that this relation is not one of a knowing
subject to a known object but a relation between being and
being. But according to Sartre, by characterizing this
relation as that of being-with, Heidegger has failed to
provide a real bridge between me and the other or to how I
encounter the other and enter into concrete relation with
him. What is needed here is, in Sartre's words, that "In
my inmost depths I must find not *reasons for believing*
that the other exists but the other himself as not being
me," the other not as an object but as another for-itself.
Such a revelation of the other occurs when I am looked at

by another who, by this very act, constitutes himself as a
subject against me and makes me aware of myself as being
an object for another. Feelings like shame -- when I am
caught by the other's glance -- show that as being-for-
myself, I am also for-others as centres of independent
subjectivity. Normally, I tend to regard the other as an
object in the sense of an autonomous centre of reference
within *my* world and "my relations with the other as object
are made up essentially of ruses intended to make him stay
an object." As a result of the "look" of the other,
however, I myself become objectified as an autonomous
centre of reference within *his* world and so feel compelled
to acknowledge the other as for-himself. The relation
between two consciousnesses is thus one of reciprocal
negation in which both affirm themselves as incompatible
absolutes. The dialectical relation between one-for-
itself and another, being based on the nihilating
character of each, is one of unresolved conflict, an
unending game of mirrors in which each is thrown back and
forth between being-for-himself and for-another. On the
plane of being, subjectivities "remain out of reach and
radically separated;" if at all some kind of harmony is to
be achieved, it can only be on the level of action, of a
common aim directed towards the accomplishment of tasks in
the world.

Sartre's philosophy is basically a philosophy of
action rather than of contemplation. The nihilating
tearing away of consciousness from the world is not a
flight into itself but only a moment in its engagement
with the world. Consciousness is wholly intention of the
world and wholly project; recovering its freedom, it
returns to the world with the intention of transforming
both the self and the world through its freely chosen
projects. Its freedom too is nothing else but pure
project or task, the task of *freeing* itself through
action. "To say that the for-itself has to be what it is,

to say that it is what it is not while not being what it
is, to say that in it existence precedes and conditions
essence...is to say one and the same thing, i.e., that man
is free." Freedom is never a possession and never empiri-
cally given. It is transcendental and total, without any
limits except that man is not free to cease being free.
Anguish in the face of such freedom may make me try to
hide it from myself by incorporating the in-itself as the
true mode of being of my consciousness but even such
escape is of my own choosing. As a nihilating power,
consciousness tears itself away from its past and,
projecting itself into goals in the future, returns to
itself in the present, the moment of presence and freedom.
Sartre rejects all forms of determinism, including the
whole psychology of passions, pushes and pulls, conscious
or unconscious. As against Freudian psychoanalysis, which
explains my present behaviour and attitudes as being
determined by my childhood experiences and the causality
of unconscious forces within me, Sartre sees in the
pattern of an individual's life the working out of a
"fundamental project" freely adopted at an early age. In
Being and Nothingness Sartre outlines a method, which he
calls existential psychoanalysis, by which we may decipher
and interpret the observable behaviour patterns of a man
in terms of the fundamental project and the categories of
being, doing, making and having. In his biographical
studies of Baudelaire and Genêt, Sartre has demonstrated
how much this approach can contribute to our understanding
of man. Our fundamental projects are ordinarily not
objectively "known" to us because we *are* that, but in so
far as we achieve reflective awareness of them in moments
of anguished crisis, we are even free to abandon it for a
new one. I may cause that "liberating instant" to arise
in which I escape the former project by relegating it into
the past as an in-itself and take up a new one, thus
bringing about a total conversion in myself. "The

extraordinary and marvellous instant", says Sartre, "when
the prior project collapses into the past in the light of
a new project which rises on its ruins and which as yet
exists only in outline...these have often appeared to fur-
nish the clearest and most moving image of our freedom."

Sartrian freedom is absolute but it is the freedom of
man abandoned in the world, freedom in the midst of
facticity. Our freedom meets obstacles all round: the
resistance of things, the particular place I happen to
occupy, the particular past that I happen to have, the
things or tools that I find around me, the presence of
others--each with his own freedom--and, finally, death.
Each of these except the last constitutes an internal
limit or condition of freedom, just as the in-itself is
the necessary correlate or object of consciousness. They
provide the medium in which freedom operates, *for* which it
can be freedom. Whether anything presents itself to me as
an obstacle or not depends, in fact, upon the ends I
choose and hence freedom is presupposed in the experience
of anything as an obstacle. My situation, far from being
an external limit to my freedom, is defined as an obstacle
by my freedom itself. There is no freedom outside of a
situation and no situation except to a consciousness free
to give it a meaning and make it his own. Death alone,
depriving me of all possibility of choice, is utterly
absurd and falls completely *outside* of my life, my
consciousness and my freedom. It is the radically
external limit to my freedom and in no way affects its
absoluteness so long as I am alive. Sartre's doctrine of
the freedom of the for-itself, condemned to choose its
projects and to structure the world, to make itself and to
create values by its acts of choice, has a far-reaching
ethical consequence. It places overwhelming moral
responsibility on man, a responsibility which is no less
absolute than his freedom. "I carry the weight of the
world by myself alone without anything or any person being

able to lighten it," for it is I and nothing foreign that has decided what I have made of myself and of my world.

Sartre's ontology recognizes, as we have seen, being-for-itself and being-in-itself, pure consciousness on the one hand and all objectivity on the other, as together encompassing the entire realm of being. A theory of pure consciousness as the absolute of existence, as pure creativity and sheer negativity, leaves no room for either pre-given essences or God in the ordinary sense. Since consciousness is utterly void of any content, no hint can be found in it of any other reality transcending it and constituting its foundation; nor is anything more basic required or indeed even conceivable. God, as Nietzsche said, is dead. And yet, as an absence he subsists, Sartre holds, integrally in our humanity as the "intention" of man, as the ideal value of a for-itself which is at the same time in-itself. "The ideal of a consciousness which would be the foundation of its own being-in-itself by the pure consciousness which it would have of itself" corresponds to the notion of God as *ens causa sui* and the realization of this ideal, Sartre says, is man's fundamental project. Man is fundamentally the desire to be God, an ideal value forever drawing him on and forever incapable of being realized. Sartre's philosophy is a humanism, a philosophy for which there is only man in his world. But by anchoring his humanism to the conception of a pure consciousness, Sartre achieves a breakthrough into a dimension which is far removed from a crude "atheism" as well as from the type of subjectivistic humanism so sharply condemned by Heidegger.

In all his writings, Sartre's sole quest is for the truth of man. But he has gone to school with Hegel and realized that all truth is truth that has become so and that it is a whole, though not as Hegel believed a whole that could be conceptually possessed at any point of time. The foundations of this truth lie in the dimension of human subjectivity examined in the earlier phases of his writings. But man's subjectivity is only one moment in the whole; it is immersed in society and its group structures, in the whole fabric of culture and history. Man fashions these through his work but he is himself fashioned by the way he responds to them and understands them. It is towards the articulation of such a total truth about man, synthesizing the subjective and the objective moments, that Sartre addresses himself in his most recent works. In *Saint Genêt*,[6] which may be regarded as marking the transition from his earlier to his later Marxist phase, we already find the original scope of ideas widened, so that the story of this poet-dramatist's liberation is told not only in terms of "existential psychoanalysis" and the other categories of *Being and Nothingness* but also takes into account the dialectical interplay between the individual and the groups, institutions, and class to which he belongs. In *The Search for a Method*, we finally see the emergence of a total framework, a kind of a philosophical macro-anthropology in which the investigation of individual subjectivity becomes one element in a larger whole comprising the entire sphere of work and culture, the life of the group and the movement of history. The one question with which Sartre is concerned in this work is "whether we have the means today to constitute a structural, historical anthropology," a comprehensive science of man in which the insights of both Existentialism and historical materialism can be reconciled and synthesized. Sartre believes that the most comprehensive framework or "totalization" as he calls it, within which we can think of man today is Marxism, but a Marxism purged of its present-day dogmatism, its mechanistic determinism and "dialectic of nature" and incorporating within it the human dimension of freedom and creativity.

The most ample philosophical "totalization" to have
been given in the recent past was Hegelianism and its
great merit was to have recognized the dialectical
relationship between knowing and being and nature of truth
as perpetually in process as History. But as Kierkegaard
saw, the rationalism of Hegel assimilates the *existing*
man, his unique subjectivity and lived experience, into a
system of ideas. Pure subjectivity can never be made the
object of knowledge and it was the merit of Kierkegaard to
have pointed out, "against Hegel and thanks to him," this
incommensurability of the real and knowledge. But while
Kierkegaard contents himself with an empty subjectivity,
Hegel reaches forward through his concepts to the
"veritable concrete," ever enriched by the constant
process of mediation, to the concrete man in his objective
reality. Marx agrees with Kierkegaard in asserting the
irreducibility of human existence to an idea and with
Hegel in his concern for the concrete objectification or
externalization of man in the world. But he reproaches
Hegel, quite correctly according to Sartre, for not taking
notice of the fact that self-externalization in the world
does not simply remain there as something to be contem-
plated as the product of man's creativity but results in
an alienation between man and his products so that his
externalization turns back against man and enslaves him.
For liberation from such alienation what is required is
not the work of the concept but "*material* work and
revolutionary *praxis*" which can bring about an objective
change in the world and enable man to live in greater
harmony with himself and with nature. Marxism thus
constitutes for Sartre a synthesis of the living truth in
Hegel and Kierkegaard and in that sense it remains "the
philosophy of our time," beyond which it is impossible to
go. Present-day Marxism, however, does not any longer
have the openness and the heuristic approach which are
essential to any living philosophy and hence Sartre
subjects it to trenchant criticism.

According to him, even original Marxism needs a more adequate theory of knowledge than Marx or Lenin have been able to provide. It will not do either to eliminate subjectivity altogether or to reduce consciousness to a simple reflection of the objective order. "Subjectivity," Sartre points out, "is neither everything nor nothing. It represents a moment in the objective process (that in which externality is internalized) and this moment is perpetually eliminated only to be perpetually reborn." In this process, both the internalization of the external and the externalization of the internal are necessary. Subjectivity or consciousness, as pure spontaneity and revealing negativity, represents the moment of freedom and *praxis*, the passage from objectivity to objectivity through internalization and choice of a personal project. This subjective or existential moment is one of immediate awareness or "comprehension," not of objective knowledge, which always presupposes it. Marxism as a system of knowledge must incorporate into itself, as its very core and foundation, this existential awareness, Sartre insists. So long as it does not provide an existential foundation for its anthropology by re-integrating man into it and by re-integrating "comprehension" into knowledge as its non-theoretical foundation, existential philosophy will continue to go its own separate way and attempt the task of constructing a philosophical anthropology in which the human reality is not forgotten. But, Sartre adds, "from the day that Marxist thought will have taken on the human dimension (i.e., the existential project) as the foundation of anthropological knowledge, existentialism will no longer have any reason for being. Absorbed, surpassed and conserved by the totalizing movement of philosophy, it will cease to be a particular inquiry and will become the foundation of all inquiry." It is not possible to attempt here anything beyond this bare hint at the direction Sartre's thought has taken in recent years.

The *Critique de la Raison Dialectique*, of which *The Problem of Method* forms only the Introduction, has not yet been translated into English, though expositions which are already available[7] give some idea of the depth, range and originality of this difficult work.

NOTES

1. *L'Imagination*, 1936; *L'Imaginaire*, 1940 (*The Psychology of Imagination*, 1949).

2. *Esquisse d'une Théorie des Emotions*, 1939 (*Outline of a Theory of the Emotions*, 1948).

3. *La Transcendance de l'Ego*, 1936-37 (*The Transcendence of the Ego*, 1957).

4. *L'Etre et le Néant*, 1943 (*Being and Nothingness*, 1956).

5. *Critique de la raison dialectique*, *I*, 1960; serving as Introduction in this work is the essay entitled, *Question de Method* (*Search for a Method*, 1963).

6. *Saint-Genêt: Comedien et Martyr*, 1952 (*Saint Genêt*, 1963).

7. Laing, R.D. and Cooper, D.G.: *Reason and Violence* (1964); Odajnyk, Walter: *Marxism and Existentialism* (1965); Desan, Wilfred: *The Marxism of Jean-Paul Sartre* (1965); Cumming, R.D.: *The Philosophy of Jean-Paul Sartre* (1965), which also contains translated extracts from *The Critique of Dialectical Reason*.

THE CONCEPT OF PROGRESS

The ideas of self-fulfillment and freedom, as possible
ends of human worldly endeavour, have provided the dominant terms in which Western man has sought to understand
himself and his place and destiny in the world since the
Renaissance. In individual life and in the collectivity,
in social and economic spheres, in political affairs, in
the pursuit of scientific knowledge and in philosophical
thinking, these ideas have formed and sustained what we
call the modern world. Both these ideas, inter-linked and
mutually dependent, presuppose a new awareness of time,
not found in classical antiquity, and a changed relationship of man to time largely determined by the process of
secularization that has marked the shaping of the modern
mind. The first of these crystallized into the idea of
progress in the eighteenth century and is very much with
us still, despite vicissitudes in the way it has been
conceived and evaluated. The second has been a moving
force of incalculable power in human affairs and
reflection on it has constituted the core of modern
philosophical thinking about man and society.

Man's new awareness of time, oriented towards a wide
open future big with infinite possibilities of fulfillment, led to the rise of the historical consciousness and,
eventually, in the last two centuries to the recognition
of historicity as a basic dimension of human experience.
In this connection, names of thinkers such as Vico and
Herder, Hegel and Croce, Dilthey and Heidegger immediately
spring to mind. The conception of human history as moving

Originally published in *Indian Philosophical Annual* 3
(1967): 20-29.

towards a worthwhile and cherished goal, as against all
cyclic theories of history, is generally traced back to
the eschatological outlook of the Jewish Prophets and of
early Christianity. Referring to the secularization of
sacred history that occurred later, Karl Loewith has
pointed out that the attempt to understand the past and
the present in terms of a future *eschaton* is at the root
of belief in progress. As he remarks, "The future is the
true horizon of history....And while the West still
remains a Christian Occident, its historical awareness of
itself is also eschatological: from Isaiah to Marx, from
Augustine to Hegel, from Joachim to Schelling." This is
also true of historical practice. The English, French and
Russian Revolutions would never have happened without the
belief in progress, and there would have been no worldly
belief in progress without the original belief in an
other-worldly or supra-mundane goal of life. In the words
of Friedrich Schlegel, "the revolutionary desire to
realize the Kingdom of God is the buoyant point from which
springs all progressive culture and the origin of modern
history." Paul's Epistles to the Thessalonians constitute
a *locus classicus* of the Christian principle of hope, of
trustful waiting and working for a future that will save
and fulfill. In recent years, Ernst Bloch, the "Marxist
Schelling" of today and no Christian believer in the idea
of Providence, has offered a monumental version of a
secularized "Principle of Hope" as the foundation of a
complete philosophical system. The theory of lived time
as developed by Bergson, Husserl, and above all,
Heidegger, provides now an adequate ontological foundation
for a conception of history of which the true element is
seen to be in the future. History is meaningful only in
the perspective of future possibilities.

The idea of secular progress emerged as a fully
developed doctrine of humanity's triumphant march towards
Utopia in the writings of eighteenth-century French

scholars Turgot and Condorcet, who lived in the sunrise of
the modern scientific spirit and, inspired by its
confident optimism, saw the Golden Age "not behind us, but
before us" and almost round the corner. Turgot spoke of
the successive progressions of the human mind, in which
"the human race, considered from its beginnings, appears
to the eyes of a philosopher to be one immense whole that,
like every individual, has its infancy and its progress."
Following him, Condorcet wrote his famous *Sketch of a
Historical Survey of the Progressions of the Human Mind,*
aptly described as the canonical eighteenth-century French
text on the idea progress. For Condorcet, the cumulative
effect of scientific knowledge assures an irreversible but
indefinite advance to a condition in which men will be
ever healthier and happier, more developed in sensibility
and reason, more equal in wealth and opportunity, more
human and rational in their conduct. This Enlightenment
idea of inevitable and infinite progress in rationality
was supplemented and enlarged in the first half of the
nineteenth century and given a more determinate goal in
the writings of Saint-Simon and his followers and of
Auguste Comte. Man was seen to be more than abstract
reason and an honourable place was given to the activist
and emotional elements of his whole nature. Progress in
the Saint-Simonian view is linear and continuous and the
law of perfectibility is absolute. It is also organic, a
harmony of complex parts, not confined to rationality but
involving an actualization of all human capacities and
held together and animated by the power of love, expanding
and diffusing through humanity in an ever-widening circle.
The final, systematized formulation of the ideas of
perfectibility and progress was given by Auguste Comte,
with whom the religion of humanity became at the same time
the religion of progress. A disciple of Condorcet and a
great admirer of Catholicism for its principles of order
and organization, Comte elaborated and gave definitive

shape to the thoughts of the French school in his system of Positive philosophy. "The fundamental march of human development," as he presents it here, is governed by the supreme "law" of progressive evolution according to which humanity advances from the theological to the metaphysical stage and achieves adulthood in the final scientific or positive stage of Western civilization. No longer sharing Condorcet's "chimerical and absurd expectations," Comte pleads for promoting the triumph of positive philosophy by completing the vast operation begun by Bacon, Descartes and Galileo, thus "reconstructing the system of general ideas which must henceforth prevail amongst the human race." Believing firmly in man's natural goodness and rationality and focussing his attention on the socio-political aspect of collective humanity, he looked forward optimistically to the immediate future as one in which human society will be scientifically organized and wars "inevitably" eliminated.

For Hegel, history exhibits the progressive self-realization of the Spirit or reason through the dialectic of its successive incarnations in individual cultures. As the sovereign reality of the world, reason brings about, through its "cunning," the accomplishment of rational, universal purposes and, eventually, of the ultimate pur-pose, the justification of God in history and the realiza-tion of His Kingdom on earth. Secular history becomes identical with sacred. Marx seeks to go beyond Hegel in his concern with the task of truly realizing reason in the realm of material and human reality and therefore issues the call for a radical break with the traditional philos-ophy of pure contemplation and for a revolutionary trans-formation of the world through *praxis*. He sees the history of all hitherto existing society as the history of class-struggles, of conflict between the oppressor and the oppressed and of man's alienation from himself and his labour. In this struggle a messianic role is henceforth

assigned to the proletariat, which will redeem and transform the world, once it has been made conscious of itself
and has become organized and politically active, and usher
in a period in which the "realm of freedom" will be
realized on earth. Marx is inspired by an eschatological
faith and his historical materialism is, as Loewith
remarks, "essentially, though secretly, a history of fulfillment and salvation in terms of social economy." In
the writings of the Jesuit paleontologist Pierre Teilhard
de Chardin we find a recent expression of this trust in a
religion of science, in which the positivist belief in
progress, the Bergsonian doctrine of Creative Evolution,
and the Pauline expectation of the coming of the Kingdom
of God and the mystical body of Christ are combined in a
strange synthesis. Condorcet, Saint-Simon, and Comte
erred not in their conception of a religion of science and
progress but in failing to see that their cult of humanity
depended upon a reinstatement, even though in a modified
form, of the very same forces of faith from which they
imagined themselves to be emancipated. And they could not
anticipate the eventual extinction of life, the destruction of the earth itself, which, modern science tells us,
must one day inevitably occur. According to Teilhard, the
basic error of all forms of belief in progress, as they
find expression in the positivistic confessions of faith,
lies in their inability to exclude death finally. Of what
use is the attainment of a centre and focal point at the
peak of evolution, when this centre must one day crumble
into dust? "Omega," the far-off, divine event, must be
independent of the collapse of the forces of evolution, a
supernatural fulfilment, beyond space and time, a
cosmo-christological metamorphosis, must occur when the
earth and mankind reach this terminal point of the
evolutionary process.

The notion of progress as a secularized eschatology
sketched above has been found unacceptable on many

grounds. Events and trends in European and world history since the eighteenth century have, in the first place, shaken that simple faith and its optimistic outlook on the future. The actual consequences of the French and later revolutions, the two world wars, the rise of new despotisms and the purges and concentration camps that accompany them, the atom bomb, all of these have more than justified the gloomy forebodings of Flaubert and Baudelaire, Dostoevsky and Tolstoy, Kierkegaard and Nietzsche. Crisis, catastrophe and extinction have over-taken civilizations and cultures in the past. This can happen again, as we learn from Spengler and Toynbee, who take, like Vico and Herder before them, a cyclic view of history. Who can predict with assurance that the complex, highly-strung civilization of today will not meet with sudden annihilation tomorrow or die of hunger a slower but more ignominious death? It is such doubts as these that have led in recent years to crises within theological and philosophical thinking and to a more deepened awareness of the difference between what humanity can achieve in its historical course, possibly but not necessarily, and what man is called upon to realize individually within the brief span of life allotted to him. The advance of scientific knowledge and technology during the last hundred years has opened out vistas of human achievement beyond the dreams of the Enlightenment thinkers of progress. But humanity is nowhere nearer perfection, materially or morally, and it has become evident that such advance, precious in itself and indispensable in the solu-tion of problems that face mankind, nevertheless, itself gives rise to further problems and threats which show up and expose man in all his finitude and neediness.

Secondly, the development of the historical conscious-ness itself has made philosophical historians more wary and critical, more sceptical of *a priori* constructions of history and speculation about last things. Historical

thinking, it was realized, must not be governed by norms
extraneous to it nor seek for a *telos* borrowed from
without. Already in the late eighteenth century, Herder
had shown that "each historical age and each people as
well as each age of the individual has the centre of its
blissfulness in itself," rejecting the Enlightenment idea
of inevitable progress from a primitive to a perfect stage
in humanity as a whole, either in respect of moral or of
rational perfectibility. As he remarked mockingly, "The
growing perfection of the whole might be an ideal that
refers to no one in particular. Well, perhaps it exists
only in the mind of God, in the Spirit of the Creator.
Now what would He be wanting with that kind of toy?" An
awareness of the illusory character of progress in world
history, of what Buckle called "moral progress," and
scepticism with regard to the validity and usefulness of
philosophical or theological interpretations of history,
in terms either of progress or providence, is clearly reflected in Burckhardt's *Reflections on History*. Attempt-
ing, like Dilthey, to comprehend the historical process in
a purely immanent manner, the only guiding principle he
insisted on was the principle of continuity, which gives
to finite man, "as he is and was and ever shall be," an
awareness of tradition and frees him in relation to it.
Continuity of historical awareness constitutes tradition
and its breakdown and replacement by a new barbarism would
be for the historical view of the world not just a
catastrophe within world history but, as Gadamer remarks,
the end of this history itself.

R.G. Collingwood has distinguished sharply between
historical progress and progress in nature or evolution
and has pointed out how the nineteenth-century conception
of progress as a law of nature was based on the misinter-
pretation of the historical process of nature. It also
failed to distinguish, as we have seen, between processes
within history and eschatological notions derived from

faith on the one hand and speculative notions concerning
the cosmos or the totality of beings on the other.
According to Collingwood, "Historical progress is only
another name for human activity itself, as a succession of
acts each of which arises out of the last...the accomplished act gives rise to a new problem...which the new
act is obliged to solve." But such progress is possible
only on the basis of historical knowledge, i.e., the
re-enactment of past experiences in the mind of the
present thinker, of a past experience known as past but
re-enacted here and now together with a development of
itself that is partly constructive and partly critical.
For Collingwood, historical knowledge is the mind's own
knowledge of itself as purposive and reflective, the
knowledge of what mind has done in the past, and at the
same time it is the redoing of this. Historical progress
is thus progress in self-knowledge. Such progress,
however, is "not a mere fact to be discovered by historical thinking: it is only through historical thinking that
it comes about at all," i.e., by the retention in the
mind, at one phase, of what was achieved in the preceding
phase in such fashion that the two phases are related not
merely by way of succession, but by way of continuity.
Whether Collingwood has said the last word on the precise
nature of this continuity is arguable but there is no
doubt that he has taken a first step that carries us
beyond Burckhardt's scepticism and beyond Loewith's Stoic
withdrawal from the historical consciousness within which
alone progress can be a meaningful concept.

There emerges thus a purely empirical view of history
for which progress presupposes a tradition of culture,
kept alive by unbroken awareness and carried foward by
incessant endeavour from generation to generation and
through continuous renewal and re-interpretation in the
light of possibilities and tasks to which the future
beckons us. For this empirical concept of progress, of

progress as fact, historical teleology is finite, intra-
mundane and dependent upon the human will to progress, be
it in the sphere of science and technology, be it in the
solution of those social, economic and political problems
where progress is both hindered and made possible, both
demanded and discouraged by the far greater pace of the
advance of science today. From the point of view of the
tradition, viz., the Western, which has generated the
concept of progress, progress in this sense is the very
condition on which the survival of that tradition depends.
And in so far as the rest of the world has become either
enveloped in that tradition or has consciously assimilated
it, it is also under the compulsion of progress, facing
the future in hope and determination and with a glimpse
into it which is content to be *ex parte, per speculum, in
aenigmate*. On the empirical level, thus, progress is
possible and necessary, in respect of both material
attainments and of man's historical understanding of
himself, as also of the freedom which is their basis as
well as conditioned by them, as Hegel and Croce, Marx and
Sartre have amply shown. In the oft-quoted words of
H.A.L. Fisher, "The fact of progress is written plain and
large in the page of history; but progress is not a law of
nature," and, as Karl Popper adds, "To progress is to move
towards some kind of end, towards an end which exists for
us as human beings. 'History' cannot do that; only we, the
human individuals can do it...progress rests with us, with
our watchfulness, with our efforts, with the clarity of
our conception of our ends, and with the realism of their
choice. Instead of posing as prophets we must become the
makers of our fate." The massive attack on the super-
stition of "historicism" by Karl Popper and against
notions of historical inevitability by Isaiah Berlin have
laid, once for all, the ghost of determinism and
prophetism in historical thinking.

To come back to our criticism of the religion of progress, the eschatological conception of progress derived from an experience of faith, in the next place, has not only no direct relevance to scientific or philosophical thinking about the future prospects of man's worldly life; by transferring it from the religious to the secular sphere it impoverishes and falsifies the meaning of that Biblical experience itself. Burckhardt saw genuine Christianity as essentially "ascetic" and other-worldly, with its hope and expectation in another world; a religion of suffering and renunciation, in permanent conflict with the *saeculum*, with a transcendent faith in a future redemption. "The crux of the modern religion of progress is not," Loewith remarks, "that it forgot the spiritual 'centre' of its secular 'applications' but that it applied an idea of progress which is anti-religious and anti-Christian both by implication and by consequences." The "pilgrim's progress" is very different from humanity's progress to perfection. The permanent centre of history where all meaning is realized is after all the human individual, suffering, striving, acting. The religious progress of the individual man, as temporally structured in his existence, converges on an ever possible moment in *his* future, in which time is fulfilled and history comes to end for him. "In every moment slumbers the possibility of being the eschatological moment," as Rudolf Bultmann remarks, and the irreligion of progress arises because the future of authentic existential time and the future of world-time, derived from it in the manner shown by Heidegger, are confused and, in consequence, the former is understood in terms of the latter. The very process of secularization which, as Loewith himself brilliantly demonstrates, led to the cult of progress, can also liberate us into the ability to re-think and reformulate the truth about time that lies hidden behind the mythical conception of eschatology, the metaphysical concept of eternity and the understanding of time in the historical consciousness. For secularization is nothing but the continued and critical appropriation of tradition in the language of the present, the demythologizing of the utterance of faith in the attempt to comprehend its truth. Loewith fails to notice this hermeneutic significance of the existential interpretation of religious experience and of the historicity that clings inexorably to the human endeavour of self-understanding and its articulation. It is this that makes him seek comfort in a revival of the cosmological thinking of the Stoics, escaping both the truth embodied in myth and religion and its faltering and imperfect but progressive comprehension through the historical consciousness.

The idea of continuous material, social and cultural progress has generally been rejected by such contemporary religious thinkers as Berdyaev, for whom it is the seductive teaching of a modern anti-Christ and who thinks of the redemption as a redemption from history, Niebuhr, who thinks of it as a new idolatry, and Dawson, for whom it is a failure to see the corruption inherent in all things. Paul Tillich admits that the "law" of universal progress as well as the circular theory of history are myths, religious symbols as he calls them, and their employment in understanding secular history is due to a confusion of dimensions. He also accepts what we have called "progress as fact," mainly within the spheres of technology, the sciences, education, and the "increasing conquest of spatial divisions and separations within and beyond mankind," each of which, however, has a non-progressive element which sets a limit to it. There is no progress in realms where individual freedom is decisive as, for example, in the moral act, the arts, philosophy, the principles of personality and humanity and the religious consciousness, though here, again, each of these has a dimension to which the concept of progress is appropriate. Beyond these "indisputable facts," as he calls them, progress is a "symbol beyond reality," a quasi-religious symbol defining the meaning and end of history itself. From the Christian perspective, the appropriate symbol for this is the "Kingdom of God" which, as a committed theologian, Tillich works out in all its implications for a theological interpretation of history, wondering yet whether this concept can provide a framework wide enough to cover the outlook of the Asiatic religions, particularly Buddhism. But, as Paul Weiss has incisively remarked, "A philosophy which fails to provide for all religions (even from the standpoint of the religion it favours) can be only an apologetic; the religion which fails to instance an independently achieved and grounded philosophy must (even from the standpoint of the philosophy it favours) be arbitrarily subjective." The empirical concept of progress is not limited, further, to the facts of progress, as in Tillich's view, and it must seek for a general explanatory principle immanent in the historical process itself. Theological interpretations of history as a whole, such as Tillich offers, depend upon experience illumined by faith and comprehended metaphysically through a presupposed notion of Being. Metaphysical interpretations of progress, affirming it in the form of a cosmic or divine evolutionism, or rejecting it in some form of non-Hegelian Absolutism or Greek and Nietzschean circularism, are all concerned with the truth of what is in its totality, with the truth of beings as such, and not with the truth of Being itself, as Heidegger has been at pains to point out. It is only in the context of an inquiry on this ultimate level, the level of what Heidegger has called the history of Being, that the true significance of progress or its absence, of the whole of what is or within it, can be laid bare. Here we can only give a brief indication of what Heidegger has to say in this regard.

Just as religious thinkers have seen behind the
outward occurrences, deeds, and ends pursued on the stage
of history the hidden hand of God, so many philosophers
have sought to formulate that hidden movement of reality
of which the externals of history can be understood as so
many manifestations. In his *Phenomenology of Mind* Hegel
has given an account of this real, hidden history behind
history as the progressive movement of mind towards
absolute self-consciousness. For Collingwood metaphysics
itself is the study of the history of the "absolute
presuppositions" upon which external progress and decline
depend and from which they flow. Nietzsche looked more
deeply, searchingly and realistically into this inner
movement of Western history and saw in it the approach of
that "uncanniest of all guests," Nihilism. Following him,
Heidegger has traced the lineaments and genesis of this
basic movement of which the outward manifestations
constitute what we cheerfully call progress and which is
no longer confined to the Western world. Accompanying
"progress" as its chill and deadening shadow is the
spiritual night falling on mankind, "the darkening of the
world, the flight of the Gods, the depradation of the
earth," as Heidegger describes it. Man has become the
subject of history, in this age of technology, objectifying the real and having it in his grip, calculating,
planning and ordering, seeking to enlarge his domain over
the realm of events by conceptualizing and representing
them. He has forgotten that in his essence he is not the
Lord of beings but the shepherd of Being and in consequence he has become enslaved and forfeited to beings.
The dimension of the Holy, in which alone Divinity can be
real to him, has vanished; Nature has turned into a mere
play of forces predictable and controllable by man; things
have become mere objects, and history the narration and
grasping of the factual and objectifiable, instead of that
invisible happening that has brought world-history to

pass. This is the price, as Karl Jaspers puts it, that the West has paid for its "progress," the price which the whole of mankind must pay in so far as it is also enveloped in this process of "civilization," i.e., Europeanization. To be aware of this bleak and cold wind blowing in the midst of "progress" is to inquire into the genesis of both; it is to inquire into the Truth of Being, into that happening of Truth from which both man and being derive their essence. It is to realize that the Western "metaphysical" tradition of thinking, conceptualizing, objectifying and being concerned with the truth of beings, is at the root of the present world-night as also of the "progress" behind which it hides itself. For, as Nietzsche saw, Nihilism is the basic happening behind Western history, its "inner logic" and, as Heidegger has laid bare in all its implications, Nihilism is only another name for metaphysics as the history of the truth of beings as such. The oblivion of the truth of Being can, however, enter into our awareness; the impoverishment and threat behind all "progress" can be experienced as such and the oblivion experienced as oblivion. While revealing beings to us *as* beings, Being conceals itself as such. But once this withdrawal of Being is realized as its way of recalling us to it, the possibility is opened for our entering into its truth again, provided only that we recognize ourselves as claimed by Being, at its disposal, and subject to its destiny. Only if we let Being in its truth be as the ultimate Identity in which we are united with all that is, is it possible to save ourselves, from the danger of "progress"; not by rejecting it or putting a stop to it but by a resigned and tranquil acceptance of it as a derivative and consequential phenomenon. Its mastery can be broken only by opening ourselves to a deeper truth lying concealed at the root of the hidden metaphysical history behind the outward history of "progress".

BEING AND NON-BEING

The basic words and ultimate concepts in which, about
which and around which the philosophizing of a people or
culture is carried on are not merely matters of remote
academic concern, and neither are the issues raised by
them resolvable through purely formal argumentation and
dialectical maneuvering. A deeper concern is at work
here, which we may seek to comprehend, even though without
the apparent conclusiveness of a logical demonstration.
For, these words and concepts are fatefully determinative,
in the last resort, of the way of being, seeing and doing
characteristic of a people's life and their historical
existence, as also of their experience of and relationship
to other cultures. Their thinking in general, not alone
their philosophical thinking, is generated from and
rendered possible on this basis; it is a culture's
characteristic response to what reveals itself in these
groundwords and concepts, and is no less limited and
restricted by them. Myth and ritual, poesy and music,
dance and holy image lay down the basic pattern of our
experience of that reality. But it is only with our
thinking response to this reality through our primordial
words that our historical existence as a cultural entity
is launched, a continued, collective life of dialogue,
conflict and self-criticism, of triumph and failure, but
also of a growing self-awareness. Such awareness then may
eventually enable us to transcend the limitation of these
formative "prejudgments," without loss of their liberating
power, and so open ourselves thinkingly to the challenge

Originally published in *Visva-Bharati Journal of
Philosophy*, 5 (1968): 15-34.

of other cultures and of other times and be prepared for
the task of freely determining our own historical life.
The term "being," with its correlate "non-being," is one
such groundword in the history of Western thought, indeed
the central directive concept of Western philosophical
thought. Its basic discipline, metaphysics, is therefore
primarily an inquiry into Being or Ontology, an inquiry
which is itself rendered possible by the fact that reality
revealed itself to the founders of this culture and this
philosophy under the aspect of Being, *as* Being. The
primordial experience which dominated and determined their
questions as well as the manner of their questioning was
the experience of this wonder of all wonders, that things
are, that they have being and are grounded in it. In what
does the being of a thing consist? What is Being itself?
How is it known and how is it related to thinking? What
are its possible modes and against what must it
be delimited?

Things come into being and pass away. Is there a
common ground from which they spring up and into which
they return? Is this ground, boundless and undifferen-
tiated, itself a thing, or is it rather the non-existent
principle (*arche*) through which each thing comes to be a
thing? All things in their totality are held within this
whole of beings. Does this whole itself have a ground
transcending it, in which case this ground cannot also *be*,
or is this whole, having nothing outside it, to be
understood entirely in terms immanent to itself as a
universal, the "beingness" that is common to all beings?
Is the world-ground to be thought of as the Being of all
that is in its totality but itself not a being? In what
terms then must this Being be conceived or spoken about,
so that one way of speaking is more adequate than another?
Or shall we speak of it as the One, beyond Being
(Plotinus) or, better still, as the Nothing (Pseudo-
Dionysus, Eckhardt), Abyss and *Ungrund* (Boehme), from

which Being itself emerges? Is it to be conceived as pure
light which causes everything as such to emerge out of
darkness and be, or as the primordial I, Reason or Spirit,
certain and secure in possession of itself as the
originative ground of everything? But, then, is this not
to conceive the ground of what *is* in terms of something
that also is, though not in the form of a substantial
entity? Perhaps there is a way of raising these questions
in a manner which is more radical, less metaphysically
"loaded" and which might enable one to incorporate all the
genuine insights of our experience of the ultimate, in the
West or East, into this questioning, yet without presuming
to adopt a position unconditioned by one's point of
departure within a tradition of thought and absolute in
its divine elevation above the finitude that attaches to
all human thinking.

This is the way taken by Martin Heidegger, for whom
the notion of Being constitutes the basic, but also the
most problematic, gift handed over as a task for thought
in the Western tradition. His point of departure
therefore is the question about the sense of Being, but
his field of exploration and interrogation is the entire
landscape of the Western spiritual adventure. On his way
back to the destination, he brings to bear upon this
notion and his questionings about it the full weight of
the philosophical and religious thinking, metaphysical or
otherwise, in this tradition, aware that his own search
may have relevance for the planetary thinking of the
future, and for the dialogue between different traditions
necessary for that. His inquiry is hence emphatically not
one into a dessicated logical abstraction but into a
notion that is comparable, in its plenitude, to the
Heraclitian *Logos*, the ideas of God and *Gottheit* in the
high tide of Medieval Scholasticism, or the Absolute of
Hegel, consummate with a richness of content derived from
both the Platonic-Aristotelian and the Judaeo-Christian

streams of the Western tradition. What Heidegger seeks
and offers is not a "conceptual analysis" of "being" but a
topology of Being, an attempt at charting a region from
which all lines of meaningfulness can be seen to emanate,
including the meaninglessness, the Nihilism, as Nietzsche
called it, in which mankind seems to be enveloped today.
For any attempt to investigate this place is bound to come
up against Not-being and the *Nihil* and to experience the
closeness of the Negative in the very Being of things,
just as, seeking to demarcate the realm of beings, one
must reckon with non-being, at the edge of the one whole
of all that is. As Heidegger has remarked,

> It is true that the Nothing appears to be utterly
> null and futile, so that even so much as men-
> tioning it by name is to do it too much honour;
> but this insignificant and common Nothing is
> nevertheless so uncommon that we encounter it in
> very unusual experiences. And what is common or
> vulgar about Nothing is only this, that it has
> the seductive power of letting itself be
> seemingly disposed of and eliminated, as a sheer
> nullity, through mere chatter. The Nothing of
> beings follows the Being of things as the night
> follows the day. Could we ever see and exper-
> ience the day as day if there were no night?
> Hence it is the hardest, but also the most
> unerring touchstone for the genuineness and power
> of thinking in a philosopher, whether he is
> aware, forthwith and from the bottom, of the
> nearness of the Nothing in the Being of what is.
> He who is denied this remains, for ever and
> without hope, banished from philosophy. [1]

It is for this reason that in approaching the question of
Being, Heidegger begins, following Hegel's admonition, by
looking Negativity squarely in the face, so that eventually he is enabled to incorporate it into the topology
of Being itself. The raising and answering of questions
pertaining to Being and Non-being, in varying perspectives
appropriate to its different periods, constitutes the
history of Western philosophy and Heidegger has only
sought to delve into the foundations of this ontological
history and point forward to a new way of thinking about

its presupposed basis. In this paper I shall be concerned
neither with this total history nor with Heidegger's
thinking on this topic directly. On the basis of the
perspective opened out by him and guided by his own treatment of the question, I attempt instead an elaboration and
discussion of Kant's views on this subject. I shall begin
with a brief examination of what Kant has to say about
Non-being and Nothing, pass on to his view of Being and
conclude with a reference to Heidegger's views on Nothing,
in so far as they are relevant to a critical appropriation
of Kant.

In the *Critique of Pure Reason,* Kant has given a table
of the division of the concept of nothing. His summary
remarks on "nothing" are attached, it may be recalled, to
the Appendix on "The Amphiboly of Concepts of Reflection"
with which the Transcendental Analytic comes to a close.
Kant appends them not because they are of any importance
in themselves but as "requisite for the completeness of
the system." That he did not altogether regard them as
unimportant is shown by the fact that in the *Prolegomena,*
he draws pointed attention to the distinction between the
concepts of "something" and "nothing," this most abstract
of ontological divisions, as he calls it, and to the table
he has constructed in the *Critique.* Kant, however, again
makes it clear that his main purpose is to exhibit the
completeness of his system of categories and how it can
provide unfailing guidance in the task of knowing with
completeness any object whatsoever of a pure concept of
the understanding or reason. Kant takes the concept of an
object in general as the higher concept and divides it
first into "something" and "nothing." "Nothing" is then
divided, "according to the order and under the guidance of
the categories"--since the categories are the only
concepts which refer to objects in general--as follows:
The first species of nothing is the *ens rationis,* an empty
concept without object. This is nothing in the sense of

"none," of the object of a concept to which no assignable
intuition whatsoever corresponds and is opposed to the
concepts of all, many and one. The second is the *nihil
privatum*, the empty object of a concept or, as Kant also
puts it, a concept of the absence of an object. This is
nothing in the sense of the negation of reality (one of
the categories of quality) as *something*. The third is
nothing in the sense of an imaginary entity, the *ens
imaginarium*, just an empty intuition without object. This
is the mere form of intuition, without substance, itself
no object, but the merely formal condition of an object.
The fourth kind of nothing is the *nihil negativum*, an
empty object without concept. This is the object of a
concept which contradicts itself and, since the concept
itself is nothing, this object is without content and so
nothing in the sense of the impossible.

It may be of some interest to inquire whether this
account, aimed at "the distinguishing of an object,
whether it is something or nothing," is exhaustive of all
possible meanings of "nothing" and whether Kant's thinking
is not determined by a preconceived notion of being which
is never explicitly stated and examined. Kant's remarks
on "none" imply that our concepts of all, many and one
remain mere *Gedankendinge* or thought entities and so
without objective reference, unless they bear upon
something given to us in intuition. We have the idea of
an All or totality of things and of the unity possessed by
this. As finite beings dependent upon something being
given to us in intuition, we are in thought at least open
to the Infinite. And yet, for Kant, this totality, either
as the whole or as the unifying ground of all that is,
remains a mere *ens rationis* to which there corresponds--
nothing. The rational entity, Kant says, is not to be
counted as possible, for it is not supported by any
example from experience, but it must not for that reason
be declared also to be impossible for it can be

entertained in thought without self-contradiction. And yet, the *ens rationis* is itself a form of "nothing," a mere fiction, i.e., itself nothing, in the first of the four senses distinguished by Kant. The third kind of "nothing" is the imaginary entity, also positively characterized by Kant as an *ens*. It is exemplified by pure space and pure time, which are indeed something, Kant admits, but as merely formal conditions of intuition, are not themselves objects which are intuited. Both the empty concept and the empty intuition are forms of nothing, though the former must not be declared to be impossible and the latter is a necessary condition of any object being given in experience. The *nihil privatum* is the negation of something determinate given to the senses. But as Kant repeatedly asserts, all true negations are nothing but limitations. Reality, or that which corresponds to a sensation in general, when combined with negation gives rise to limitation, i.e., to "something," which is thus inclusive of the limiting negation, as Plato declared, even if we understand reality to mean, with Kant, the "what," the *Sachheit* of anything. Reality and negation are taken by Kant as concepts representing being and non-being, respectively, in time. Further, negation here is to be understood not as logical negation, which does not properly refer to a concept but only to its relation to another concept and is therefore quite insufficient to determine a concept in respect of its content. The negation is transcendental, for it refers to such content as can be thought *a priori* as belonging to a predicate, and it signifies the not-being in itself of this content. Reality, on the other hand, is transcendental affirmation, "which is a something the very concept of which in itself expresses a being." The *nihil negativum*, finally, is total nothingness, an *Unding*, because the impossible object of a self-cancelling concept. That of which the concept contradicts itself, for Kant, *is not*

and not a something, as yet indeterminate, but awaiting
conceptualization. Kant also completely disregards the
possibility, later envisaged by Hegel, that contradiction
may inhere in the content of the concept itself or that
the self-contradictory concept may, instead of being
totally self-annulling, be the positive indication of a
more adequate determination. Here then would be a nothing
incorporated within being itself and a negativity inherent
in "the labour of the concept."

Kant's views on "something" and "nothing" are derived
from and based upon his conception of knowledge as
resulting from a combination of intuition and concept;
where one of these is lacking we get a form of nothing.
Further, "anything" and "nothing" are conceived as sub-
classes of the concept of an "object in general," taken
problematically, as opposites *within* this wider class. An
object is a thing as "represented" in an intuition and as
conceived in relation to a subject which "represents" it
in a concept. For Kant only that counts as something
which can be in the mode of an object. But this leaves
open the possibility of a nothing as the other to all
"objects" as not a sheer nothing and yet not an object.
This becomes obvious in Kant's treatment of the imaginary
entity and the rational entity, as has been adumbrated
above. Pure space and pure time are imaginary entities
intuited in pure intuition. They are nothing in the sense
of not being objects, but as given in such intuition they
are still something. Although what pure intuition
discloses is not intuited thematically in the manner of
our apprehension of something that is simply given and
actually there, such intuition is not altogether vacuous.
What is intuited in pure intuition is the pure, unthe-
matic, unobjectifiable "look" or aspect which constitutes
the horizon within which empirical intuition can operate
and have objects disclosed to it. The "derivative
intuition" of finite beings has this in common with the

intuitus imaginarius of a divinity that, through the
activity of pure imagination, it can creatively project
the horizon within which a particular entity given by
sense may then be taken up. Human intuition is dependent
upon something given to it, whereas Divine intuition is
itself creative of what is apprehended in such intuition.
What the formative giving of pure finite intuition itself
gives is not a thing and yet not nothing, something and
yet a nothing. It may be argued in like manner that an
empty concept without object, i.e., the *ens rationis*, is a
nothing also in another sense than that meant by Kant.
The mere concept, to which no assignable intuition
corresponds, is a representation nevertheless and what is
represented in it is unity in a multiplicity, a rule and
the way it functions. Nothing in this sense is also a
something, though not as an object which can be given
directly in intuition.

In two passages in the *Critique of Pure Reason*, Kant
speaks of this something-nothing as an X and calls it an
"object":

> 1. All representations have, as representations,
> their object, and can themselves become objects
> of other representations. Appearances are the
> sole objects which can be given to us imme-
> diately, and that in them which relates
> immediately to the object is called intuition.
> But these appearances are not things in them-
> selves; they are only representations, which in
> turn have their object--an object which cannot
> itself be intuited by us, and which may,
> therefore, be named the non-empirical, that is
> transcendental object = X. [2]

> 2. All our representations are, it is true,
> referred by the understanding to some object; and
> since appearances are nothing but representa-
> tions, the understanding refers them to a
> *something*, as the object of sensible intuition.
> But this something, thus conceived, is only the
> transcendental object; and by that is meant a
> something = X, of which we know, and with the
> present constitution of our understanding can
> know, nothing whatever, but which as a correlate
> of the unity of apperception, can serve only for

the unity of the manifold in sensible intuition.
By means of this unity the understanding combines
the manifold into the concept of an object.[3]

The X is "object in general," not a general object,
entity or essent confronting us. Other than all essents
and constituting the horizon of objectivity as such,
within which any essent can be apprehended thematically as
an object standing over against us (Gegen-stand), this X
is, as sheer horizon, a nothing that transcends all
essents. It cannot be "known," as objects are known in
direct apprehension, and yet it is disclosed as that
through which essents become manifest. It is for this
reason that Kant calls such disclosure "transcendental
truth," for it is a form of knowledge of which the truth
lies in letting things be encountered and "known" in
experience as "objects." "All our knowledge," Kant says,
"is contained within this whole of possible experience,
and transcendental truth, which precedes all empirical
truth and renders it possible, consists in this general
relation to that experience."[4] The "nothing' transcending
all possible objects, it must now be obvious, is no other
than the being of these essents themselves and what Kant
calls "transcendental truth" refers to this ontological
domain, "an island enclosed by nature itself within
unalterable limits." No wonder he goes on to speak of
this realm, this "land of truth-- enchanting name!" as
being "surrounded by a wide and stormy ocean, the native
home of illusion."[5] What first seems to be a "nothing,"
when "to be" is to be given as an object, exhibits itself
as the very being of objects and the transcendental ground
of our knowing them. But this very Being, as Kant's
doctrine of Transcendental Illusion teaches, turns again
into a "nothing" when it is taken apart from all relation
to our knowledge of these objects, as subsisting
independently in the fashion of *a* being or essent.

Our knowledge of beings (essents), ontic knowledge,
depends upon a prior comprehension of their being. Kant
abandons "the proud name of an Ontology"[6] in favour of the
title "transcendental philosophy" because he rejects the
claim of traditional ontology to have, through pure
reason, direct and unconditional knowledge of the realm of
Being. Man is dependent upon something being *given* in
intuition, but knowledge of what is thus given (i.e.,
ontic knowledge) is possible only through the *a priori*
"knowledge" of Being, which transcends all beings. This
is ontological knowledge, but it has only an "empirical
use," for it is knowledge of the being of all beings as
encounterable in experience and hence "relative" to
experience. Pure intuition, pure imagination and pure
apperception in their unity constitute, as Heidegger has
remarked, "the pure act of objectification (*das Gegen-
stehenlassen von*...) which thus first makes manifest such
a thing as the horizon of objectivity in general. And
because pure knowledge in this way first opens up the free
space necessary for a finite being, i.e., the space in
which 'all relation of being and non-being'[7] occurs, this
knowledge must be termed ontological."[8] This was also the
concern of "the transcendental philosophy of the
ancients."[9] The *Critique of Pure Reason,* however, is "a
treatise on method, not a system of the science itself,"
as Kant expressly says, and what it accomplishes is the
exhibition of the inner possibility of Ontology or
metaphysica generalis. There is little that is directly
said about Being, that nothing-something in the light of
which beings are known. What was his conception of Being
and what were the limitations within which his conception
moved? The best known of his somewhat episodic remarks on
Being occurs in the course of his discussion of the
arguments for the existence of the *ens realissimum,* in the
section entitled, "The impossibility of the ontological
proof of the existence of God." Kant says here:

"Being" is obviously not a real predicate; that
is, it is not a concept of something which could
be added to the concept of a thing. It is merely
the positing (*Position*, from Lat. *positio* and
equivalent in Kant's use to the German *Setzung*)
of a thing, or of certain determinations as
existing in themselves.[10] In logical usage, it
is merely the copula of a judgement. The
proposition, "God is omnipotent" contains two
concepts, each of which has its object--God and
omnipotence. The little word "is" adds no new
predicate, but only serves to posit the predicate
in its relation to the subject.

What is of primary significance here is the onto-
theological context in which Kant offers his view of
Being, here as well as in the pre-Critical essay, "The
only possible principle for the demonstration of the
existence of God." This may serve to remind us that in
the tradition of Greek-Christian metaphysics, the
Aristotelian question, "What is being (*ti to on*)?"
necessarily takes the two-fold form of an inquiry into
beings as such (*on he on*) as well as an inquiry into the
highest being (*to theion*). The metaphysical inquiry into
the being of what is (the essent) is, in other words,
simultaneously ontology, which is concerned with beings in
general, and theology, which deals with what can be said
to be in the highest, most complete sense. In both cases,
the being of all that is (beings or essents) is conceived
as the ground of essents, whether as the underlying basis
by virtue of which the essent is as such, or as the
highest being which causes everything to come into being.
For Kant also the ideas of the *ens necessarium, ens
originarium, ens summum, ens realissimum, ens entium*
constitute the theological background of what he has to
say about being (*ens*). Although, according to Kant, "the
ideal of the supreme being is nothing but a *regulative
principle* of reason, which directs us to look upon all
connection in the world *as if* it originated from an all-
sufficient necessary cause,"[11] yet he also speaks of such
ideas as "unsubstantial and baseless for the merely

speculative reason," which "feels indeed no loss in allowing them to vanish entirely."[12] And although the objective reality of the supreme being cannot indeed be proved and "it remains a mere ideal, it is yet *an ideal without a flaw*, a concept which completes and crowns the whole of human knowledge."[13] It is a fiction, an illusion which nevertheless is "indispensably necessary if we are to direct the understanding beyond every given experience (as part of the sum of possible experience), and thereby to secure its greatest possible extension, just as, in the case of the mirror-vision, the illusion involved is indispensably necessary if, besides the objects which lie before our eyes, we are also to see those which lie at a distance behind our back."[14]

As Heidegger has observed, the need to think that "God is" is the secret spur that drives the thinking of the *Critique* and subsequent works of Kant. Is God a being? Or is God the same as Being? Is Being itself also one more being or is it rather the other to all possible beings, in the light of which all beings are revealed as such? Is "to be" the same as to be an "object" for a knowing subject? How far can we conceive a supreme being as the existing ground and substratum of everything? Can Being itself be conceived, in the last resort, as ground? Kant's intense awareness of the unresolved problematic character of this notion--which he rejects for pure speculative reason, and for that alone--is vividly expressed in this passage in the first *Critique*:

> Unconditioned necessity, which we so indispen-
> sably require as the last bearer of all things,
> is for human reason the veritable abyss.
> Eternity itself, in all its terrible sublimity...
> is far from making the same overwhelming
> impression on the mind; for it only *measures* the
> duration of things, it does not *support* them. We
> cannot put aside, and yet also cannot endure the
> thought, that a being, which we represent to
> ourselves as supreme amongst all possible beings,
> should, as it were, say to itself: "I am from
> eternity to eternity, and outside me there is
> nothing save what is through my will *but whence
> then am I*?" All support here fails us.[15]

How problematic indeed the whole situation, in respect of
Being as supreme being and ground of things, must have
been for Kant can be realized when we recall that he was
confronting a legacy of thought which combined in itself
the Eleatic-Aristotelian notion of Being and the Christian
conception of God as Creator *ex nihilo* and, more
immediately, the legacy of an Aquinas, for whom, as for
Augustine, God and Being were the same. As Gilson has
remarked, in good Christian doctrine the first or proper
name of God is Being and this name denotes His very
essence, in such fashion that in Him essence and existence
are identical. The further view of St. Thomas that God as
Being is the pure act of existing, the conception of being
as act, being understood in the verbal sense of being, is
so foreign to Kant's subjectivistic way of thinking and to
his view of being as the "objectivity" of objects that it
is completely disregarded by him, and we have to wait
until Hegel and Heidegger to take serious note of the
dynamism inherent in the notions of Being and Non-being.
In terms of Kant's "transcendental theology," if we ask

> whether there is anything distinct from the
> world, which contains the ground of the order of
> the world and of its connection in accordance
> with universal laws, the answer is that there
> *undoubtedly* is. For the world is a sum of
> appearances; and there must therefore be some
> transcendental ground of appearances, that is, a
> ground which is thinkable only by the pure under-
> standing....[But] what this primordial ground of
> the unity of the world may be in itself, we
> should not profess to have thereby decided, but
> only how we should use it, or rather its idea, in
> relation to the systematic employment of reason
> in respect of things of the world....This idea is
> thus valid only in respect of the *employment* of
> our reason *in reference to the world*. If we
> ascribe to it a validity that is absolute and
> objective we should be forgetting that what we
> are thinking is a being in idea only.[16]

Kant clearly perceives that being is such only in relation
to beings, and that is the great insight of transcendental
philosophy. But like Aquinas he conceives Being as an

individual, as a being--and only as such can God be
conceived--and he is therefore forced to reduce it to a
demand of reason, a mere nothing. Thinking within the
Christian framework, he never allowed himself the
possibility of raising the question of Being in
independence of the theological problem of God. For the
same reason, he missed the insight that Being *as* Being,
independently of the notion of God, may be power and act
in relation to beings, without itself being conceived as *a*
being. For Kant, the activity is all on our side and
consists in our "employment" or "use" of reason; what
alone bothers Kant is how *existence* can belong to this
primordial ground, not how, if this ground "undoubtedly
is," as he admits, it must be conceived as generative, in
some sense, of both existence and *our* manner of comprehending it, and how if the ground is the ground of all
that is (exists), it cannot itself be an existing ground.
Kant is not only insensitive to the notion of Being as
pure act but does not question how the being of all beings
can itself be a being. In European thought the demand for
conceiving an ultimate ground in terms of a being beyond
substantial being (*epikeina tes ousias*) and of not-being
has been persistently felt and voiced by the protagonists
of apophatic or negative theology, from Plotinus to
Nicolas Berdyaev and Henry Dumery in our day, by the
German speculative mystics and by thinkers such as Jacob
Boehme and Schelling. Kant had a lively and deep sense of
the abyss before which reason stands and could not shake
it off, for deep calls unto deep, *abyssus invocat abyssum,*
as the old saying has it. But he was too much the
prisoner of his own Enlightenment presupposition as to the
nature of pure thought as "critical" and as "reason" to
have any use for these speculations. He could only shrink
back in horror from this shadow thrown by his own rationalistic, subjectivistic prejudice and make room for faith
as the repository of all that proved recalcitrant to
thinking conceived as reason.

To come back to Kant's statement of his "thesis," as
Heidegger has described it.[17] Kant denies here that
"being" is a real predicate, not that it is a predicate;
and he asserts that it is mere or pure positing
(*Position*). Kant here repeats what he already wrote,
about twenty years earlier, in the pre-Critical essay
mentioned before, except that the denial refers now, not
just to a predicate, as in the earlier essay, but to a
"real" predicate. A "real" predicate is one that belongs
to the *res*, the content or the "what" of a thing, which
can be represented in a concept. But such representation
by itself does not imply that the thing is or exists nor,
if it does exist, does its "what" or concept come to
include any additional attribute thereby. Being is not
real, in Kant's sense, i.e., does not pertain to the
"what" of anything. But though to say of a thing that it
is does not give us any further information about the
thing as such or about its "what," it does tell us *that*
this thing, this something as an object, is or exists.
Being as pure position cannot be spoken about in terms of
the 'what' or concept of an entity, for it is not part of
the object, but means the positedness of something in an
act of representation which is positing in character.
Kant goes on to speak of "the logical use" in which being
is merely the copula in a judgment, which only posits the
predicate in its relation to the subject. Where, however,
it is not merely the relation between subject and
predicate that is posited but the thing itself is posited
in itself, "being" is used in a different way from its
logical use and means existence as, for example, in the
sentence, "God is." Being in this use is described by
Kant as the "Absolute positing of a thing," in which, as
he puts it, "I go beyond the concept, not to another
predicate not contained in the concept, but to the thing
itself with just the same predicates, neither more nor
less; only the absolute position beyond the relative is

thought in addition."[18] It should, however, be noticed that even in "absolute position," i.e., in the objective or ontic use of being (as Heidegger calls it to distinguish it from the logical use), a relation is posited, giving to the "is" the character of a predicate, even though not a "real" one. This is the relation between the positing subject and the object, with the subject-predicate relation interposed across that, as Heidegger puts it. Thus the copula "is" has a richer meaning in the objective use than in the purely logical.

In the pre-Critical essay, Kant declared that the concept of "is" was so simple that nothing could be said towards explicating it and that in this case "the nature of the object in relation to the faculty of our understanding does not also allow of a higher degree" of clarity than that provided by the determination of being as position. In the *Critique,* however, he sees that "to be" *can* be explained further but that to do so we must not consider being and existence solely in their "relation to the faculty of our understanding." This further elucidation is given in connection with a discussion of possibility, existence and necessity as modes of being. So long as we seek their definition, Kant says, solely in pure understanding, they cannot be explained save through an obvious tautology and that if all sensible intuition, the only kind that we possess, is removed, not one of these concepts can be shown to be really meaningful.[19] "To be" is indeed to be posited by an operation of the understanding but such positing requires that something should be *given* through sense affection, on which the positing can catch and so set it up as an object standing over against us. Being thus is positedness, but it is the positedness of an affection. In order, however, that the streaming multiplicity of presentations given in sensible affection should find a halt and come to a stand in the form of objects standing over against us, it is necessary

that it be ordered and connected together. This connecting can only be accomplished by the faculty of understanding, which is characterized by a mode of representation which Kant calls "synthesis." Such synthesis is
positing (*Position*) in the manner of a proposition, i.e.,
a judgment, through which alone thus what is given in
affection is known as an object. The "is" as copula here
means something more than "the representation of a
relation between two concepts," in which, according to
logicians, the nature of a judgment truly consists. As he
himself declares, Kant could never find this view satisfying, for its leaves undetermined the nature of this
"relation" and says nothing about the basis on which the
predicate is posited of the subject. The subject of the
proposition can be this basis only when it is at the same
time an object for a knowing subject. Kant, therefore,
says, "...a judgment is nothing but the manner in which
given modes of knowledge are brought to the 'objective'
unity of apperception. This is what is intended by this
little word of relation 'is,' employed in it to distinguish the objective unity of given representations from
the subjective."[20] The copula "is" is now seen to include
in itself the sense of unity, of a gathering and binding
together, that inter-relatedness of being and unity which
was already noticed by Parmenides and Heraclitus in the
first Western speculations about Being.

The "is" signifies a combination of the propositional
subject and predicate in the object and, along with that,
the unity which combines the given manifold. This unity
does not itself arise from a combination. Kant says,
therefore,

> This unity, which precedes *a priori* all concepts
> of combination, is not the category of unity...
> the category already presupposes combination. We
> must therefore look yet higher for this unity,
> namely in that which itself contains the ground
> of diverse concepts in judgment, and therefore of
> the possibility of the understanding, even as
> regards its logical employment.[21]

Upon this primordial synthetic unity of transcendental apperception rests the very possibility of understanding and therefore, as Heidegger puts it, it is that *hen*, the *Logos* of which Heraclitus spoke, from which arises all *syn* (together) of every *thesis* (positing). In this "principle of the original *synthetic* unity of apperception" lies, according to Kant, "the first pure knowledge of understanding," through which the being, i.e., the objectivity, of the essent regarded as object is rendered possible. Consistently with his premises, however, the location of this primordial unity is shifted to the "I" as subject and being, with its different modalities, is determined in terms of its relation to the understanding. For Kant, being as positedness is the positedness of something given and hence the objectivity of objects as disclosed to a thinking subject; it is with reference to such a subject that being derives its meaning as position.

A glance at Kant's treatment of those principles of pure understanding which he calls "Postulates of empirical thought in general" will show that this conception of being as positedness is also borne out in the case of the modalities of being. The three postulates, referring respectively to possible being, actual being and necessary being, are as follows:

> 1. That which agrees with the formal conditions of experience (in respect of intuition and concepts) is *possible*. 2. That which is bound up with the material conditions of experience (sensation) is *actual*. 3. That of which the connection with the actual is determined in accordance with universal conditions of experience, is (exists as) necessary.[22]

In conformity with Kant's thesis that "being" is obviously not a real predicate, the modalities of being also say nothing about *what* the object is but, as Heidegger puts it, only give information about the *how* of the relation of the object to the subject, for which reason they are called modalities. As Kant himself says, "The categories

of modality have the peculiarity that, in determining an
object, they do not in the least enlarge the concept to
which they are attached as predicates. They only express
the relation of the concept to the faculty of knowledge,"
i.e., to understanding in its relation to affection.[23]
The predicates of modality posit "certain determinations"
of the object, for they tell us something about the object
in itself, i.e., about the object as such, though not in
respect of its "what" or reality. Being as possible,
actual or necessary, in other words, is not a real or
ontic predicate but a transcendental or ontological
predicate. "Agreeing with," "being bound up with," and
"connection with" are the relations posited by the various
modalities as requirements for the possible, actual and
necessary existence of objects. Being, as positedness,
thus, is the pure relation of the objectivity of objects
to the subjectivity of the knowing subject and
possibility, actuality and necessity signify the position
of the various modes of this relation. The pure synthesis
of transcendental apperception is the primordial act of
thought as an element in knowledge, the original "thesis"
of human subjectivity from which arise the various
modalities, determining what "to be" means, along with its
different modes.

Why must we distinguish between possibility and
actuality and what is the basis of this distinction?
Towards the close of the *Critique of Judgment*, Kant
remarks in a Note (Sec. 76), "It is for the human
understanding inescapably necessary to distinguish between
the possibility and actuality of things. The reason for
this lies in the subject and the nature of his faculty of
knowledge." The need for this distinction lies in the
fact that for knowing anything we require two quite
disparate functions, understanding for concepts and sense
intuition for objects which correspond to them; were our
understanding intuitive, it could have no objects as

actual, and concepts (which concern only the possibility of objects) and sense intuition (through which alone something is given, but without being determined as an object) would both become superfluous. In regard to the basis of the distinction, Kant goes on to say, "Now, all our distinctions of the merely possible from the actual rests on this that the first signifies only the positing of the representation of a thing in respect of our concept and of the faculty of thinking in general, whereas the latter means the positing of the thing in itself (beyond our concept)." This not only confirms that for Kant being is positedness and possibility and actuality different modes of positing but shows that in the very nature of the being of things, as Kant conceives it, there inheres this necessary distinction between possibility and actuality.

Kant "explains" being as pure position and thus "locates" its meaning in positing as an activity of human subjectivity. That from which, or in terms of which, being gets its meaning is its location and to ask about the geography of this location (*Ort*) is to attempt to determine the context from which "positing" itself derives its meaning.[24] "The crossbearings" of this region have been traced by Kant, as Heidegger has pointed out, in the Appendix to the *Transcendental Analytic* entitled "The Amphiboly of Concepts of Reflection" to which attention has already been drawn earlier. Being as position, i.e., as the positing and the positedness of objects, has been explained with reference to the different relations to the faculty of knowledge. These relations are reflexive relations, for they refer to "the act by which I confront the comparison of representations with the cognitive faculty to which it belongs," which Kant calls "transcendental reflection" and which is concerned, not with objects directly, but with the experiencing subject. Being, in other words, has been explained in terms of that location to which reflection is the appropriate cognitive

response. The further exploration of this region consists
of an examination of the "concepts of reflection," in a
reflection on reflection which constitutes for Kant the
ultimate *locus* (*topos* or place) of human subjectivity as
defined by its relation to what is given in sense
affection. The principal concepts of reflection mentioned
by Kant are those of identity and difference, of agreement
and opposition, of the inner and the outer and of the
determinable and the determination (matter and form) and
hence the final location of the sense of being must be
found in terms of the distinctions contained in them.
Amongst these transcendental concepts of reflection, the
contrasting pair of matter and form is the most basic. As
Kant himself declares, "These two concepts underlie all
other reflection, so inseparably are they bound up with
all employment of the understanding. The first (matter)
signifies the determinable in general, the second (form)
its determination."[25]   And it is in terms of these that
Kant has "explained," as we have seen, the meaning of
"possible being" and "actual being," the one referring to
the formal, the other to the material conditions of
experience. "Form" is determination, depending upon the
spontaneity of the understanding, and "matter" the
determinable, presented through the receptivity of sense-
perception. Thus, for Kant, "to be" means to be posited
and the latter itself gets its meaning from the innermost
core and location of human subjectivity, i.e, from a
thinking of thinking which is intrinsically bound up with
sense-perception.

Western speculation about Being has taken a great
stride forward in Kant's reflections on Being, for he has
demonstrated that the being of things is not itself a
thing and not objectively given, that it belongs to a non-
objectifiable realm of its own; he has seen something of
the complex structure of this realm and in particular its
character as unifying and enabling, but he has also

exhibited how all talk of Being is meaningful only in the
context of our experience of beings. We have "knowledge"
of beings but only in the light of a prior conception of
their being. Kant has also stated his "thesis" about this
prior conception and told us that being and non-being lie
in the objectivity of beings, i.e., in their being experienced as objects and also that such experience is grounded
in the depths of our own subjectivity, i.e., in our own
being, conceived as *subject*. But Kant does not inquire
into the basis of this prior conception itself, does not
ask as to the presupposed sense of being which makes it
possible for being to be determined in terms of position,
positing and positedness. He has made it evident that the
being of things gets its sense from beyond it, i.e., from
what he calls its "transcendental location," the thinking
of thinking as conditioned by sense. But he does not ask
why, in Heidegger's words, "in determining the positedness
of what is posited, the former emerges as subject in a
two-fold form, once as subject in relation to a predicate
in a proposition and again as I-subject in its relation to
the object. What does it mean for being to be determinable in terms of the *subiectum* or, to use the Greek
expression, of the *hypokeimenon*?" Heidegger's own answer
to this question is that the sense of being tacitly
presupposed in all "metaphysical" thought, including that
of Kant, is that of constant presence, which is then
interpreted as what lies in front (*hypokeimenon*), as what
has been laid down, put down, represented and posited.
Once it has been seen that positedness and objectivity are
themselves derived from being understood as constant
presence, it becomes also clear that being in this primary
sense cannot be explained in terms of and through
reflection (thinking of representational thinking), nor
can it be located as to its origin and meaning in the
human subjectivity.

The specific interpretation of being, including man's being, as subject, presupposes being as presence. Is it possible to think about, or locate the sense of, being and non-being, presence and absence, not in terms of human subjectivity nor indeed in terms of any essent but in themselves? Is it possible to think about and determine the sense, not of beings as beings, but of Being itself as Being? To ask this, as the metaphysical tradition of the West has never done, is to raise, with Heidegger, the question of Being and so inquire, beyond the truth of beings, into the truth of Being itself, from which all presence and absence flow and are sustained as such.

The history of ontology begins with Parmenides' sharp *krisis* or separation between being and non-being, with his assertion that only being is and that non-being is not and with his prohibition to let thought travel on the way of nothingness. Plato laid unfilial hands on the pronounce-ment of "father Parmenides" by taking this way and sought to "establish by main force that what is not, in some respect has being, and inversely that what is, in a way is not." In his account of the "great refusal,"[26] Whitehead follows him, in this century, in insisting that every event is decisive in proportion to the importance (for it) of its untrue propositions, and that each eternal object which is synthesised *qua being* is also synthesised *qua* not-being. The Platonic perplexities over being and non-being, handing over to posterity the logical problems of negation and existential judgment, and his character-ization of the sensible world itself as *me on* (non-being, not utter nothing) did nothing, however, to overcome the dualism of Being and Non-being generated by Parmenides' delimitation of Being against Non-being. The dark shadow of Non-being, looming as the unthought and unthinkable Other to Being in the background, deepened with the arrival of Christianity. The idea of creation *ex nihilo* added to the notion of non-being (*genesis* and *phthora,*

change and otherness) the dimension of Nothingness in the
interpretation of world and man, giving rise to the need
for justifying the very existence of things in their
totality. The Spanish philosopher Xavier Zubiri has
described this happening in the following words:

> The Greek is alienated by the world because of
> its *changeability*. The European of the Christian
> era is alienated by its nullity or, better still,
> its *nihility*....For the Greek, the world is
> *something* that changes; for the man of the
> Christian era it is a *nothingness* that seems to
> be or exist....With this change of perspective
> being comes to mean something *toto caelo*
> different from what it meant in Greece: for a
> Greek, being means to be there, at hand; for the
> Western European, being means, first of all, *not
> being nothingness*....In a certain sense, then,
> the Greek still philosophizes *from the point of
> reference of being*, and the Western European
> philosophizes *from the point of reference of
> nothingness*.[27]

It is against this theological background that we must
understand the notion of Non-being as Nothingness, like
the problem of Being, if we are to make sense of the
question raised by Leibniz, "Why is there something rather
than nothing?", later repeated by Schelling and taken up,
in our own day, but in a transformed sense, by Martin
Heidegger in the context of his inquiry into the sense
of Being.

   While asking this question, Heidegger does not
inquire, like Leibniz, into the sufficient ground of
essents, itself essent, but into the Being of beings,
problematically and tentatively conceived as the
transcendental ground of beings. Leibniz's question
already presupposes the Christian answer, as also the
principle of sufficient reason, first explicitly stated by
himself as the central principle underlying all
metaphysical inquiry. Setting aside the testimony of
revelation as inappropriate to philosophical thinking and
seeking to discover the possibility and structure of
transcendence within man himself, Heidegger asks whether

and how man can reach out beyond himself and all essents, what it is that manifests itself to him in this act of transcendence and how far this is to be conceived as the ground of all essents. The "metaphysical" inquiry into the essent *qua* essent is an inquiry that seeks to comprehend the essent by going beyond it and Heidegger also begins his questioning with an examination of the nature of that transcendence. But though his question is posed in the manner of the metaphysical tradition, he answers it in a quite different way, for according to him, that *to* which we transcend in going beyond all essents is not God--Himself an essent, albeit the highest one--but that which is the other to, or the other of, all things, the nothing. But this nothing, far from being absolute non-being, is the "not" of beings only when regarded in terms of the latter; though it constitutes an experience necessary to make us aware of the limits of the meta-physical concern with essents, the nothing shows itself, once this insight is attained, to be only the veil of Being itself. Seeking to discover a transcendent ground for all that is, we find ourselves confronting the abyss of nothingness. For Heidegger this leads to the insight that this negativity of transcendental experience is an experience of non-being as the inescapable correlate of the subjectivistic will to ground beings, to go beyond them only to have beings all the more firmly in our grip. As he has remarked,

> Non-being as the "not" of beings is in sharpest opposition to mere nullity. Non-being is never sheer nothingness and it is as little a something in the sense of an object; it is Being itself, the truth (disclosure) of which is only then made over to man when he has vanquished himself as subject, i.e. when he no longer represents the essent as object.[28]

The encounter with the "not" of essents enables us to shed our self-will, to see things in their true being and the "not" itself as a manifestation of Being and integral to

it. The experience of this "not" is the surrender of the
"metaphysical" will to possess and ground, to secure and
certify; it is the abandonment of all hope and all desire,
the suspension of all willing and all knowing and hard as
cutting ourselves loose from the last shore, as the aged
Schelling saw. In the latter's words, "What is needed
here is to leave *everything*, not merely, as we are wont to
say, wife and child, but everything that *is*, God Himself,
for in this respect even God is an essent. He who would
place himself at the starting-point of a truly free
philosophy must hence lose God Himself. Here it is true
that he who wants to retain it shall lose it and he who
loses it shall find it."[29] With such surrender, the abyss
of non-being is seen to be a "not" clinging to Being
itself as its veil.

Neither of Being nor of Non-being can we say that it
is (for only beings are) and yet, as Heidegger puts it,
"It gives (*Es gibt*)" both.[30] We shall not ask here, with
Heidegger, how both derive simultaneously from the mystery
of truth and the mutual owning of man and Being in the
Ereignis, to which Heidegger is finally led in his
"topology" of Being. Instead, let us examine briefly the
notion of Non-being as the veil of Being. If Non-being is
not sheer nothing, it must belong to Being itself as a
negativity inherent in it. Its origin cannot lie
ultimately in human subjectivity, either as privation or
negation, as an illusory projection of thought or figment
of the imagination, as little as the way Being is revealed
to man can be regarded as his invention. The "not,"
Heidegger says, never arises from the no-saying of negation, for every "no," which does not misinterpret itself
as wilful presuming on the power of subjectivity to posit,
is really our response to the claim of the naughting that
resides in Being itself and which reveals itself as the
"not". Every "no" is only the affirmation of Non-being.

Because the naughting occurs in Being itself, we
can never perceive it as something clinging to
the essent. But this impossibility is no proof
that Non-being has its origin in no saying. This
proof appears sound only when the essent is set
up as the objective (counterpole) of subjectivity. From this alternative it is then con-
cluded that every "not," since it is never manifested as something objective, must necessarily
be the product of the act of a subject....The
naughting prevails in Being itself and by no
means in the human being, in so far as this is
conceived as the subjectivity of the *ego cogito*.[31]

In the absolute idealism of Hegel and Schelling, negativity is for the first time taken up into the innermost
happening of Being, but it is conceived there as "negation" because Being itself is for them of the nature of
Will, a character which was soon to emerge to the surface
as the will-to-power, along with Being itself as the
Nihil, in the explicit metaphysical nihilism of Nietzsche.

Being, as presence, and Non-being belong together in
the same location *(topos)*, according to Heidegger, and
both are consequent on the "metaphysical" quest for
transcendence and ground. The "not" as absence, and as a
possibility inherent in presence itself, is the nihilistic
spectre lying in wait at the heart of all "metaphysical"
thinking as such, for such thinking is concerned solely
with the essent, and with *its* being only as it transcends
and grounds it, and not with Being itself in its own
truth. From the perspective of the latter, however,
"metaphysics" is not due to man's making but is one way in
which Being conceals itself as such from man in the
process of revealing the essent as such to him. The
unhiddenness or disclosure of the essent as such is the
happening of metaphysics. In this happening, Being itself
is disclosed as the being of beings, while staying away in
its own truth, remaining hidden as Being and denying
itself as such. Non-being as the veil of Being is not
another entity, as little as Being itself, with which
Being covers itself up; it is this staying away itself, as

which Being discloses and gives itself to us. This is the
negativity inherent in Being, the "not" which derives in
the ultimate resort from the nature of truth itself. For
truth in the primordial sense is unhiddenness rooted in
hiddenness, revelation anchored to concealment. Metaphysical thinking of every form, but especially the
Cartesian-Kantian variety of subjectivism, is rooted in a
disclosure in which what remains hidden is precisely this
"not," this contrariety in the truth of Being as such. In
Kant's conception of Being as positedness, the presupposed
view of being as constant presence, underlying the entire
metaphysical tradition, remains the basis. But if, as
Heidegger maintains, being and nonbeing are not simply
equivalent to presence and absence, if being is conceived
as rich with the opponency of refusal and bestowal
intrinsic to it, it can no longer be regarded as amenable
to "pure reason" and its concepts, nor can presentedness
in pure intuition exhaust the full richness of Being.
Further, if the primacy of the present in all presence is
presupposed, unquestioningly and unjustifiably, as
Heidegger insists, in the Greek experience of Being on
which the whole metaphysical tradition rests, Being as
thus inclusive of the "not" must also be regarded as
incorporating within itself the full reality of time as
the unity of the past, present and future. Finally, if
"to be" cannot be thought of as something apart from the
human essence but only as mutually related and ingressive,
as Heidegger has demonstrated, it necessarily evades metaphysical thought, whether conceived as *theoria* or as
reflexio, giving no promise of the assurance and certitude
in our thinking about Being so relentlessly pursued by Kant.

Transcendental illusion, Kant says, mocks us with a
reality where none is to be found.[32] According to him,
the illusion is natural and inevitable, and it rests on
subjective principles, which it foists upon us as
objective. As he declares in a well-known passage,

> There exists, then, a natural and unavoidable
> dialectic of pure reason--not one in which some
> sophist has artificially invented to confuse
> thinking people, but one inseparable from human
> reason, and which, even after its deceptiveness
> has been exposed, will not cease to play tricks
> with reason and continually entrap it into
> momentary aberrations ever and again calling for
> correction.

Where is the locus of this "entirely natural antithetic"?
Does it lie in the positing, thetic character of reason or
does it derive, more primordially, from the contrariety of
Being as such, or, in the last resort, from the revealing-
concealing mystery of truth itself? Is the transcendental
dialectic merely negative, or does it not rather lead to a
more positive location of this transcendental untruth
(illusion) within transcendental truth itself and at one
with it as its own disessence?

NOTES

1. *Nietzsche*, 1:460.
2. *Critique of Pure Reason*, A 108f.
3. Ibid., A 250.
4. Ibid., A 146, B 185.
5. Ibid., B 294f.
6. Ibid., A 247, B 303.
7. Ibid., A 110.
8. *Kant und das Problem der Metaphysik*, 82.
9. *Critique of Pure Reason*, B 113.
10. The translation is N. Kemp Smith's. In the original
the sentence runs: "*Es ist bloss die Position eines
Dinges, oder gewisser Bestimmungen an sich selbst.*" Max
Müller translates this as "It is merely the admission of a
thing, and of certain determinations in it." According to
Heidegger's commentary in *Kants These ueber das sein*,
"certain determinations" are the modalities of the thing
as it is in itself, i.e., as object.
11. *Critique of Pure Reason*, N.K. Smith's translation, 517.
12. Ibid., 513f.

13. Ibid., 531.

14. Ibid., 533f.

15. Ibid., 513.

16. Ibid., 565ff.

17. *Kants These ueber das Sein.* The discussion of Kant's view of Being in this paper is based on this essay by Heidegger.

18. *Kant's gesammelte Schriften, Akademieausgabe,* vol. ?, 73; see also vol. 18, no. 6276.

19. *Critique of Pure Reason,* B 302 and B 302a.

20. Ibid., B 141f.

21. Ibid., B 131.

22. Ibid., A 218f., B 265f.

23. Ibid., A 219, B 266.

24. For Kant's remarks on "transcendental location (topic)" and its difference from "logical location (topic)" see *Critique of Pure Reason,* A 265f., B 324f.; for his discussion of "definition" and "explanation," see A 730, B 758. Following him, Heidegger distinguishes between *Erklaerung* and *Erlaeuterung* and derives both from *Eroerterung.* For further elucidation of these distinctions, see Otto Poeggeler's *Der Denkweg Martin Heideggers,* 280-296 and the author's *The Philosophy of Martin Heidegger,* 58 and 387.

25. *Critique of Pure Reason,* A 266, B 322.

26. *Science and the Modern World,* Mentor ed., 143ff.

27. Quoted by Julian Marias, *History of Philosophy,* 105-196.

28. *Holzwege,* 104.

29. Schelling, *Ueber die Natur der Philosophie als Wissenschaft,* quoted in Walter Schulz, *Der Gott der neuzeitlichen Metaphysik,* 57f.

30. *Zur Seinsfrage,* 38.

31. *Humanismusbrief,* in *Platons Lehre von der Wahrheit,* 112-114.

32. *Critique of Pure Reason,* B 530, A 502.

33. Ibid., A 298, B 355.

PROBLEMS OF INTER-CULTURAL UNDERSTANDING IN
UNIVERSITY STUDIES OF RELIGION

The question of the study of religions in Indian
universities has to be raised within the context of the
cultural situation prevailing in the world today generally
and in this country in particular. And since the
religious tradition that constitutes the predominant
strand in the cultural fabric of India is Hinduism, I, as
a Hindu coming from the Holy City of Varanasi and from the
Banaras Hindu University, can only raise it from this more
particular and specific point of view. It is only when we
speak from such concrete *points* of view that we save our
talk from running into abstract generalities, evading the
real issues that confront us, and come to grips with the
actual and the problematic. Far from limiting or
narrowing our inquiry, or encapsulating us within the
particularity of our cultural horizon, such points of
view, along with the presuppositions and prejudices that
inevitably go with them, alone provide the vantage point
from which a problem can be seen as real and meaningful to
us. As a student of "understanding" (*Verstehen*), I am
aware that "all understanding, irrespective of whatever
object it refers to, is ultimately religious", as Van der
Leeuw puts it, and also that the modern phenomenon of
"comparative religion" can itself be profitably approached
as a species of such "understanding." In what follows, I
shall accordingly seek to explore the subject of inter-
cultural and religious understanding from the perspective

Originally published in *Ānvīkṣikī: Research Bulletin of
the Centre of Advanced Study in Philosophy*, ed. by N.K.
Devaraja. Banaras Hindu University 1 (1968): 78-93.

of philosophical hermeneutics in so far as it is relevant
to our present task and to our concrete situation. The
factors that enter into and condition the particular
situation in this country may be broadly divided into two
groups: those that involve the Indian's relation to his
own religious tradition and those that concern the
contemporary impact upon this of other world-religions and
traditions. As implied by our perspectivistic approach
and as I hope to show more explicitly in the course of
this paper, the first of these is the more basic task for
us in India and in consequence any intelligent formulation
of the question which concerns us must be sought in terms
of that rather than in terms of an abstract and general
comparison of different religious traditions. The primary
task which faces us in this country today is, I submit,
the task of a critical and creative understanding of our
own religious traditions. This is not a merely
"academic," ivory tower pursuit but a necessary effort at
self-understanding upon which depends not only the sense
we have of our own identity but also what we strive to
become in the future in a world in which barriers of time
and place, of memory and hope, are breaking down, in which
we are slowly becoming enveloped in a common destiny.
This is both a threat and an opportunity. Among the
leading Christian thinkers of the West, at least, one
finds notable examples of intense and searching efforts
towards such self-understanding. That these efforts are
inseparably linked with the general intellectual climate
of the present and with a sincere striving towards a
dialogue with other religious traditions is evident from
the emergence of the new discipline of Comparative
Religion. In this paper, I should like to dwell at some
length upon the self-criticism and reconstruction that go
hand in hand with it. I should also like to say a few
words as to why I think that we in this country must learn
from this pre-occupation of Western theologians and

religious thinkers and why, before undertaking to formulate a conceptual frame-work or formula for a possibly
universal religion, we must take upon ourselves the more
humble task of self-examination and self-understanding, in
explicit awareness of all that such a task involves.

Lest I may have given the impression of conceiving too
narrowly the objectives of instituting religious studies
in Indian universities, I hasten to add that I consider
the very first of these to be a better knowledge of "the
faith of other men" and of other religious traditions, a
knowledge which is not merely scientific but insightful
and an understanding awareness of what is other. The
second task before such studies here is a similar comprehending knowledge of religions that have, on the one hand,
taken root in India, e.g. Christianity, Islam and Zoroas-
trianism and, on the other, those that have grown from
within our own tradition, e.g. Hinduism in all its variety
of sect and cult, Buddhism, Jainism and Sikhism. The
third aim, referred to earlier as the primary task before
us, is that of self-understanding of a critical appropriation and reconstruction of our own religious tradition in
its unity, in the perspective of our present cultural
situation and of our participation in the secular, scientific and technological adventure of man in the present
day world. Only after this return movement to ourselves
can we, in the last place, go on to the task of constructing a broad enough frame of reference for all religions,
in terms of which we can comprehend their variety, and of
reawakening an understanding of the sacred as an ineluctable and basic dimension of our experience, of our very
being as necessarily involved in Divinity. A fifth task
suggested by the Education Commission refers to religious
instruction and I shall say nothing about it here.

It may appear that the fulfillment of the first task
is an easy matter, requiring only a study of readymade
textbook material on the religions of the world. But

obviously a study which seeks to *comprehend* from within
the faith and traditions of other men must go much further
than acquiring mere information *about* them. It must
strive to comprehend the other in its otherness, let it
speak to us in its difference from us and allow it to lay
hold of us in its claim to truth. I make bold to suggest
that such an approach to what is other is somewhat alien
to the genius of our entire tradition and the task
therefore correspondingly difficult and against the grain
for us; also that we cannot take the first steps towards
an understanding of other religious traditions unless we
first notice and acknowledge understandingly this more
basic difference at the root of the cultural traditions of
East and West. In its understanding of both itself and
the other, India has followed the way of growth through
absorption and assimilation, rejecting what could not be
appropriated without its own disintegration, accepting
from other cultures whatever could be suitably transformed
to become part of its living body. The Indian cultural
tradition thus has retained its identity and continuity
but it has at no time *defined itself* in relation to the
other, nor acknowledged the other in its unassimilable
otherness, nor in consequence occupied itself with the
problem of relationship as it arises in any concrete
encounter with the other. It is true that much of the
purely philosophical activity in this country has been in
the past concerned precisely with this task of analysing,
demarcating and defining the metaphysical presuppositions
of the principal religious trends that were of indigenous
origin here. But this led only to the fixation and
hardening of a number of rival "positions," to the emergence of an extraordinarily energetic analytical thinking
in which the logical implications of each were meticu-
lously worked out, and to the development and co-existence
of independent "religions." The other was allowed to
live, mostly in peace, but without any effort at mutual

dialogue and understanding. In the second place, neither in religious thinking nor on the strictly philosophical level was there any explicit intellectual attempt within our tradition, in the long history of its encounter with Christianity and Islam, to understand them in their difference or to let them address us in their truth. The strategy was one of defense through insulation rather than one of active grappling or dialogue and this was perhaps made necessary by the exigencies of historical circumstance and, partly at least, by the very nature of these alien incursions and their uncomprehending claims.

The Western approach, in this respect, has been markedly different. As Karl Loewith has remarked: "The experience of the essential difference between Orient and Occident has laid the foundation of the entire history of Europe and put its stamp on it." Ever since the Greeks attained a sense of their own individual identity through their encounter with the Persians, from whom they distinguished themselves as from their Barbarian other, this process of delimitation and exclusion has been continuous. The West's relationship to other cultures is determined by its characteristic mode of thinking in concepts, that "enormous power of the negative" of which Hegel speaks in the *Phenomenology of Mind* and which constitutes that "energy of thinking", the intellectual activity of making distinctions, of dividing and separating, in which lies, according to Hegel, "the most amazing and the greatest power and work of the understanding." This negative, separative intellect of the West does not leave the world as it is, but works it over, changes it, analyses it into its elements, puts them together again and in this manner makes it its own. As the power of the negative, the understanding also objectifies everything, and is thus enabled to change and direct the course of the world. For Hegel, the crucial mark of the European spirit, as against the Oriental, is this capacity to turn everything into an

object standing over against it and thus to appropriate it
to itself as its own other. The peculiar freedom of the
European spirit lies, according to him, in "being with
itself in being different," as mediated by the negative
activity of the mind. Tne European spirit puts the world
over against itself, makes itself free from it, annuls
this opposition again and appropriates the other to
itself. In this mastery through objectification,
abstraction and conceptualization, there is nothing, as
Hegel proclaimed, which can present itself to this spirit
as a barrier that cannot be surmounted. Otherness is
overcome here through being grasped, comprehended, by the
objectifying concept.

It is not enough that we in this country should unreflectively assimilate, in our concern and need for participation in the economic, political and social efforts of
the modern world, this mode of thinking, indispensable as
the basis of all scientific and technological achievement.
Such assimilation, if it is not to insinuate into our very
being an alien force bound to disrupt and eventually
master it, must appropriate this other through the Western
way of conceptualization and in full awareness of its
otherness. A clear understanding of this peculiarly
Western attitude to the other is, more specifically, a
necessary first step towards an appreciation of its religious tradition and of the contrast between knowledge and
faith (*Wissen* and *Glauben*) which is characteristic of it.
The Western conception of knowledge and of faith have a
common origin in the mode of thinking peculiar to the West
which has been described above. To quote Loewith again:

> Both, scientific knowledge and faith, have before
> them a determinate object, and all determination
> is a delimitation or negation (*determinatio est
> negatio*), i.e. stating definitely that it is thus
> and not otherwise. We know something when we
> know something determinate and we have faith in
> something when we have faith in something
> determinate, e.g. in God's revelation in Christ.
> And we know something and have faith in something

when we do *not* know something else or have faith
in something different. The European perceives
all that is indeterminate and unlimited as
something *not yet* determined or indeterminable,
which can always be grasped more definitely and
more determinately.

This is how the West understands the other and this is how
it has in the main understood itself so far. To understand the religious traditions that have come to us from
the West, we must understand, not just their religions but
also, first and foremost, their way of understanding
themselves as well as others, the self-understanding of
their faith as well as the way in which it defines itself
and its aims in relation to other religious traditions.

Hegel has given classical expression to the West's
understanding of itself and its characteristic mode of
thought. His understanding of the "Oriental spirit",
however, summing up and making explicit the Western
approach to the Orient, is itself predetermined and
restricted by the limits imposed upon it by this very mode
of thought and of the way it understands itself. Judging
Eastern philosophy and religion in terms of the *not yet*
determined, he notices only a lack in the Orient. He
fails to see that this lack is at the same time, in the
words of Loewith, the Orient's great merit and its subtle
superiority, which consists in the fact that it acknow-
ledges the undetermined and indeterminable *as such* and is
thus capable of taking it, in an attitude of natural
attunement and precisely in its indeterminateness, as the
starting point and goal of a complete and well-rounded
knowledge. Maurice Merleau-Ponty also refers to Hegel as
one "who contrasted the Western idea of truth as the total
conceptual recovery of the world in all its variety to the
Orient, and who defined the Orient as a failure *in the
same understanding*." He recognizes it as a prejudice to
treat all other modes of thinking as only distant
approximations of conceptual understanding and to force

every other type of thought to the alternative of
resigning itself to being a first sketch of the conception
or disqualifying itself as irrational. He admits, even as
a Westerner, that "the Orient's 'childishness' has something to teach us, if it were nothing more than the
narrowness of our adult ideas" and that in these cultures
can be found

> a variant of man's relationship to being which
> would clarify our understanding of ourselves, and
> a sort of oblique universality. Indian and
> Chinese philosophies have tried not so much to
> dominate existence as to be an echo or sounding
> board of our relationship to being. Western
> philosophy can learn from them to rediscover the
> relationship to being and the initial option
> which gave it birth, and to estimate the
> possibilities we have shut ourselves off from in
> becoming "Western" and perhaps reopen them.

But even Merleau-Ponty agrees with the Hegelian, Western
claim, reaffirmed by Husserl, that the "historical
entelechy" of the West requires and authorizes it to
understand other cultures and that it is "committed to the
onerous task of understanding others," not necessarily in
order to destroy them but to face up to the crisis they
are going through and to rediscover the source from which
they derive and to which they owe their long prosperity.

This whole enterprise of "understanding," it would
seem, is a characteristically Western one. It must be
added, however, that it is also a recent one, even in
Western history. If the Orient has followed the path of
pre-conceptual absorption and insulation, the Occident has
also, until recently, treated the other merely as its own
negation, without caring to determine it in itself or
seeking to understand it from within. May it be that the
emergence of "understanding" heralds a new mode of
thinking without objectifying, more appropriate to this
new venture in mutuality. What is significant of the
present situation, inter-culturally speaking, is that with
all our difference, and despite our long indifference to

the enterprise of mutual understanding, we are now
actually participants in a world-embracing process which
can become aware of itself through a dialogue which has
already started and in which the difference between East
and West is becoming growingly blurred. So far, we have
been mostly engaged in exploring other cultures and
religious traditions with a view to discovering points of
similarity, if not just confirmation of basic insights in
our own. In doing so we have been guided and impelled by
the inner genius of our own cultural tradition. It is
time that we opened ourselves to the differences now,
coming to closer grips with the truth of those other
traditions, and turn the monologue of the past into a real
dialogue. Perhaps the other may then present itself to us
a truer face, come nearer to us and help us in comprehending our own selves, somewhat differently perhaps but
certainly more deeply and truly. True dialogue is less a
telling each other than a questioning of each other and it
never leaves us where we were before, either in respect of
our understanding of the other or of ourselves.

Most of what has been said above applies to the second
task confronting religious studies in our universities,
the task namely, of understanding the other within the
complex fabric which is the heritage of the Hindu student
of religion, with which he must come to terms from the
vantage point of his own belongingness to his specific
religious tradition, in the process widening and correcting this perspective itself. The attempt to grapple
with this task has already over a century's history behind
it and most of the great leaders of this country's
national renascence have contributed to it. It still
remains, however, for our universities to take up the task
in an organised, systematic way and devote to it the
scholarly, dispassionate and patient labour that it
requires. Much of what has been accomplished in this
field has been done by Western scholars and there is no

reason why we should not also bring to bear upon this task
the same detached and disciplined academic energy and
attention. In Professor Murti's classical study of
Madhyamika Buddhism we have already a model to inspire
scholars here.

To come to the third and central point, the task of
understanding our own religious and cultural tradition.
It is obvious that as intellectuals living in the world of
today, we are shaped not only by our own cultural heritage
but by three other forces to which we cannot close our
minds: the scientific and technological requirements of
today, along witn the general outlook and way of thinking
that sustain them; the pervasive secular cultural climate
of thought, expressed by the single word modernity, in
which we are enveloped; and the free encounter with other
traditions, religious and cultural, which has not only
become possible for us now but which constitutes an
obligation and a challenge coming to us from humanity's
new vision of a world community. It is in this new
context, the context of present, contemporary life, that
we are required to understand and re-appropriate our
tradition and make it truly our own. And we have to do
this not merely as scholars dedicated to the academic
pursuit of a "subject," nor in the interests of any sort
of a "traditionalist revival," nor indeed because any
special sanctity attaches to the past as past, but out of
a passionate concern with our present religious life. The
attempt to recapture what once was, the voice that was
once heard and the event that once happened, in the
perspective of an open future that can be ours, is the
only way in which we can be liberated into and for our
true present and see our religious present for what it
really is.

In the cultural history of Europe, the central problem
of the modern age has been posed by the coming into
existence of modern science, and since the seventeenth

century the principal task of its philosophy has been to
reconcile this new power of knowing and making with the
entirety of man's experience of life and his image of the
world and of himself, to a ceaseless wrestling with the
problem of revising his understanding of himself,
including his relationship to the heritage of his own
past, classical as well as Christian. What is important
for us in this country to realize is that as an integral
factor of our life now, scientific activity and outlook
cannot be kept apart, in another compartment as it were,
from our traditional culture, intellectual or religious,
that the scientific way of thinking, if it is not to be a
frail and superficial possession, must permeate all our
intellectual activity and that in consequence we are
placed under the obligation of a continued examination of
the nature of this way of thinking as well as of revising
and re-comprehending our tradition from the perspective of
our altered awareness. An instructive example of such an
experienced requirement in the field of recent religious
thought is Rudolf Bultmann's wrestling with the mytho-
logical elements in the New Testament and more radically
projected, in Dietrich Bonhoeffer's programme of reinterpreting Biblical concepts. The self-comprehension of
faith, this basic concept of Bultmann's theology, is
different from the metaphysical concept of self-
consciousness (as Gadamer has been at pains to point out),
and refers to the historical and hermeneutical task of
comprehending, in the context of the scientific temper of
thought today, the encounter with unobjectifiable
happening of revealed faith in the Christian tradition.
The pursuit of science is not just the specialized
preoccupation of a few professional scientists, nor a mere
skill, nor a stocking of expert knowledge about the
"material" world. It is a way of looking at things, an
attitude of mind and a habit of thinking, leaving nothing
unsubjected to its scrutiny, generating again and again

trends and movements exemplified by the Enlightenment of
the eighteenth century, criticising, debunking and
replacing concepts no longer capable of ordering our
experience in the manner demanded by its own inner logic
and commitments. The birth and death of gods, the rise of
new cosmologies, the criticism of superstitions--e.g. Pico
della Mirandola's attack on astrology during the Italian
Renaissance--a radical transformation of religious
concepts bearing on the forces which determine the affairs
of men and their regulation, all of these illustrate the
extent to which science transforms the whole of human
thought and existence. It is only when we have fully
opened ourselves to its impact and submitted to its
discipline that we can realise the magnitude of the task
of a renewed understanding and interpretation of our
cultural tradition and its special importance in this
country. No facile compromise or reconciliation,
miscalled "synthesis," but a relentless exposure to the
tension between the scientific consciousness and the
legacy of tne past is the way we can learn to address the
right questions to our religious tradition and be rewarded
by the answers truly adequate to our present situation.

Edward Shils, in his remarkable studies entitled, *The
Intellectual between Tradition and Modernity: the Indian
Situation* and *The Indian Intellectual*, has analyzed in
detail the whole nest of problems that face an ancient
tradition-bound society, such as ours, which seeks to
transform itself into a modern society. The pattern for
this has been laid down for our age by "Western civilization," with its educational, social, economic and
political thinking, its concepts of freedom, organization,
industry and rational administration, its scientific and
humanistic thought, its creative adventures in art,
literature and ideas. This complex of idea, sensibility
and practice has generated an international community of
intellectuals, a world-wide climate of opinion and a new

way of thought, expression and approach to our concrete
worldly problems which is characteristic of what Shils
calls the modern intellectual tradition, as against
India's own "great tradition of Brahmin intellectuality."
This modern tradition of intellectual work in literature,
science and scholarship has not yet succeeded, Shils
insists, in finding a firm foundation in India. Yet, in
so far as we are pushing on towards the goal of modernization and thus sharing in its world-wide intellectual
base, we are bound to experience the tension between the
claims of our traditional culture and the impulsion toward
modernity, as also a sense of alienation and distance from
our cultural past.

Without such experience of alienation, the question of
"understanding" could not have arisen and it is only when
"religion" becomes, as Professor Wilfred Cantwell Smith
has so well said, one aspect of life among others, merely
one facet of life alongside many others, instead of being
coterminous with human life in all its comprehensiveness,
that the "study" of religion arises. This fragmentation
of "an earlier cohesiveness or integrity of man's social
and personal life, once religiously expressed and
religiously sanctioned," generates the secular quest of
religious "understanding," just as the rise of "the
aesthetic consciousness," in Gadamer's sense, represents
an alienation from that immediacy of living in which art
was once man's way of experiencing the Divine and of his
response to it. Understanding seeks to overcome this
alienation by letting tradition speak to us once again in
all its revelatory power, without any attempt at reviving
a past mode or form of life, in the world of today,
fragmented, secularized and "modern," and in its language.
As a people striving to participate in the heightened,
incredibly complex and differentiated consciousness of
this world of today, we can neither go back to any epoch
of our past nor regain the immediacy of a bygone form of

consciousness. It is therefore all the more incumbent
upon us, if not indeed the only possibility open to us, to
strive to recapture, from the perspective of our own
station in time and place, the truth revealed and yet
hidden in our religious tradition and express it for our
time, for ourselves. Of the many elements in our
religious tradition calling for understanding, i.e., for
re-interpretation and reformulation, I may refer to two,
by way of example. The worship of "the many gods" is in
this country not just dead tradition or evocative poetry
but part of the life of many, a living reality of their
world, not yet overpowered by modernity. Does this
so-called polytheism, this worship of the graven image,
not have a profound truth of its own? Is there not here
something to understand, something which we can make our
own? Is not such understanding likely to make us more
explicitly aware of those presuppositions or prejudgments
which have been responsible for relegating such experience
of Divinity to an inferior level of the religious
consciousness? Can we not learn something, to this end,
from the history of *Mythos-Forschung* from Schelling to
Walter F. Otto and Karl Kerenyi, from Hoelderlin, from
Cassirer and from Martin Heidegger's re-opening of the
question of "God and the gods"? Another example is the
place, authority and understanding of revealed truth,
along with the role and significance of language in the
happening of such truth. Both in the Indian and Western
traditions there is a long history of logos-speculation
which is profoundly relevant to the task of a mutual
understanding, comprehensive of the very foundations of
each. We can learn something here not only from the long
tradition of the Christian doctrine of incarnation and the
word that became flesh, of the logos-mysticism of men like
Hamann and Boehme, Cusanus and Eckhart, but also from the
approach to language inaugurated by Heidegger and taken up
in the philosophical hermeneutic of Hans-Georg Gadamer and

in the theology of language as developed in the recent Protestant thought of an Ebeling and a Fuchs. Revelation, Incarnation, the Word, are root ideas in our own religious tradition, though in respect of them we are not only more "alienated" but have perhaps lost all living sense for them, as also the language in which to think about them. The recovery of the meaning of these for our present religious consciousness, their re-appropriation through understanding, is a major task for the study of our religious tradition in our day. From the vantage point of this renewed understanding we may then begin to inquire whether, and in what respects, the Christian doctrine is different, whether, and in what sense, the idea of "historicity" constitutes the crux of this difference. The rise and development of the historical consciousness during the last two hundred years, I may add here in passing, constitutes an integral element of modern intel- lectuality. This further contributes to the experience of alienation mentioned above and forces upon us a reflective relationship to the witness of past modes of life and thought, thus enabling the adoption of a critical attitude towards ourselves as taken up in a historical process. Our relation to tradition can no longer be one of conser- vation alone or determined by the rationalistic ideal of a total assimilation of fact into the concept, much less of an unreflective immersion in it.

In the third place, the free encounter with other traditions made both possible and necessary in today's planetary civilization provides an unparalleled oppor- tunity to reawaken, in Whitehead's words, the sense of vast alternatives, magnificent or hateful, lurking in the background, and awaiting to overwhelm our safe little traditions, which was lost by the moderns. We must realize that every tradition "only presents one finite aspect of the many-sided modes of importance which are pressing upon the outskirts of human consciousness."

Such expansion of understanding is not merely a "prime
necessity" for the survival of civilization; it is the
only safeguard against the dogmatism which paralyses
self-criticism and halts the emergence of novelty in the
patterns of conceptual experience, congealing tradition
into a lifeless burden, a deadening deposit which hides
and chokes up the very wellsprings which bestow the
dimension of the Holy and the quality of piety upon our
experience. What is needed here is that spirit of joyous
adventure which boldly marches out into the unfamiliar and
the alien, without fear of self-loss, and returns to
itself with enhanced understanding of itself, changed and
yet the same. Like all understanding, the understanding
of our cultural tradition is inescapably dialectical in
character and presupposes a going out of oneself, the
encounter with the other and the strange, and a return to
oneself. The encounter itself has the structure of mutual
questioning, presupposing mutual openness and so an
acknowledgement of the other as question-worthy, not its
dismissal as questionable. And, as Heidegger has said,
the wandering out in the direction of what is different
and question-worthy is not mere adventure but a homecoming. The way to what is closest to ourselves is the
longest way back and into the remote, back to the
nourishing well-head and away to distant regions. Only
thus can we truly come home to ourselves, understand and
be ourselves, and enter into the legacy of a vision that
is neither distorted nor blurred. This nisus towards the
goal of a *world-community* cannot reach its end through any
sort of *Herschaftswissen*, or any sort of cultural and
conceptual conquest, nor merely through a peaceful
co-existence of religious traditions, but solely through
this reaching out to the other in active understanding,
and in the service of a Truth which will perhaps never
shed its mystery but to which each tradition bears witness
and is in this united with each other.

The basic principle of all interpretation is that we must understand a text from and out of itself and the hermeneutic rule for this is that the whole must be understood in terms of the parts and the latter in terms of the whole. And we understand the text not by transposing ourselves into the mind of the author but by sharing the meaning of what he says and allowing for the possibility of its being true. Its goal is reached when we arrive at some kind of understanding with the text (person or tradition), with respect to the matter or meaning, with its claim to be valid. Our understanding of this meaning is in the first instance distorted, but also made possible, by our preconceptions and anticipations. Only our openness for what the other says and our willingness to listen to him, can guarantee that the encounter will lead us to an awareness of these precon- ceptions and thus to understand it, without bias, in the otherness of what it means. This circularity in the movement of understanding (from whole to part and back and from text to reader and back, in regard to form and con- tent respectively) is governed by the basic presupposition that only what really possesses a perfect unity of sense is comprehensible. This "anticipation of perfectness", as Gadamer calls it, grants to the text from the very first the possibility not only of expressing a meaningful whole but of uttering a truth that could deepen, widen or correct our own vision of the reality which is at bottom our common concern. The distance of time or cultural space is not a gulf over which understanding seeks to throw a bridge but is "the carrying ground of the process in which our present understanding is rooted" (Gadamer). This is what makes understanding a creative and unending processes. And it presupposes receptiveness for the other, preparedness for a radical suspension of our prejudgments, a spirit of questioning, i.e. of laying open and keeping open possibilities which were hitherto beyond

our ken, mindfulness of the historicity of our own way of
understanding and an awareness of the fact that in our
attempt to understand the past, history itself is
effectively at work. He who seeks to understand, his own
tradition or that of other cultures, can do so only from
his own particular standpoint; his "prejudices" not only
restrict his vision but enable it. In the act of understanding, this vision is both enlarged and corrected, at
the same time making the seeker explicitly aware of these
"prejudices," which are not just peripheral but constitute
the very core of our particularity. The critical awareness of these prejudices alters, however slightly, this
core itself and all understanding, therefore, changes us
and presupposes a readiness for that. But all understanding, in the next place, also changes what is understood. We never understand either our own cultural past
or that of other traditions as they understood themselves,
but always differently and in the context of our present
way of life, in terms of which understanding translates
it. Understanding thus is never mere repetition or
reaffirmation of what has been; it is itself a movement,
an event in cultural history, generates true novelty and
thus remoulds tradition. No culture is an island enclosed
within its own horizon, though all cultures and traditions
have their being within such horizons. It is of the very
essence of the "hermeneutic experience," i.e., the
explicit comprehension of the voice of the past and the
other, that in it the horizons, within which both he who
seeks to understand and what is understood exist, open
out, move towards and fuse with each other, in however
small a degree. This is a movement towards a higher
generality, but it is an unending movement, and towards a
universality which can emerge in the concrete only dimly,
imperfectly, without foreknowledge of its true shape. The
problem of intercultural understanding as a movement of
living thought is not the problem of discovering a formula

for the "other" culture, or of grasping it in a concept, but of a mutual sharing of horizons, however slightly. Understanding in this context is not to be taken as a psychological process or occurrence but solely in terms of the matter or reality comprehended, with the fusion of horizons implied in it, and in this sense the movement of understanding is a movement in the very substance of this reality. The two partners in the dialogue of thought that is understanding, are not so much the agents of this process as themselves taken up in it and carried by this movement. "They do not so much lead as they are led by it," in Gadamer's words, and "mutual understanding or its failure is like something that has happened with us....The dialogue has its own spirit and the language which is employed and formed in it bears a truth of its own, i.e. discloses something, makes something emerge, which henceforth is." Understanding is thus a dynamic and creative process, and what is understood in it is this movement of truth towards novelty. Language is the medium in which this movement is accomplished, leading to the forging of a new and common language, which alone enables participation in a common meaning and a common truth in its actuality. For it is not we, but language that speaks. Self-understanding is thus inseparable from the understanding of the other, and it reaches its fulfillment only with the fashioning of a language which mediates us with the other and our present with our past.

The final task for religious studies in our universities is a purely theoretical one, in the narrow sense of the term, and its scope is covered by what is called the philosophy of religion. In so far as each religion is particular, concrete and individual, its study implies investigation of a mass of empirical material or factual information. The problem of conceptualizing this, in explicit comparison with and in the context of similar material in the other religious traditions and with other human sciences such as psychology, sociology and anthropology, comes first. Next, we have the philosophical problem of analysing and systematising the most general religious concepts, of building up a framework allowing for all religions--showing how they are possible--and of examining the truth-claims of each. To the extent to which these problems are adequately solved, we have the promotion of inter-cultural understanding, if only on the plane of abstract conceptualization. Finally, there is the problem of examining our religious life and ideas on a level deeper than the "metaphysical," beneath or beyond the level of that objectifying, presentational thinking which has brought, if Heidegger's analysis is to be accepted, the spectre of Nihilism, that uncanniest of all guests, into our midst. This is the problem of seeking for a name for that which evokes piety in the men of today, of discerning the truth that bears it, of taking note of its remoteness and nearness from us, of learning to speak about it in a manner which will bring men of different faiths and traditions nearer and not divide them, which will make us sightful, not merely for "our" faith but for the reality to which we respond by faith or its lack, and which is ever with us, even when manifest only as its own absence. For, what we understand, in the last resort, is not men but, through their doings, feelings and sayings the matter or *Sache*, the truth that shines through these and to which they bear witness. The collaborative striving for seeing this truth is at the time the problem of finding a language that goes beyond the opposition of East and West, beyond the clash of cultures and the conflict of tongues. This is the encounter and dialogue on a level beneath the emergence of difference, insight into the true nature of these differences, and a step taken beyond them. It is a task to which our very finitude commits us, never terminating so long as the human spirit endures on earth.

I have dealt in this paper with four tasks for university studies in religion and I have tried to show how in each case the basic problem is one of "under-standing." The fifth task pertaining to religious education is no exception to this. In all understanding, the moment of what may be called "application" is essential, i.e., the comprehension of a general utterance in terms of my own particular present. In such mediation of the religious tradition and the present consciousness lies precisely the function of religious education.

UNDERSTANDING AND TRADITION

Recent philosophical thought has been marked by a
growing awareness of the role of tradition in moulding our
experience of the world and of ourselves and in determining both the manner and content of philosophical
reflection on experience. Along with that has gone a
recognition of the particularity and uniqueness of
traditions and a quest for the hidden logic of their
historical development. Western philosophical thinkers
like Edmund Husserl, Martin Heidegger and Maurice
Merleau-Ponty, for example, all philosophize with an
explicit awareness of the fact that they stand within a
particular tradition of thought, the Occidental.
Furthermore, they not only reflect on the basis of this
tradition, so that the questions they raise and seek to
answer have a necessary reference to that tradition; they
also exhibit a relatively novel concern within philosophy
for this fact itself as being integral to that quest for
universality which is of the very essence of philosophical
thinking. What we call progress in philosophy depends in
large measure on the continued exposure and overcoming of
our naivety, of what is at any stage taken for granted and
remains implicit. Philosophical claims to universality,
not only in individual thinkers but also in entire traditions are themselves rooted in presupposed particularities
of vision and what was once regarded as an obvious,

Presidential address in the Metaphysics and Epistemology
section of the Indian Philosophical Congress, Dharwar,
1969, originally published in *Ānvīkṣikī, Research Bulletin
of the Centre of Advanced Study in Philosophy,* ed. by N.K.
Devaraja. Banaras Hindu University, 2 (1969): 117-136.

straightforward and absolutely valid affirmation turns out
to have been "rendered possible" by certain implicit
presuppositions. A significant advance in present-day
philosophical awareness consists in the growing sense of
such particularity and limitedness, in the asking of new
sorts of questions engendered by this and in the quest of
a wider generality of thought and utterance which is not
yet unmindful of the particularities it seeks to transcend
and of the fact that such transcendence always remains
relative to the particulars which constitute its point
of departure.

In his last work, *The Crisis of the European Sciences
and Transcendental Phenomenology*, Husserl speaks of the
"inborn telos" of European man, since the birth of Greek
philosophy, to desire to live as men inspired by
philosophical reason and be able to live only as such. He
asks whether this urge towards the infinite movement from
latent to manifest reason and this striving for self-
regulation through the presence in him of the authentic
truth of humanity itself is a mere historical-factual
delusion, a merely fortuitous acquisition of a type of man
accidentally emerging in the midst of other peoples and
races and of other historical developments, or is it
rather that in the Greek man there comes into view for the
first time what is intrinsic to humanity as such as its
very entelechy? What is at stake in the present-day
crisis in "the European sciences" is reason and
rationality, this specific entelechy of European man
itself, and upon its power to sustain itself and prevail
will depend, Husserl asserts, the decision "whether
European humanity carries within itself an absolute idea
and is not a merely empirical anthropological type like
'China' or 'India', and whether, furthermore, the
spectacle of the Europeanization of all other parts of
mankind reveals the sway of a significance which is part
of the meaning of the world itself, and not just an

unmeaning, historically accidental emergence." In the
Vienna Lecture on the crisis of European man and philosophy, out of which the larger "Crisis" volume developed,
Husserl speaks again in similar fashion of the uniqueness
of Europe and of the spiritual telos of European man.

> There lies (in our own Europe) something unique,
> which all other human groups, too, feel with
> regard to us, something that, apart from all
> considerations of expediency, becomes a
> motivation for them--despite their determination
> to retain their spiritual autonomy--constantly to
> Europeanize themselves, whereas we, if we
> understand ourselves properly, will never, for
> example, Indianize ourselves. I think that we
> feel (and with all its vagueness this feeling is
> not without its own justification) that in our
> European humanity there is an innate entelechy
> that thoroughly controls the changes in the
> European image and gives to it the sense of a
> development in the direction of an ideal of life
> and of being, as moving towards an eternal pole.

The term "philosophy" itself is for Husserl a proper name
denoting that "completely new kind of attitude of
individuals towards their environing world" resulting in a
"completely new type of spiritual structure, rapidly
growing into a systematically rounded cultural form that
the Greeks called philosophy."

In Heidegger's thought, philosophical reflection is
even more explicitly and prominently linked with the
specific Greek-European tradition, and the tradition-bound
character of thought itself, the cultural particularity of
its origin and historical unfoldment, emerges vividly and
sharply into view. Heidegger does not merely assert
dogmatically, "However and whatever we attempt to think,
we can only think within the bounds sketched out by tradition. Its presence reigns when it frees us from thinking
back to a thinking ahead which is no more planning. Only
when we turn thinkingly towards what has already been
thought, shall we be used for what has yet to be thought."
The whole movement of his thought, all along the way, is a
massive demonstration of this claim as well as a long

drawn out exercise in uncovering the facticity and
historical particularism that has ever clung to the
Western philosophical tradition. His thinking is thus
basically a critique of this tradition, oblivious so long
of its own particularism, and at the same time an attempt
to develop a way of thinking for which that tradition will
provide a liberative rather than a restrictive basis for
future planetary thought. "Metaphysics" is for Heidegger
only another name for "Occidental thought in the entirety
of its essence" and his quest for the way back into the
ground of metaphysics, his attempt to take the step back
that leads out of metaphysics into its essence and source,
his overcoming metaphysics, are all attempts at making
explicit the particularistic, historically rooted
presuppositions in which that specific mode of thinking
has been based and thus at dispelling the illusion of its
apparent universality and necessity. Philosophical
thinking itself, as he analyses its nature, is a specific,
historically conditioned mode of thinking about man, world
and Being, Greek in origin and proper to the West, and not
just thinking *simpliciter* about these ultimates. As he
puts it in *What is Philosophy?*

> The word *philosophia* tells us that philosophy is
> something which first determines Greek existence.
> Not merely that--*philosophia* determines also the
> inmost distinctive feature of Occidental-European
> history. The phrase "Occidental-European
> Philosophy" which one so often hears is in truth
> a tautology. Why? Because "philosophy" is in
> essence Greek--Greek in the sense that in the
> origin of its essence philosophy is of the sort
> that it has first claimed the Greeks in order to
> unfold itself. To say that philosophy is in
> essence Greek is the same as to say that the
> Occident and Europe, and they alone, are in their
> inmost historical course originally "philo-
> sophical." This is proved by the rise and domi-
> nation of the sciences. Because they originate
> from the inmost Occidental-European course of
> history, namely the philosophical, therefore they
> are today in a position to give their specific
> stamp upon the history of man on the whole
> earth....The word *philosophia* appears as it were

as the birth-certificate of our own history; we
might even say, as the birth-certificate of the
contemporary epoch in world-history which calls
itself the Atomic Age.

It is as an invitation to Western thought to shed its
particularism of tradition that Heidegger declares, "The
thinking of the future is no longer philosophy, because it
thinks on a level deeper than metaphysics, which term also
means the same."

I do not propose to discuss here either the contrasting assessments of the Western philosophical heritage
by Husserl and Heidegger or their differing evaluation of
the significance of the Oriental traditions, in the
perspective of our present and ongoing search for self-
understanding and of an ultimate framework of meaning upon
which that rests. Nor do I intend here to track down the
changing presuppositions behind Western thinkers' understanding of the significance of their own philosophical
tradition relatively to the Oriental, first explicitly
stated by Hegel, repeated by Husserl and subjected to
critical scrutiny more recently by Heidegger and Merleau-
Ponty. The views quoted above open out a fascinating and
challenging domain of questions, of central philosophical
importance and vital to our own self-understanding as
legatees of another heritage than the Western but as also
having an inescapable share, in the present and for
tomorrow, in what both Husserl and Heidegger call "the
Europeanization of the earth." Instead of discussing
these on the present occasion, I should rather like to
draw your attention to this basic fact, as it seems to me,
of the rootedness of philosophical thought in a cultural
matrix, to the fact that human reflection on the basic
problems of life and experience, the very fabric and
character of that experience itself, is always embedded in
a context of tradition. This gives it a factual and
historical dimension requiring what has been called
understanding (*Verstehen*) and interpretation in recent

thought on the foundations and philosophical significance
of the human sciences (*Geisteswissenschaften*). Further,
and principally, I should like to speak at some length on
what understanding means in this context, leaving it for a
future occasion to discuss what this conception of the
role and significance of understanding implies for a more
broadly conceived theory of experience itself. In what I
have to say on these questions, I may add, I am indebted
to the ideas of Martin Heidegger and Hans-Georg Gadamer,
two contemporary thinkers who have contributed significantly to our knowledge of the place of understanding in
that self-awareness of tradition which is so intrinsically
a part of philosophy itself.

The human sciences are concerned with aspects of
experience which in the main lie outside the scope of the
exact sciences, and include, in Gadamer's words, the
experience of philosophy, the experience of art and the
experience of history itself. They deal, thus, with that
dimension of experience in which a truth is disclosed to
us and an awareness of reality is made available to us
through the vehicle of tradition which is not accessible
through the methods of the exact sciences and is not
verifiable by them. Systematic reflection on the epistemological problem of the nature and validity of knowledge in the human sciences began with the reaction,
during the last decades of the nineteenth century, against
the prevailing positivism in philosophy and the claim of
the exact sciences to be the model and norm of all knowledge whatsoever. Wilhelm Windelband and Heinrich Rickert
of the South-West German Neo-Kantian School sought to
justify the independent epistemological status of the
cultural sciences as against the natural sciences by
pointing out the differentiating features of the fields to
which each kind addressed itself. The former, Windelband
pointed out, are "ideographic" and concerned with individual happenings and processes, whereas the latter are

"nomothetic" and concerned with universally valid laws.
Rickert held fast to the dualism of natural and cultural
sciences, considered the individual and singular character
of the processes dealt with by the latter as being due to
the connection of facts with value-systems and in general
sought to ask, after the manner of Kant, how a science of
historical knowledge is possible and, conceiving historical knowledge after the pattern of knowledge in the
natural sciences, attempted to provide an epistemological
foundation for it. It was, however, Wilhelm Dilthey, the
philosopher of life, who saw vividly and clearly that
human life and thought are embedded in tradition and
history, who wrestled massively with the problems this
raised for the distinctive methodology of the human
sciences and who first grasped, even though in a fumbling
and groping fashion, that the philosophical foundations of
these sciences cannot be laid through a narrowly conceived
theory of knowledge, as it became prevalent with the "back
to Kant movement" in German philosophy. What he was
concerned with was the full and concrete movement of human
life, as expressed and embodied in literature and art, in
philosophy, religion and history, whereas, as he declared,
"in the veins of the 'knowing subject' constructed by
Locke, Hume and Kant runs no real blood." The decades of
hard work which Dilthey devoted to laying the foundations
of the *Geisteswissenschaften* (a term which became current
in German thought since the translator of Mill's *A System
of Logic* first mis-rendered the phrase "moral sciences" by
this term) represents, as Gadamer has pointed out, a
continuous effort to grapple with the logical demands
raised for these sciences by the famous last chapter of
Mill. Even though unable to liberate himself completely
from the hold of the natural science model of knowledge
and from the notions of method implied in it, he nevertheless saw that the dogmatism of Mill's insistence on
induction was the outcome of a lack of historical

awareness, that the key to the specific kind of knowing
involved in the human sciences lay precisely in the
historical dimension of life and in the fact that these
sciences were concerned with historical processes and with
the way our present consciousness is determined by what is
transmitted to us from the past. Keeping in view this
distinctive and essential dimension of human experience,
Dilthey sought to do for the historical human sciences
what Kant had done for the science of nature and for "pure
reason," namely to write a critique of historical reason,
and to formulate categories appropriate to "life," i.e.,
to human experience as determined by historical tradition
and man's own inner historicity, as against the abstract
categories of pure reason operative in the scientific
knowledge of natural processes. He went beyond the Neo-
Kantians in conceiving experience not in a narrow
"epistemological" framework but as part of the process of
living itself, as *Erlebnis* or felt and lived experience
and as that fusion of memory and expectation in the
present which is implied in the historicity intrinsic to
human living and experiencing as such.

Dilthey thought of life, along with its historical
expression and objectification, through which alone it can
be understood, as a text which must yield its meaning from
within itself and for which the appropriate cognitive
operation is understanding rather than explaining, as in
science, or subsuming conceptually the particular under a
universal. World-history is for him, in Gadamer's words,
a great obscure book, the collective work of the human
spirit composed in the languages of the past which has to
be understood, as one understands a text handed down from
the past. Dilthey, it should be recalled, was the
biographer of the theologian Friedrich Schleiermacher and
profoundly influenced by his work on Hermeneutics, "the
art of understanding" anything that exists in written form
and even what is orally communicated, not just the

interpretation of the Holy Bible, to which this term was originally restricted. By giving to the problem of understanding a central position in his work, Schleiermacher transformed this ancient auxiliary discipline providing a method to be applied by the philologist or the theologian, into the philosophical theory of the nature and scope of the activity of understanding itself and thus laid the foundations on which Dilthey, Heidegger and Gadamer have built. It is significant to note that according to Schleiermacher hermeneutics is the art not so much of producing understanding where there was none before as of avoiding misunderstanding. He believed that misunderstanding arises of itself and that "understanding has at every step to be deliberately desired and pursued." His conception of a universal hermeneutics or theory of understanding is based on the realization that the experience of strangeness and alienation and thus the possibility of misunderstanding, in respect of what is transmitted to us from the past, torn from the world to which it originally belonged, is universally present. The quest of understanding presupposes such a sense of alienation and remoteness from tradition and does not arise so long as we unreflectively live under its domination, or fail to see the novel present as it actually is and claims us. As for the phenomenon of understanding itself, Schleiermacher thought that it consisted in transporting ourselves into the psychology of an author, into the individuality of his frame of mind, tnrough the reproduction in our minds of his original act of creation, through a sort of reversal of the original process of composing, and in the last resort, through a congenial divination of his creative individuality.

This psychological interpretation of the nature of understanding in the sense of the re-creation of an original creation is open to the charges both of psychologism and of an inadequate conception of our

relationship to our past. The first, psychologism, has
been a constant challenge to philosophers, so diverse in
temper and approach as Bradley and Frege or Husserl and
Wittgenstein, since its emergence in British Empirical
philosophy and is by now a dead horse. In the present
context, the problem is: when we understand a human
document expressive of a thought, deed or experience, is
that which is understood a particular, factual mental
process, or is it a meaning, with the moment of ideality
and impersonality attaching to it, that we comprehend and
share? Do we understand a text, as a vehicle of meanings,
or the mind of the author, the *mens auctoris*? Or, is the
true object of understanding not even the text but,
through the text, the truth it seeks to disclose to us?
As in a conversation, do we not rather understand each
other in respect of the subject matter talked about than
pry into the subjective processes occurring within us?
Where a considerable distance of time separates us from
the author of a text, understanding aims, according to
Schleiermacher, at equating ourselves with the *author* and
putting ourselves in his position, to which the putting
ourselves in the position of the original *reader* is a
preparatory act. Is the latter not equally, even more
basically part of the attempt to understand?
Schleiermacher was not unaware of the fact that the
reproduction can never amount to identification with it
and he therefore laid it down as the aim of the hermeneutical enterprise to understand a writer better than he
understood himself. This formula, which has been
subsequently interpreted in a variety of senses, contains
the core of the hermeneutical problem. It is obvious that
the deliberate activity of reproducing the original
creative act can bring into consciousness a great deal of
which the author himself was unaware, as happens, for
example, in literary criticism. To understand an author
thus includes understanding his unconscious intention and

rendering explicit the implications of what he said. But
is this superiority of the critic and interpreter to be
understood in a psychological sense or in the sense of a
better knowledge of the subject matter dealt with by the
author? Is it legitimate, in other words, to take a text
purely as a document expressive of the author's mind, in
isolation from its claim to lay bare and communicate a
truth? Is understanding a sort of psychoanalysis? The
opposite extreme of such a psychological claim to
understanding in the sense of knowing better, we may add,
is frequently found in the practice of philosophers, from
Aristotle to Wittgenstein, and is exemplified by the
following assertion of Kant:

> I need only remark that it is by no means
> unusual, upon comparing the thoughts which an
> author has expressed in regard to his subject,
> whether in ordinary conversation or in writing,
> to find that we understand him better than he has
> understood himself. As he has not sufficiently
> determined his concept, he has sometimes spoken,
> or even thought, in opposition to his own
> intention.

In the case of the philosophical tradition as such, the
emphasis is all on the subject-matter, the truth of a
thought, and on conceptual clarity and consistency in
dealing with it. Further critical analysis can always
lead to new logical insights and a later thinker may be
able to see what the earlier has said in the light of a
truth hidden from himself. Some such principle is
involved not only in the notion of philosophy as primarily
critical and analytical and is itself determined by the
rationalistic ideal of a total and supra-historical
conceptual transparency. Even in a thinker like
Heidegger, for whom philosophical reflection is itself a
"hermeneutics of facticity", the understanding and
interpretation of finite, tradition-centred thought, the
principle of the unthought in what a philosopher has
actually thought appears to be based on the assumption

that in some sense to understand an author is to understand him better than he understood himself. But "better," in this case, is historically meant and is an admission of the limits imposed upon a thinker by his temporal situation within a tradition; every great thinking, Heidegger asserts therefore, understands itself best within the limits marked out for it.

These considerations throw light also on the erroneous notion of understanding as reproduction. What is allegedly reproduced in understanding is never meaningful today in the same way as it was when first produced, and when its original meaning is sought to be grasped in isolation from the historical process which has nourished it and kept it alive and from our own place in the present, it can only amount to the re-evocation and transmission of a dead meaning. Hegel had better insight into the futility of all attempts to restore the past and of the true task of the thinking spirit in relation to the past, for, as he saw, the nature of the spirit as historical, as which alone can it come to full awareness of itself, consists, not in the restitution of what is gone but in its reflective mediation with our present experience. The historical distance which separates an author and his interpreter introduces a necessary difference between what the author may have meant and what the interpreter understands. The author, Chladenius even roundly said, need not know the true meaning of his own text at all. In Gadamer's words, "Every age has to understand a text passed down to it from the past in its own way, for it is part of the totality of the tradition, in which that age is materially interested and within which it seeks to comprehend itself." The real meaning of a text need not be restricted to what the author "intended," nor to what the first readers understood, for it is also determined by the historical situation of the interpreter and thus by the entirety of the objective

process of history. The meaning of a text always
surpasses and overflows its author and understanding is
therefore never merely reproductive but always contains an
element of creative productivity. Understanding, strictly
speaking, is not understanding better but understanding
differently and with that excess of meaning which accrues
from the existence of a historical tradition itself.

Dilthey followed Schleiermacher in regarding understanding as the reproduction or re-experiencing of the
inner world of experience of another, but was led by his
own persistent questioning to overcome the psychologism
infecting the earlier view. According to him, the human
sciences owe their distinctive character to the fact that
their procedure is based on the systematic relation among
life, or lived experience, expression and understanding.
What is to be recaptured in understanding, through its
expression, is an *Erlebnis*, immediate and pre-reflexively
given, not as an object standing over against my apprehension but as an occurrence in which content, existence
and awareness are not yet distinguished. But as he saw
more and more clearly, what is significant in such lived
experience is not merely its subjective reality but the
fact that it represents a unit of meaning. As he
remarked, "That which in the stream of time forms a unity
in the present because it has a unitary meaning is the
smallest entity which we can designate as a lived
experience." It is these unities of meaning--conceived by
Dilthey as temporal, reaching out to the future in
anticipation and back to the past in recollection--which
we grasp in the act of understanding and which become
accessible to us not in introspection but only through the
interpretation of their expression and objectification in
history and tradition, and through an interpretation,
moreover, which is itself in terms of historical rather
than abstract and static categories. The knowledge of man
is the knowledge of everything in which the human spirit

has expressed itself, and the mode in which we have such
knowledge is understanding, which, as Dilthey said, has
its true object in the objectification of life itself.
According to him, "What man is and what he wills, he
experiences only in the development of his nature through
the millenia and never completely to the last syllable,
never in objective concepts but always only in the living
experience which springs up out of the depths of his own
being." Despite the fact that Dilthey conceived his quest
as one for objectively valid knowledge in the human
sciences, after the Neo-Kantian model, he could not fail
to realize that the knowing subject, the historian seeking
to understand, does not simply stand over against the
historical flow of life which is the object of his
inquiries but is himself also borne on the same movement
of historical life. But the implications of this for the
nature of understanding as itself shot through with
historicity were to be drawn only later by Heidegger and
Gadamer, thus exhibiting man's relationship to tradition
in a radically new perspective.

Dilthey asserted that universally valid synthetic
judgments are possible in historical knowledge because man
himself is essentially historical, in the very opaque
depths of his being, because here, as Vico said long ago,
man is both the maker and the investigator of history, and
subject and object in this case have thus a common nature.
But this does not yet answer the question how on the basis
of the experience of single individuals we can rise above
to historical experience. As Gadamer has remarked, the
fabric of inter-relationships in history must in the end
be understood as a systematic complex of meanings which
basically transcends the horizon of the lived experience
of individuals. History is concerned with structures
transcending what can enter into the experience of single
individuals or what others may understand through
reproduction in their own experience. The meaning which

is to be understood here is not only not objectively given
but is something that goes beyond the collective
experience of all possible subjects, and the question is
how such transsubjective meaning is at all knowable.
Erlebnis, regarded non-psychologically as a unity of
meaning, cannot provide the basis for historical understanding, and it cannot do this, moreover, because every
Erlebnis is itself already determined *a priori* by pre-
existing historical realities such as society, state and
the entire heritage of the past. Nor can the concept of
"expression," objectifying the structural inter-relations
of lived experience, provide the adequate field to which
understanding and interpretation may address themselves,
for if the movement of history exhibits an excess of
meaning, and discloses a truth, beyond all that can be
apprehended within the experience of individual human
beings, how and what does this express, and can it be
regarded as "expressed" at all, in Dilthey's sense, unless
we posit an ideal subject and a supra-individual *Erlebnis*?
It is not surprising, therefore, to find that Dilthey
extended Hegel's concept of the objective spirit to
include art, religion and philosophy itself, which were
for the latter constitutive of Absolute spirit. For
Dilthey, they were not immediately revelatory of truth but
forms in which life expresses itself, and the historical
consciousness therefore remained the only access to what
metaphysics so far had been the means of knowing, the
achievement of absolute and infinite self-transparency of
spirit. Can, however, historical understanding take the
place of the absolute self-knowledge of the spirit through
concepts? Contrary to the claims of Ranke, Droysen and
Dilthey, a historical consciousness aware of its own
historicity can never rise above history, nor shed its
linkage with the particularity of its place in the
movement of history. As pointed out above, for Dilthey
the object of understanding is the world of history

regarded as a text to be deciphered; everything in history
is comprehensible, for it is all text, as Gadamer comments, and historical inquiry is a matter of decoding the
alphabet of history and thereby acquiring objective and
universally valid knowledge of the past rather than
gaining historical experience aware of its own finitude.
The epistemological Cartesianism in which he remained
caught up and the vain aspiration after total clarity,
rational transparency and de-mythologizing which he shared
with the thinkers of the Englightenment, prevented him
from seeing the true historicity of our experience of
history itself, the finitude infecting it, and led him to
conceive the act of understanding both subjectivistically
and ahistorically.

We cannot deal here with the early Husserl's contribution to the phenomenology of understanding, including
his doctrine of the intentionality of consciousness which
deeply influenced Dilthey, nor with the implications of
his theories of anonymous and implicit intentionalities,
or horizontal intentionality and of the life-world, for
the phenomenon of understanding in relation to the
historical tradition and to human experience generally.
Heidegger's own views, central to this topic, will be
assumed as familiar and mentioned here in the most summary
fashion. The radical critique of subjectivism in modern
philosophy he launched, the temporal interpretation of
Being and man and in general the re-opening of the
ontological dimension in philosophical inquiry are all
reflected in the conception of the nature and role of
understanding. In his existential analytic of *Dasein* in
Being and Time, Heidegger has laid bare the ontological
structure of man, and this includes understanding as an
intrinsic constituent of man's being-in-the-world. As
thus conceived, understanding is not just one method of
knowing but the basic mode of man's being-there itself,
tne primordial cognitive openness to his being-in-the-

world or, in Kantian terminology, the condition of the
possibility of all actual ways of knowing open to man and
thus prior to them. According to this transcendental
interpretation of understanding, it is no longer, in
Gadamer's words, "the resigned ideal of man's experience
of life in the dotage of the spirit, as with Dilthey, but
it is also not, as with Husserl, an ultimate methodological ideal of philosophy as against the naivety of simply
floating along the stream of life, but is on the contrary
the original form in which man exists as being-in-the-
world." Understanding is no longer a methodological
concept or a mode of knowing distinct from scientific
explaining and specific to the human sciences alone, but
is conceived as the primordial mode of being of human life
itself. In this deeper sense, understanding is not just
passive awareness but man's potentiality to be, in this
way or that; it is man himself in his essence as possibility. Further, all understanding is intrinsically of
the nature of project, not in the sense of thinking out
plans for the future but as the very mode of being of man
as possibility and as essentially ahead-of-himself. By
virtue of its character as project--which for Heidegger is
always a thrown project determined by the temporal
modality of the past and in conformity with the facticity
attaching to all existence--understanding is itself that
basic movement of transcendence which lifts us above bare
entities to their being, i.e., that dimension of ultimate
meaning from which they derive their character as such and
so. From this perspective, it also becomes evident that
understanding is not the detached contemplation of a
meaning factually out there but is always self-understanding:
whatever and whenever we understand, we always do this in
terms of projecting ourselves on our own possibilities.
The thrownness and projectivity intrinsic to understanding
reflect the temporality of man's very being as care and
render it obvious how belongingness to tradition is just

as originally and essentially part of the historical
finitude of man as the projective and creative movement
towards his own future possibilities. In all understanding and interpretation, thus, the totality of this
existential structure of thrownness and projection, of
facticity and existentiality, is at work.

Heidegger's discussion of the relation between
understanding and interpretation or explication in *Being
and Time* is also of considerable importance in clarifying
a disputed question in hermeneutic theory: are these two
different and independent activities and can one take
place without the other? Interpretation, according to
Heidegger, is grounded on understanding and is only the
explicit cultivation and carrying through of the latter.
It is not a subsequent and additional act of taking notice
of what has already been understood but is an explication
of the possibilities projected in understanding and a
constitutive moment in the unfoldment of the latter as the
awareness of something as something. We shall notice
below how explication involves language and how all understanding necessarily occurs within the medium of language.
Of capital importance for the theory of understanding is
Heidegger's analysis of the circularity of understanding.
According to the principle of "the hermeneutic circle,"
recognized as basic in the methodology of interpretation
and exegesis by the predecessors of Schleiermacher, the
parts of a text must be understood in the context of the
whole and the whole in the light of the parts. Schleiermacher applied this principle in the psychological sense
already mentioned above, but he also saw it as a universal
feature of the phenomenon of understanding as such. To
understand is always to execute an unending movement from
the whole to the parts and back again in an ever widening
circle until the relatively total meaning is in our grasp.
But neither the subjective nor the objective interpretation of this circle, the one in terms of comprehending the

author's mind and the other in the sense of a detached, uninvolved grasping of the text as an objective whole of meaning within its historical context, really touches the core of the matter. Beyond having this purely formal character, understanding is circular also in respect of the content or subject matter we seek to comprehend.

The marvel of understanding, which is no mysterious communion of souls, consists in the sharing of a common meaning and its aim is the achievement of agreement between oneself and another, or coming to an agreement with another, in respect of a content, through the unending circular inter-play between the implicit pre-suppositions with which we read a text and the meaning which it conveys to us. This is what Heidegger means when he says,

> Interpretation is never a presuppositionless grasping of something which is already given. When in the particular and concrete case of explication as attempted in "exact" text-interpretation, one appeals to the authority of "what is really there," this apparent what-is-really-given-there is nothing but the presupposition, unexamined and taken for granted, with which the interpreter approaches a text and which is necessarily the starting point in all interpretation.

All understanding has this "pre-structure," as Heidegger has called it, in consequence of which the interpretation of something as something is basically and *a priori* grounded in the pre-possession or prior intention, the pre-view, the sight which we bring with us, and the pre-conception or anticipation with which we inescapably confront a text. And the meaning of the text is "not something that mysteriously clings to it, lies hidden behind it, or hovers somewhere in a parenthetical realm" but is rather that which emerges through the interaction between the text and the reader's fore-structured project of understanding. The circle of understanding is thus not, in Gadamer's words, of a formal character, is neither

subjective nor objective, but is descriptive of the fact
that understanding consists in the inter-play between the
movement of tradition and the movement of the interpreter,
a to-and-fro movement between text and interpreter,
between understanding its meaning and self-understanding.
According to Heidegger's interpretation of the circle, as
he says, "the understanding of a text is necessarily
governed by the anticipatory movement of pre-structured
understanding. The circle of whole and part is not
dissolved in a completed act of understanding but is on
the contrary truly and authentically executed." The
circle of understanding is thus not at all a "methodological" circle but refers to an ontological property of
the structure of understanding itself, such that to
understand is always to be involved in the unending inter-
play of the whole which is tradition, and the part, which
consists of the unconscious presuppositions with which the
interpreter approaches it. There is no understanding which
is presuppositionless and the anticipation of sense which
governs our understanding of a text is not, as Gadamer
says, an act executed by us as subjects, is not the act of
our subjectivity, but is rather an ingression into the
process of tradition in which the past and the present are
continuously mediated. It is itself determined by the
community and mutuality which binds us with tradition, a
community which is not just a pre-given fact but is in
constant formation in consequence of our participation in
the process of tradition through understanding.

Presuppositions, pre-judgments and prejudices do not
merely restrict our understanding, or necessarily falsify
it, as is generally supposed, but also enable it and are
constitutive elements in it. The prejudice against prejudices in general is, as Gadamer has pointed out, the basic
presupposition of the Enlightenment, manifesting itself in
the rejection and criticism of all authority, especially
that of the religious tradition of Christianity, as a

source of prejudices and is expressed in Kant's formulation at the commencement of his article, "Answering the
question, what is Enlightenment?" Have the courage to use
your *own* understanding; according to this principle, not
tradition but reason is the ultimate source of authority
and final arbiter; what is written down in books need not
be true, for we are capable of knowing better. The
Romantic glorification of tradition and myth, of the past
and the remote, was itself based on the presuppositions of
the Enlightenment, with only the values reversed, and
ultimately led to the emergence of historicism, for which
the last step in the liberation of the human spirit from
enslavement by dogma lay in gaining objective knowledge of
the historical world, thus relegating everything in tradition which cannot stand up to the scrutiny of reason to
the world of the past and interpreting it "historically,"
i.e., in terms of bygone, pre-rational modes of thought
and living. The objectively historical way of understanding tradition is thus the consummation of the spirit
of the Enlightenment, robbing tradition of all potency and
authority and holding up before us the image of a disenchanted, de-mystified and rationalized world which is only
a reflection of the historically generated, subjectivistic
prejudice against our own rootedness in the past and the
naivety of our presumption to have elevated ourselves
above the concrete, historical flow of life and thought.
For, as Gadamer remarks, "The idea of an absolute reason
is in no sense a live possibility for historical mankind.
Reason is for us conditioned and bound up with historical
realities, not master over itself but ever dependent upon
the data to which it applies itself." In reality it is
not to us that history belongs but we who are owned by
history and hence, he adds, the pre-judgments of an
individual, far more than his judgments, constitute the
historical reality of his being. There is no absolute
antithesis between tradition and reason, for the former

depends upon its continuity, not upon the sheer inertia of
physical persistence but upon our rational affirmation
and critical appropriation, as much as all revolution
and innovation.

The hermeneutic act of understanding, we remarked
earlier, comes into operation with a sense of alienation
from tradition, with a sense of its otherness from our
present and remoteness from it. The task of understanding, which does not begin so long as we just live it
out unreflectively and without question, is to overcome
this alienation by making us explicitly aware of those
unconscious presuppositions through which the past is ever
operative in our present experience and ways of thinking
and speaking. And it does this when we open ourselves to
the voice of tradition, let it speak to us and confront us
with its claim to communicate a truth. "We can never
bring a presupposition in front of us as it were," Gadamer
remarks, "so long as a presupposition is in unbroken and
unnoticed play, but only when it is so to speak provoked
and irritated. What has the power to act as such an
irritant is precisely the encounter with tradition."
Through such encounter we are enabled to draw out our
presuppositions into the open, suspend their blind
operation and bring them into play, explicitly as questions, against the truth-claim of what is said in a text
handed down from the past. We can then see our relationship to tradition as a game in which we are partners with
it, or as a dialogue into which we enter with it, not only
putting questions to tradition but allowing ourselves to
be questioned in turn by it. The authentic character of a
game lies in the fact that here the partners are caught up
in a movement which transcends the subjectivity of each of
them and which is governed by its own inner law. Phenom-
enologically, play and the kind of understanding that
happens in a conversation or when we occupy ourselves with
a traditional text, have a common structure, as Gadamer

has well brought out. As in conversation, when we argue a
point, the give and take of understanding a text occurs in
the medium of language, we may in fact say, as the give
and take of language itself. In a dialogue, each speaker
plays a language-game of his own to begin with and the
authenticity of the dialogue depends upon the extent to
which they gradually surrender themselves to the sway of a
language-game that encompasses them both and which is not
identical with either of their separate games--and thus in
the end let a new common language emerge, and with it a
new horizon of meaning and a new truth that was not in the
possession of either before. It is in this sense that
when we allow ourselves to be addressed by tradition and
play the game of understanding, we participate in a creative process in which new horizons of meaning, resulting
from a fusion of our present horizon and that of a past
world, new ways of speaking and a new truth emerge, not as
something made *by* us but as that which moulds and shapes
us and enables us to live by. The refusal to play this
game is a surrender to philosophical naivety and, beyond
this, it is to let tradition operate blindly and as a
natural force in the form of our own presuppositions and
so to allow our past to creep up towards us as our own
future and take us by surprise.

Just as explication or interpretation is inseparable
from understanding and is an integral moment in it, so
also is application; comprehension, explication and
application together constitute in their unity the fully
executed activity of understanding. We do not really
understand and explicate a text, whether philosophical or
literary, legal or scriptural, so long as we take it only
as an historical document and do not translate it so that
it speaks to us in our present concrete situation, so
long, in other words, as it is not applied to the
historical point where we stand, here and now. Every
encounter with tradition, unfolded explicitly and with

historical self-consciousness in understanding, involves
an experience of the tension in the polar relation between
the text and the present moment, a tension which arises
from the application of what is said in the text to the
present and which understanding then seeks to overcome.
In this manner, tradition, of which our understanding is
itself a moment, is continuously mediated with the present
and is ever renovated, corrected and transformed through
projects of understanding that drive it forward into a
future which holds no more terrors, and understanding
itself is seen as that creative moment of heightened
awareness in which the past transforms itself into a
future truly its own.

Gadamer's explication of the phenomenon of understanding, and his application of this to the philosophical
present of the West as it has attained self-awareness in
the thinking of Heidegger, is determined by an attitude
towards the Western tradition which he shares with Husserl
rather than with Heidegger in its disregard of the existence, claim and world-historical viability of other
traditions. Perhaps it is for the Oriental thinker
himself to seek to achieve clarity about the obscurity and
ambiguity of the situation in which he finds himself today
in respect of his own tradition, however feeble its
breath. We in India can begin to do this only by squarely
facing the issues posed for us by the fact that for us our
own tradition is no embalmed mummy, or not yet, and that
it is still alive in us, for good or ill, as shaping our
attitudes and ways of thinking and speaking; and that, on
the other hand, we live and think in a world which is
under the sway of what we still experience as an alien
destiny. Do we also experience the tension between these
two, and have we attempted to examine the structure of
this field of tension? Have we realized the full otherness of that destiny and investigated, on our part, the
nature and logic of the tradition that has engendered it?

In regard to our own tradition, we have two hundred years
of apologetic, reform and re-interpretation behind us,
since our entry into modernity. But how far have we been
able to achieve that distance from our past which can
enable us to bring before our view and comprehend the
inner, dynamic structure of this tradition from the perspective of the present? The present self-understanding
of the West has been mediated by the dialectic of Athens
and Jerusalem, of the Enlightenment and the Romantic
movement, of this whole past with the scientific, technological present. Can we simply turn our backs on our
own past, just discard it, and appropriate the final
fruits of Western self-understanding as *the* inner telos of
man universally and as such, or shall we reject the
spiritual-philosophical endeavour of the West altogether
as of no consequence and seek to entrench ourselves into a
specifically Indian philosophizing, in the language of the
past and supposedly undistorted by the alien world of
meanings embodied in the English language we employ for
the purpose? Or shall we begin to *understand* both in
their mutual otherness, to learn the language of each and
so to evolve ways of thinking and talking which will be
truly appropriate to our membership of both worlds,
striving in such fashion to transform it into one? I for
one have no doubt that we can gain some help in this
direction if we pay more attention to that moving image of
the West's self-understanding which constitutes its
tradition as also to the ways in which Western scholars
have been seeking to understand our own.

THE PROBLEM OF PHILOSOPHICAL RECONCEPTION
IN THE THOUGHT OF K.C. BHATTACHARYYA

Classical Indian philosophy is rich in examples of the
attention given by Indian thinkers to conceptual problems
arising from their concern with a truth that saves and
liberates. In the Vedānta tradition specifically we have
the two-pronged enterprise of developing a mode of
thinking which is both a hermeneutic and an analytic, both
an explication of what found utterance in the "beginning"
and an analytic of the concepts required for such
explication, the two held together by the unity of a
historically unfolding system. Picking out examples at
random, one may mention the exegesis of *tat tvam asi* in
the *Upadeśasāhasrī* of Śaṁkara and Sureśvara's attempt, in
the *Naiṣkarmyasiddhi*, to inquire into the logical structure of this type of scriptural utterance. What kind of a
sentence is this, in respect of its logical form? Is it
descriptive of a reality standing over against us, to
which it can correspond, or is it more like a call that
awakens a sleeper, thus negating an existent state or
belief, rather than affirming a state of affairs, unless
the way we can be brought to see our true selves be itself
spoken of as a possible state of affairs? Examples of the
more analytical kind of thinking are the conceptual
investigations of "self-luminosity" by Citsukha and of
"falsity" by Madhusūdana, not to speak of the sustained
probing into the nature of the self and of illusion in the
school of Śaṁkara and into what Brahman means by Maṇḍana
and in all schools of Vedānta.

Originally published in *Philosophy East and West*, 24
(1974): 59-70. Reprinted from *Philosophy East and West* by
permission of the University of Hawaii Press.

It would certainly be a task worth undertaking to
determine how, in terms of our present "modern" ways of
thinking and speaking, a philosophical vision has been
developed through conceptualization of religious
experience in the tradition of classical Advaita; what
epistemological, metaphysical, and logical problems have
had to be tackled in the process and why--and to investigate, finally, what light these results, achieved in
this particular religio-philosophical tradition, may throw
on the general problem of the process of symbolization
involved in the conceptualization of truth as disclosed in
religious experience. Implicit in such an enterprise,
however, is the naive belief that the terms in which this
"general problem" is posed provide the standard frame of
reference, the failure to see that categories like
"religion," "philosophy," "religious experience" and
"conceptualization" themselves derive from one particular
tradition, and that they have become questionable even
within that tradition itself. How adequately do the
expressions "religious experience" and "philosophical
vision" represent the self-understanding of the Indian
tradition? Did Indian thinkers understand their task as
one of bringing to the concept specific modes of
experience, and were they concerned with experience and
its conceptual mastery in the way Western thinkers have
always been?

I should like to focus attention here, instead, upon
this last set of questions, upon the hermeneutical task of
understanding the past in terms of the present, of
translating from one to another, and of the impingement of
one tradition upon another. This is not a matter of
merely peripheral relevance to the problem of gaining
access to alien modes of religiousness and of their self-
understanding, but is an intrinsic dimension of the self-
understanding, and thus the very existence and continuity
of every tradition as such. The continuity of a tradition

is one of changing interpretations, of reconception, and
of translation; and in the religious sphere is made
possible by our openness to the past utterance or event,
by letting it claim us in the present and by the faith
that it can become meaningful to us, speak to us, here and
now. But to such faith there always corresponds a predicament. For *homo religiosus*, it is not merely the
existential predicament of finding himself caught in the
necessity of taking account of time and of gathering
together the past and the future in the living present.
It is also, more concretely, the predicament of being torn
between languages and modes of thought, between worlds,
some dead, some alive yet different, others not yet born.
In the Indian religio-philosophical tradition, as in
others, there have been a number of historical nodal
points where such faith and such a predicament has
exhibited itself in dramatic fashion from early Vedic to
late classical Brahmanism and medieval "Hinduism." One
may investigate each of these transition points to determine the quality and the power of faith exhibited, to
analyze the precise character of the predicament and
challenge--linguistic, conceptual-philosophical and
cultural--and of the creative response by which a new
pattern of meanings and a new self-understanding was
generated and handed down to posterity. One fascinating
inquiry of this type would be to study the fateful deci-
sions made from time to time in the long conflict between
classical Sanskrit and the vernaculars and dialects, the
religious significance of the emergence of Sanskrit as a
medium of both religious symbolization and philosophical
understanding and of its eventual abandonment, in the
latter role, in favor of regional languages and dialects.

Much more significant and relevant to our present
concern, however, is the predicament into which a Hindu
seeking to formulate a philosophical vision has been
thrown by India's entry into modernity since the days of

Rammohun Roy. The coming of modernity to India signified not merely the impingement of an alien world of knowledge, ideas, and ideals upon the Indian consciousness but of a world which was itself rapidly reaching out toward a newly conceived future, as well as spreading out its tentacles to encompass the whole world. Under the colonial origins of his modernization, the Indian encountered "philosophy" and "religion" and began forthwith the long journey of reinterpreting his tradition in terms of these Western categories. More importantly, he began thinking about it and reconceiving it in the English language, not just to expound it to English scholars but as the principal medium of his own self-understanding. Such self-understanding was reflected back in new meanings being given to ancient words in the Indian languages, and it also expressed itself in the way traditional meanings were themselves reflected in his use of concepts embedded in English words. In this interplay between the one and the other, between the traditional and the modern, between one's own and the alien, between the present and the past, what was happening to the truth of that tradition itself and to its manner of speaking to us? Was it being gradually covered up and hidden from our view, or was it being brought now to shine forth, at least in promise, in its real purity? How far were the thinkers engaged in the task of reinterpreting their tradition aware of the two players in this game, in their specific distinctness as well as in their mutuality? Did they, in the strength and lucidity of their faith, see that in understanding their tradition in this new fashion, symbolizing its thought in a novel way and for a new age, they were letting a new truth emerge out of this meeting of the past and the present? How clearly did they see that the voice of tradition speaks historically, in varying tongues, and what it says to us depends largely upon our relationship, not merely to our present but to the future as it rushes on toward us?

In one of his brilliant and penetrating studies of
Hinduism, the Indologist Paul Hacker has pointed out how
in the work of men like Bankim, Vivekananda, and
Radhakrishnan modern Hindu thinking has remained a hastily
improvised mixture of traditional heritage on the one hand
and, on the other, of Western and Christian ideas
impinging upon it with inescapable urgency, without any
real fusion of the two and often at the expense of the
heritage of the past, preventing the authentic Hindu
heritage as such from emerging in its real significance
and thus becoming truly effective. More pointedly, he
says there, "Excepting perhaps for Aurobindo Ghose and a
few other, less known thinkers, [Indians] have in general
not succeeded till today in thinking the Indian tradition,
Western and Christian influences, as well as the
requirements of the contemporary situation in their
togetherness and in a unified manner."[1] He admonishes
Indian thinkers, therefore, to overcome now the memory of
the colonial epoch which has so deeply wounded the Indian
spirit and gain back the greater tranquility and inner
self-collectedness requisite for undertaking the task of
seeing, in sober clarity, the multiple and manifold
forces, and sources of insight, still alive and operative
in the spiritual and intellectual space of India and of
orienting itself anew.

Not the least distinguished of these lesser known
thinkers was Krishna Chandra Bhattacharyya, who lived and
thought, like Gandhi, Aurobindo, Tagore, Nehru, and
Radhakrishnan, during the terminal phase of the colonial
epoch. For him, as for these others, the wounds inflicted
by this epoch were not just a memory that darkened their
thinking, as Hacker would seem to imply. As the purest,
most philosophically disciplined and "critical" *thinker* of
them all, he took upon himself this wound at its sharpest
and most intense moment and turned it into an instrument
of lucid vision. By his deep, unbroken faith in the voice

of his spiritual and philosophical tradition, he trans-
muted this wound into the sovereign tranquility and
collectedness of spirit of a true thinker and gained that
rare intellectual honesty that drives a thinker on to
raise new questions and find new answers.[2] He was thus
enabled to search with profound penetration into the truth
of his own tradition and at the same time be genuinely
open, as few Indian thinkers have been, to the call of the
modern, as gathered together in the thought of the
greatest masters of modern Western thought--Kant and
Hegel. What is uniquely characteristic of Bhattacharyya
is the fact that in his massive venture of reappropriating
and critically reinterpreting the Indian philosophical
past in the language of "modern" Western thought, he did
not falsify his understanding of either by an uncritical
superimposition of the one upon the other or by a naive
identification of concepts belonging to these different
traditions. His thought thus embodies and exemplifies the
entire problematic of the hermeneutic enterprise, the
coming together of two intellectual worlds in the act of
understanding, in all its creative significance and power.

Bhattacharyya sought neither to construct a system of
speculative thought nor to create a comprehensive philosophical world-view encompassing all of man's religious
and philosophic experience. His was an enterprise of
genuine spiritual humility, for he only sought to wrench
meaning from an antique philosophical tradition for
himself, to render it meaningful to himself as a thinker
and thereby perhaps also to others. But he thought in the
English language, and wrote in a language which bears a
heavy imprint of the work of Kant and, to a lesser degree,
of Hegel, both of them German thinkers who were available
to him, moreover, in hardly adequate or elegant English
translations. Beyond this, his language strains to
express concepts embedded in the Sanskrit of his own
scholarly tradition, giving to his style and idiom a power

of generating, for the sensitive and educated philosophical ear, echoes emanating from the most diverse
regions of the spirit. The difficulty and occasional
obscurity of his writing is a reflection of the intensity
of effort he spent in bringing about a fusion of intellectual horizons (*Horizontverschmelzung*, as Hans Georg
Gadamer has described it in his *Wahrheit und Methode*), the
horizons of past and present, of the West and India, the
distinct horizons within the Indian philosophico-religious
tradition itself. It is in such fusion, made possible by
creative effort toward a novel understanding, that the
essence of the hermeneutic experience consists, according
to Gadamer. K.C. Bhattacharyya's work exemplifies and
expresses, as hardly any other philosopher's, this kind of
experience in which a tradition achieves new self-
understanding and in which new truth is born.

Although Bhattacharyya wrote extensive studies seeking
to reinterpret the Sāmkhya and Yoga systems of philosophy
also, he considered Advaita Vedānta as the supreme
expression of the religious quest of freedom in the Indian
tradition. As he remarked, "This philosophy is the most
satisfying formulation of the distinctive spirit of
Hinduism, and in this sense it may claim to be a synthesis
of other systems of Indian philosophy, which all seek to
formulate this spirit; and it has also explicitly
influenced the historical evolution of Hinduism."[3]
Bhattacharyya points out that "Vedānta is primarily a
religion, and it is a philosophy only as the formulation
of this religion. All religion makes for the realization
of the self as sacred, but the religion of Advaita is the
specific cult of such realization understood explicitly as
self-knowledge, as sacred knowledge, and as nothing but
knowledge."[4] The self, which is to be known, is accepted
in the first instance in faith; this faith is "confirmed,
clarified, and formulated by reason" and is in this manner
"inwardized into a vision." This work of reason,

essential to the completion of the process of self-
knowledge in Advaita, may be called philosophy. And
philosophy, as thus understood, is hence "not only an
auxiliary discipline, but an integral part of the religion
and its characteristic self-expression."[5] For Bhattacharyya, Advaitism is thus religion and philosophy in one.

Advaita is religion in the sense that its central
content is given to thought "by something other than
thought and other than sense."[6] The content, in other
words, is here revealed or presented to thought by the
Upaniṣadic Word and is accepted in faith as a demand to be
fulfilled or realized through thought. Such thought,
however, is for Vedānta "itself an emanation of faith,
being spiritual thought that is utterly distinct from
secular thought...."[7] In this respect, Vedānta differs
from the approach of the Sāṁkhya, for which "metaphysical
thought is nothing other than secular thought,"[8] in which
the natural or secular unfolds into the spiritual.
Bhattacharyya describes the Sāṁkhya, therefore, as "a
religion of reflective spontaneity or spiritual natural-
ness,"[9] in which secular thinking, initiated by the
experience of pain, is directed to the service of freedom
from sense and thus itself functions as spiritual
thinking. The metaphysics of Sāṁkhya springs from this
religion and its organon is reflection as the spiritual
process of freeing from sense. The religion of Yoga, as
Bhattacharyya calls it, differs from both of the above and
centers around the discipline of the will as the means of
freedom. "The free realising of freedom is regarded in
Sāṁkhya and Vedānta as a knowing process and in Bhakti-
systems as a feeling process. In Yoga it is taken as
literal willing,"[10] but as willing in its essential or
spiritual form, that is, as will not to will, will to
retract willing.

The category of the "spiritual" plays a pervasive role
in Bhattacharyya's thought, though a precise definition of

what he means by this term is hard to find in his
writings. It may be pointed out, however, that this term
is used by him to express the traditional Indian notion of
adhyatma as integrating the various aspects of existence;
this usage being another example of his practice of
clothing and expressing traditional Indian thought-
schemata in English, "modern," terms, thereby giving them
new meanings not readily intelligible to the reader
unfamiliar with the Indian tradition. The concepts of
adhyātma, adhibūta, adhideva, and *adhiloka* are traditional
Indian ways of marking "the distinctions among the several
aspects of existence" and Bhattacharyya's first published
work, *Studies in Vedāntism,* gives ample evidence of the
effort he spent in making intelligible this ancient,
Upaniṣadic thought-schema in "modern" terms. In the
second place, his use of the term "spiritual," we may
conjecture, also indicates his dissatisfaction and
uneasiness with the concept of "religion," which he found
hardly adequate to explicate what Vedānta, Sāṁkhya, Yoga,
and the Bhakti systems are about. They are all
"religions" and yet in a sense "transcend the sacred" and
"supersede religion." The category of the "spiritual" is,
for Bhattacharyya, the ultimate, comprehensive category,
of which the "religious" is one mode and manifestation,
and which expresses itself in its highest form in a
consciousness which can only be described as "super-
religious." For example, the consciousness of the
overpersonal Self as identical with I is described by
Bhattacharyya as "the religious form of the spiritual
consciousness,"[11] so that the investigation of the
religious consciousness becomes merely a part of the more
comprehensive discipline, the philosophy of the spirit,
which is a "study of all contents enjoyed in explicit
reference to the subject I."[12] Super-religious spiritual
activity, in which willing is absolutely disinterested,
transcends all activity conceived as religious, for its

final objective is the absolute transcendence that is freedom or *mokṣa*. As Bhattacharyya says, "All activity for *mokṣa* (as distinct from *svarga*)--activity as opposed to self-surrender--where the good is conceived as absolute and not as coordinate with evil, not, in other words, as satisfying an interest, is super-religious. Self-knowledge, for example, is a super-religious good in Vedānta; so is bhakti in Vaiṣṇava systems."[13] In its final stage, Yoga also culminates in such super-religious activity. According to Bhattacharyya, further, the "spiritual" is itself a concept that points beyond itself. The philosophy of the spirit (including that of its expression in the religious form), in which there is a necessary reference to the subject or "I", culminates in the philosophy of truth. Here, we reach the region of the absolute, of "transcendental consciousness," in which even the "I", as the symbol of reality, is negated. In the religious consciousness there is experience of self-abnegation but no theoretic denial of the subject *I*. From the perspective of the absolute, of which there is no "enjoying" experience as there is of the overpersonal reality in religion, and of which the positive character "is expressible only by the negation of *I* (or more accurately, by 'what I am not'),"[14] the subject or the individual self is unreal, for the absolute alone *is*. But when "we say that the absolute *is*, we mean by 'is' not reality but truth. Reality is enjoyed but truth is not. The consciousness of truth as what is believed in but not understood either in the objective or in the subjective attitude, as not literally speakable at all but speakable only in the purely symbolistic way, is extra-religious or transcendental consciousness."[15]

In Bhattacharyya's description of the Vedānta as "primarily" a religion, there is implicit thus a critique of religion as a central concept handed down to us by the Western tradition. In what sense, we may now go on to

ask, is Advaita a "philosophy"? It is obviously not
philosophy in the pure Greek sense of autonomous, open
questioning pursued with a view to the attainment of
contemplative vision, of truth as *theoria*. The primordial
gesture of thinking here is not one of questioning, as
with the Greeks, but of hearing, to use Heidegger's
language, and the piety of thought, for Vedānta thinking
emanates from faith in a revealed content presented to
thought and demanding intellectual clarification, but
eventually calling for a "spiritual knowing" in which the
activity of thought terminates. Bhattacharyya antici-
pated, in large measure, the critique to which the central
metaphysical tradition of the West has been subjected in
the philosophy of the recent past, in particular by Martin
Heidegger. He pointed out that "The attitude of metaphysics like that of the sciences including psychology is
objective. It seeks to know reality as distinct from the
knowing of it, as objective, at least, in the sense of
being meant."[16] Metaphysics, and with it logic and
epistemology, belongs to what he called the "philosophy of
the object," object being defined as what is meant, which
is comprehended within and by no means exhausts the realm
of the significantly speakable. The concern of Vedānta,
however, is with the subject or subjectivity conceived as
conscious freedom or felt detachment from the object.
This cannot come within the purview of "metaphysics" for,
as he says, "There is properly no metaphysic of the
subject and the apparent problems about the existence of
the subject and its relation to the object are really
illegitimate."[17] And yet, the subject and its positive
freedom to refer to the object are both speakable, "and it
is from the speakable that we must start in philosophy."[18]
In the *Critique of Pure Reason*, Kant opened up a whole
realm of what is speakable and is not yet objectively
meant, namely, the realm of the "transcendental." It is
not surprising that, of all Western philosophers,

Bhattacharyya felt himself closest to Kant, took his own point of departure on crucial issues from Kant and developed his thinking in constant debate with Kant.

As mentioned above, Bhattacharyya agreed with Kant in rejecting "the so-called metaphysic of the soul." According to him, the subject is a believed content, is problematically spoken as "I" and is not meanable or is not a meant something. But, he points out

> The understanding here is not a mystic intuition though it may point to its possibility, nor the intuition of a meaning that can be a term of a judgment, nor yet the thought of a meaning that is not known because not intuited or that is known without being intuited. It is somewhere midway between a mystic intuition and the consciousness of a meaning, being the believing awareness of a speakable content, the negation of which is unmeaning and which, therefore, is not a meaning. What is claimed to be mystically intuited is speakable only in metaphor which presents a contradiction in meaning and what is affirmed or denied in metaphysic is a meanable. The subject as I is neither contradictory nor meanable and the exposition of it accordingly is intermediate between mysticism and metaphysic. As, however, the subject is communicable by speech without metaphor, it cannot be taken as falling outside philosophical inquiry. [19]

The philosophical inquiry into the modes or functions of subjectivity or into the ways in which the "I" relates itself freely to the object, and thus may also freely detach itself from it, cannot, however, be content with, far from identifying itself with, the form which transcendental reflection takes in Kant. Bhattacharyya chides Kant for his "persisting objective attitude." The interest of Kantian epistemology, he says, "is still in the object, in the knownness or objectivity of the object which it seeks to understand theoretically as knowing. It does not abandon the objective procedure of metaphysics and the sciences, even though it sets itself to correct the conceit of independent objectivity." [20] It is this that leads Kant to deny self-knowledge and also to

disbelieve in "the possibility of a spiritual discipline
of the theoretic reason through which self-knowledge may
be attainable."[21] The Kantian analysis misleads insofar
as it presents the knowing function "as an objective
meaning and does not recognise that it is believed without
being meant."[22] Kant's epistemology, further, is reduced
to nothing more than a philological study, an enquiry into
the significance of the mere phrase "knowing *of* object,"
"unless it is consciously viewed as rooted in the faith in
the facthood of the knowing function and unless the
so-called deduction that it presents is definitely known
to be not inferential and not literally meant but to be
the symbolisation by logical form of what is immediately
believed as spiritual fact."[23] According to
Bhattacharyya's formulation of the Vedantic view, "the
subject is known though neither thought (meant) nor
intuited. It is known as what the speaker of *I* is
understood to intend by it. The understanding is a direct
believing in something that is not meant but revealed as
revealing itself....The subject is thus known by itself,
as not meant but speakable, and not as either related or
relating to the object."[24] The knowing function represents a positive mode of the freedom of the subject to
relate to the object without getting related to it and is
itself not "known" but only believed, though more
indubitably than the knowledge of a meant object.

The task of philosophy, in this view, is the symbolic
elaboration of these believed or felt subjective functions
"the speaking creation of a system of subjective functions
or the symbolising elaboration of the positive freedom of
the subject."[25] This is "a special study," "a new
philosophical study," not envisaged by Kant, which is
"intermediate between the recognition of the subject
purely through the intention of the word *I* and the
inferential inquiry into the reality behind the meant
object which is called metaphysics."[26] To this discipline

Bhattacharyya gives the name of spiritual or transcendental psychology because it seeks to elaborate, into a
system of symbolisms, the believed but not known facthood
of the knowing function and of subjective function in
general. It is a discipline of the theoretic reason, of a
sort inadmissible to Kant, because it investigates the
ways in which the subject freely relates itself to the
object. But it is a spiritual discipline in the sense
that the inquiry into the subject's positive freedom of
relating, into the objective attitude, is in the service
of a cultivation of the subjective attitude, or that of
realizing or inwardizing the subject's negative freedom
from all objectivity. Spiritual psychology is thus conceived of by Bhattacharyya as a philosophical study based
on the method of spiritual introspection, in which one
becomes aware of the subjective functions of relating and
detaching, that is, of the modes of freedom, as distinct
from psychological introspection, which is only concerned
with the consciousness of psychological abstractions like
the knownness and feltness of an object considered in
isolation from the object itself. In this discipline the
subjective attitude is symbolized by the objective attitude from which it seeks to be freed, for the modes of
subjectivity are nothing other than the modes of freeing
oneself from the modes of objectivity. The business of
spiritual psychology, Bhattacharyya says, is not to
explain or to solve a problem but "to interpret empirical
psychology in terms of the positively felt and believed
freedom of the subject from objectivity"[27] and, secondly,
"to elaborate modes of freedom that have no reference to
object at all."[28] As he explains, "In the objective
attitude, the knownness or feltness of the object appears
positive and knowing or feeling appears as its problematic
negation. In the subjective attitude, the case is
reversed: freedom is positively believed and the related-
ness of the object to the subject--its objectivity--

appears as constructed, as not belonging to the object...
and is thus understood as the self-negation or alienated
shadow of the subject."[29]   In his Amalner lectures of 1929
entitled, *The Subject as Freedom*, Bhattacharyya has provided "a rough sketch of transcendental psychology, conceived of as the legitimate substitute for the so-called
metaphysic of the soul,"[30] elaborating the stages of
freedom from objectivity and suggesting "the possibility
of a consecutive method of realising the subject as
absolute freedom, of retracting the felt positive freedom
towards the object into pure intuition of the self."[31]

In consequence of Bhattacharyya's attempt to rethink
the Advaita as "philosophy," the concept of philosophy
itself undergoes a far-reaching transformation at his
hands. The call to thinking comes no longer from a sense
of wonder, as with the Greeks, nor from the need for a
rational justification of established doctrine, as in the
European Middle Ages, nor from the sense of doubt and the
self-assertion of the human will, as in modern philosophy,
but as a demand for making true in one's personal experience a truth heard once as eternally valid and accepted
in faith, as the call to "know" and to be one's self as
absolute freedom through the activity of a faith-full
thinking. In a modern Indian thinker like Bhattacharyya,
open to the highest reaches of the Western philosophical
tradition, the demand springs from the awareness that
ancient texts communicate truth to us only insofar as we
are able to translate them and rethink what they say in
the language and idiom of the present, that a truth, to be
eternal, must be ceaselessly reinterpreted and reformu-
lated and thus made to withstand the exigency of time. It
springs, above all, from the need for a creative response
to the encounter of two traditions, each speaking a
different language, each constituting a world-horizon in
its own right, and of which a certain degree of fusion can
be brought about only by the faith that the utterance of

one's own tradition can sustain itself and even find a
more satisfying articulation in an alien medium, in an
alienated age.

For thinking the "demand" is, as Bhattacharyya puts
it, "that the subjective function being essentially the
knowing of the object as distinct from it, this knowing
which is only believed and not known as fact *has* to be
known as fact, as the self-evidencing reality of the
subject itself."[32] "*Was heisst Denken?*" asked Heidegger,
for the first time explicitly in the history of Western
thought and sought to give an answer adequate to the
unasked question behind the entire philosophico-religious
tradition of the West. Bhattacharyya's thinking, as also
his concept of thinking, gave explicit and appropriate
place to the notion of a "demand," which presupposes faith
in the source of the demand, the recognition of it as in
some sense sacred, and one's response in the act of
thinking as itself religious, as an act of truth and of
truing. As in the thinking of Heidegger, a concept of
thinking is developed here that sheds the traditional
Western dichotomy of theory and practice and of faith and
philosophy, for which thinking itself becomes the highest
form of practice, a process of self-knowledge that is at
the same time a transformation and fulfillment of self,
generated and sustained by faith in the Vedic word. For
Bhattacharyya as for Heidegger there is nothing more
questionable and question-worthy in philosophy than the
nature of philosophy itself. As the former remarks at the
beginning of one of his most seminal essays, "The Concept
of Philosophy," "an explication of the concept of philosophy appears to me more important than the discussion of
any specific problem of philosophy."[33] Coming, however,
as he does from another tradition and inspired by a
different concern than Heidegger's, Bhattacharyya
preferred to retain for his thought the terms "philosophy"
and "subjectivity" rather than rejecting them, along with

some others, as inappropriate on the basis of a historical critique such as Heidegger's.

It may appear incredible that so keen a student of Hegel as Bhattacharyya should have remained unappreciative of the dimension of historicity intrinsic to philosophical understanding, and not so mindful as he might have been of the historicity of his own understanding, both of his own tradition and that of the West, and so of his whole enterprise of interpretation. This failure was due, it may be surmised, in part to the ahistorical climate of philosophical thought at the time in the English-speaking world in general and of its reception of Hegel in particular and in part to the ahistorical bias of the Indian tradition itself. Beyond this, however, it was a legitimate reaction on Bhattacharyya's part to an unbridled historicism that claimed to "explain," and thus to bury, the past historically without concerning itself with the possibility that in them truths may have found utterance that still speak to us and challenge us to renewed thinking. Bhattacharyya was fully aware of the dangers of such historicism, and he reacted sharply on finding how "history thus sits in judgment on philosophy." As he remarked:

> There is the danger, no doubt, of too easily
> reading one's philosophic creed into the history,
> but the opposite danger is more serious still.
> It is the danger of taking the philosophic type
> studied as a historic curiosity rather than a
> recipe for the human soul, and of seeking to
> explain the curiosity by natural *causes* instead
> of seriously examining its merits as philosophy.
> This unfortunately is sometimes the defect of
> Western expositions of Eastern philosophy
> and religion.[34]

To the present-day reader, Bhattacharyya's work would also appear to be insufficiently sensitive to the role of language in thought, to the particularity of languages and the way they embody, not just express, concepts. He sought in his thinking to provide "problematic construc-

tions on Vedantic lines intended to bring out the relations of the system to modern philosophical systems."[35]
Had he experienced the full impact of Husserl's
phenomenology, or written after the later Wittgenstein and
Heidegger, would Bhattacharyya not have concerned himself
more centrally with the historical and cross-cultural
determinants of his own understanding of the Indian and
Western philosophical traditions?

NOTES

1. "Schopenhauer und die Ethik des Hinduismus," *Saeculum*
12, no. 4 (1961):398-399. My translation.
2. It is interesting to note that, like Tagore,
K.C. Bhattacharyya was linked, through his grandfather,
with some of the pioneers of the "Bengal Renaissance."
Umakant Tarkalankar, as the grandfather was called after
his academic title, was a teacher of Joshua Marshman and
William Ward of the Serampore Mission College and was held
by them, along with William Carey, in the highest respect
as their guru. Cf. Pravas Jivan Chaudhury, "Krishna
Chandra Bhattacharyya: A Biographical Sketch," in *Krishna
Chandra Bhattacharyya Memorial Volume*, ed. S.K. Maitra, et
al. (Amalner, 1958), i.
3. Gopinath Bhattacharyya, ed., *Studies in Philosophy*, 2
vols (Calcutta, 1956), 1:122.
4. Ibid., 1:118-119.
5. Ibid., 1:119.
6. Ibid., 1:150.
7. Ibid.
8. Ibid.
9. Ibid., 1:147.
10. Ibid., 1:285.
11. Ibid., 2:114.
12. Ibid.
13. Ibid., 1:289.

14. Ibid., 2:116.

15. Ibid.

16. Ibid., 2:25.

17. Ibid., 2:27.

18. Ibid., 2:26.

19. Ibid., 2:24-25.

20. Ibid., 2:30.

21. Ibid., 2:31.

22. Ibid.

23. Ibid.

24. Ibid.

25. Ibid., 2:27.

26. Ibid.

27. Ibid., 2:29.

28. Ibid.

29. Ibid., 2:29-30.

30. Ibid., 2:3.

31. Ibid., 2:33. The phenomenological mode of thinking and "doing" philosophy, apparently so close to Bhattacharyya's concerns, had at this time not yet assumed the status of a "modern philosophical system." Even those of Husserl's writings that were published during his lifetime remained inaccessible to the English-speaking student until the appearance of *Ideas* in 1931, one year after the publication of *The Subject as Freedom*. Bhattacharyya read this work in the same year "and recognised a similarity in the general attitude and method between himself and the German thinker." Cf. Pravas Jivan Chaudhury, op. cit., v.

32. Ibid., 2:32.

33. Ibid., 2:100.

34. Ibid., 1:1.

35. Ibid.

THE WILL TO INTERPRET AND INDIA'S DREAMING SPIRIT

An important development in contemporary philosophy is
the emergence of what may be called philosophical hermeneutics or, alternatively, hermeneutic philosophy. This
is concerned not so much with the art or methodology of
interpreting texts as with understanding and interpreting
as themselves basic moments in man's very way of being
human, as forms of be-ing and happening rather than as
operations directed at an objectively given entity or
happening. Wilhelm Dilthey is here the pioneer, but it is
to Martin Heidegger that we owe the basic insights, to
Hans Georg Gadamer the explication and working out in
elaborate detail the implications of these insights and to
Paul Ricoeur the continuation, in the Franco-American
milieu, of this novel mode and dimension of philosophical
thinking. The future alone can show how far and in what
manner Heidegger's call to a planetary thinking, as
against or rather beyond Western "philosophizing", is
heard and turns out to be capable of realization. But in
one respect at least this hermeneutical mode of thinking,
based on Heidegger's critique of the traditional Western
notions of Time, Being, Truth and Man, seems to be immediately helpful. It promises a new sort of freedom and
renewed hope to the Indian thinker reflecting on, and out
of, his own tradition, to the Indian willingly partici-
pating in the larger movement of world civilization and in
the international community of modern scholarship and yet
unwilling to be totally swept off his feet by them. It
enables him to turn a fresh look at the beginnings of his

Unpublished lecture given in the Franklin J. Matchette
Series, Boston University, April 10, 1974.

own tradition, in some measure estranged from it and yet owned by it, to rethink its cumulative transmission through successive transformations down to the present and revaluate it in respect of its truth claims. An awareness of that whole dimension or form of experience which Gadamer has called *hermeneutische Erfahrung*, he finds, strengthens him against what he has long experienced as a relentless pressure, carrying myriad threats, from the West, and it also brings to him the assurance of an unending possibility of creative endeavour in relation to his tradition in the future.

To a certain extent and in its more popular expressions, this new trend of thought is perhaps a Western response to a new awareness of the "eternal East" in the Western soul, of this Western dream, and to the historical termination of the colonial epoch in the age of Western dominance; to an awareness of the dreaming East awake and no longer willing to exist only as a dream within the Western dream-world. Henri Baudet has described how the European imagination has reacted to what he calls "the West's great retreat from Asia and Africa within the space of less than a generation", and Mircea Eliade has repeatedly spoken of the need of a "creative hermeneutics" as the only adequate response to the cultural and religious pluralism of the present. To quote:

> After the Second War, an encounter with the "others," with the Unknown, became for Westerners a historical inevitability. Now, for some years Westerners have not only felt with increasing sharpness what a confrontation with "outsiders" means; but have also realised that it is they who are being dominated. This does not necessarily imply that they will be enslaved or oppressed, but only that they will feel the pressure of "foreign," non-Western spirituality. For the encounter--or shock--between civilizations is always, in the last resort, an encounter between spiritualities--between religions. A true encounter implies a dialogue. In order to begin a valid dialogue with non-European cultures, it is indispensable to know and understand these

> cultures. Hermeneutics, the science of inter-
> pretation, is the Western man's reply--the only
> intelligent reply--to the demands of contemporary
> history, to the fact that the West is committed
> (one might be tempted to say "condemned") to a
> confrontation with the cultural values of the
> "others"....The will properly to understand the
> "other" is rewarded by an enrichment of the
> Western consciousness....might even lead to a
> renewal in the philosophical field.

The "other" here, it is worth noticing, is still part of
the Western dream, for which hermeneutics is also a
science of interpretation, an effective instrument for
decoding, unmasking and mastering an unconscious, anxiety-
generating content, in the manner of psychoanalysis, and a
means of achieving cultural totality, if not wholeness, by
assimilating the other as an element in a total dream
image. Strange hermeneutics, in which a valid dialogue
can begin only after understanding has first been
achieved, rather than being itself the locus or the play-
ground in which understanding has its very being. It is
true, as Eliade says, that "Today history is becoming
universal for the first time." But, we ask, must it bring
in its wake the spectral corollary of a "planetary"
culture, as envisaged by him--or by Teilhard de Chardin or
W.I. Thompson--and are Oriental spiritualities destined to
survive only as elements within a planetized culture, to
assist in the birth of which he invites historians of
religion to contribute?

At the level of religious thought, this quest for
universality, completeness and self-sufficiency in the
West goes far back to, and would seem to be rooted in, the
thinking of the Church Fathers and in the explicitly
formulated principle of "utilization" or *chrêsis*, as
another Catholic scholar, the Indologist Paul Hacker, has
not only described but energetically commended as the
central motivating principle in a religious hermeneutics
of the "other". Hacker has drawn attention to the
phenomenon of what he calls "reorienting assimilation of

foreign materials" in the Old and New Testaments and shown
how in the writings of the Church Fathers the Christian
attitude to the religions of the Gentiles found explicit
formulation in the principle of *chrêsis*. The principle is
implied in the ideas of Justin and Clement and in Origen's
symbolical interpretation of the *spolia Aegyptorum*. In
Gregory's meditation on the Life of Moses three symbols
exhibiting the role of pagan culture in theology are
presented: Pharaoh's daughter, Moses' wife and the
Egyptian treasures, each pointing to the legitimacy of
assimilating the contents of pagan culture. Finally,
Augustine (*De doctrina Christiana*, book II, chapters
40-41) expounds the doctrine of the Egyptian treasures and
of their utilization by Christians, explaining how the
liberal arts and moral concepts to be found among the
Nations constitute their gold and silver which the
Christian is to appropriate to himself, for the gentiles
are unlawful possessors of those treasures and misuse them
perversely and illegitimately. In his discussion of the
views of Karl Rahner and Raimundo Panikkar and of the
implications of the Second Vatican Council, Hacker has
offered his own explication of this principle:

> The practical attitude toward non-Christian
> religions consists mainly in what the Fathers
> called *utilization* (*chrêsis, usus justus*).
> Utilization connotes, (1) that the assimilated
> elements are made subservient to an end different
> from the context from which they were taken, (2)
> that they can be taken over because some truth is
> contained or hidden in them, (3) that they must
> be reoriented in order that the truth might shine
> forth unimpeded.

Hacker addresses himself to the community of believers,
just as Eliade spoke in the name of Western culture, to be
enriched by assimilating "the spiritual universes that
Africa, Oceania, Southeast Asia open to us." He is
therefore not interested in the question whether this same
threefold hermeneutical process may not be at work,
"illegitimately" perhaps, from his point of view, in the

development of these other traditions too, and be adopted
as the creative task of men of faith everywhere, in
relation to *their own* traditions. If it were not for the
fact that the former is professionally a historian of
religion and the latter a distinguished Indologist, I
might have little justification for eavesdropping on what
is said *entre nous*. But both are engaged in scholarly
work in the *Geisteswissenschaften*, work which in its
claim, authority and appeal encompasses East and West,
Christian and non-Christian alike. Or, does the claim to
objective knowledge in such humanistic scholarship, with
its methodologies validating its claim, have something
illusory, dreamlike about it, no more than the pursuit of
a phantom, as Gadamer has put it? Is the "other" present
there only as an object of such scientific knowledge? For
Hacker, the impeccable scholar of Advaita Vedānta,
Indology is a *Fach*, a field of specialized research, a
Wissenschaft with a simple but severely austere methodology for investigating alien texts for the sake of what
is objectively present in them, with all "interpretation"
ruled out of court and its place taken by theological
"utilization". "A text," Hacker says, "does not answer us
like the partner in a conversation. It says, irrespective
of what question the interpreter approaches it with,
always the same, and the interpreter must, *nolens volens*,
let that text speak out with its fixed and established
words." This "*zu Wort kommen*" of the fixed words of the
text, a text belonging to an alien tradition, presumably
occurs by way of translating from the Sanskrit into a
Western language, and is for Hacker a strictly "static"
procedure. Dynamism is introduced into it, he tells
Panikkar, only when the interpreter takes up a stand *vis a
vis* the text, outside its heathen context, exposes its
"daemonic ambiguity and barrenness in that soil and then,
by an act of *chrêsis*, transplants any grains of logos-seed
he picks up there into the soil where alone they can

blossom and bear fruit--in the garden of the Church. The
Hindu Indian can only say amen to this noble enterprise,
for this kind of taking away enriches the other without
leaving the donor any poorer. He too is enriched by the
knowledge that somewhere there is a garden in bloom and is
strengthened in his hope that he too may some day learn to
tend his own garden better. Only, he feels a little left
out in the cold, somewhat bewildered and helpless, to
overhear that in order to grasp the truth in a text that
speaks to him directly, without translation, he must first
secure an Archimidean point outside the entire context of
his tradition. Or is this a hermeneutic only of the
"other," and confined to the foreign, with another, less
urgent hermeneutic for one's own tradition on the shelves?
What is it to understand, oneself or the other, and what
is it to understand a text generally? Is there not a
dynamic moment inherent in all understanding, so that to
understand is not just an independent preliminary act but
is inclusive of interpretation and application as necessary and constitutive moments in the total act, as Gadamer
has shown? Is there such a thing as an objective, unchanging meaning "contained" within a text? Was Heidegger
wrong in holding that all understanding is, as such,
interpretative, or when he said, "Whenever something is
interpreted as something, the interpretation is founded
essentially upon fore-having, fore-sight, and fore-
conception"? As he pointed out,

> An interpretation is never a presuppositionless
> apprehending of something presented to us. If,
> when one is engaged in a particular, concrete
> kind of interpretation, in the sense of exact
> textual interpretation, one likes to appeal to
> what "stands there," then one finds that what
> "stands there" in the first instance is nothing
> other than the obvious undiscussed assumptions of
> the person who does the interpreting.

Must we all think of our relationship to our traditions in
terms of reified entities called "religions," and is there

nothing to be learned here from the liberating insights of
Wilfred Cantwell Smith?

Philosophically more significant, and for our present
purpose closer to the heart of the matter, is the
following classic formulation of the Western concern with
understanding, and its approach toward, the Orient by
Maurice Merleau-Ponty:

> Like everything built or instituted by man, India
> and China are immensely interesting. But like
> all institutions, they leave it to us to discern
> their true meaning; they do not give it to us
> completely. China and India are not entirely
> aware of what they are saying. What they need to
> do to have philosophies is to try to *understand*
> themselves and everything else. Although these
> remarks are commonplace today, they do not settle
> the question. They come to us from Hegel. He
> was the one who invented the idea of "going
> beyond" the Orient by "understanding" it. It was
> Hegel who contrasted the Western idea of truth as
> the total conceptual recovery of the world in all
> its variety to the Orient, and defined the Orient
> as a failure in the same understanding....Hegel
> and those who follow him grant philosophical
> dignity to Oriental thought only by treating it
> as a distant approximation of conceptual under-
> standing. Our idea of knowledge is so demanding
> that it forces every other type of thought to the
> alternative of resigning itself to being a first
> sketch of the concept or disqualifying itself as
> irrational. Now the question is whether we can
> claim as Hegel did to have this absolute know-
> ledge, this concrete universal that the Orient
> has shut itself off from. If we do not in fact
> have it, our entire evaluation of other cultures
> must be re-examined.

Speaking of Husserl's more open attitude in this regard,
Merleau-Ponty adds, however, "Yet the fact remains that
the West has invented an idea of truth which requires and
authorizes it to understand other cultures, and thus to
recover them as aspects of a total truth." As a "historical entelechy" and as itself a historical creation,
the West is "committed to the onerous task of understanding other cultures," though it can learn from Indian
and Chinese philosophers "to rediscover the relationship

to being and the initial option which gave it birth, and
to estimate the possibilities we have shut ourselves off
from in becoming 'Westerners' and perhaps reopen them....
This is why we should let the Orient appear in the museum
of famous philosophers." Merleau-Ponty, too, does not
"settle the question," and still shares, along with
Husserl, the basic presuppositions of Hegel as to the
reality and significance of the East for Western man.

It was Hegel who described India as "the land of
imaginative aspiration," as "a Fairy region, an enchanted
World," "the region of phantasy and sensibility," as
exhibiting the unearthly beauty of a woman in the days
which immediately succeed childbirth, or of women during
the magical somnambulistic sleep, connecting them with a
world of super-terrestrial beauty. "Such a beauty," he
says, "we find also in its loveliest form in the Indian
world; a beauty of enervation in which all that is rough,
rigid, and contradictory is dissolved, and we have only
the soul in a state of emotion;" "the charm of this
Flowerlife...in which its whole environment and all its
relations are permeated by the rose-breath of the soul,
and the world is transformed into a Garden of Love." This
India of the German Romantic imagination, projected by
Hegel on to a distant geographical region, represents for
him "the character of Spirit in a state of Dream," a
character which constitutes "the generic principle of the
Hindu Nature." Hegel goes on to explain, "In a dream, the
individual ceases to be conscious of self *as such*, in
contradistinction from objective existences. When awake,
I exist for myself, and the rest of creation is an
external, fixed objectivity, as I myself am for it." "The
dreaming Indian" has not only never awakened into the
sphere of Understanding, where the self, existing for
itself, stands over against the objective world; he is
lost in his dreams. The Hindu Spirit revels in the most
extravagant maze through all natural and spiritual forms,

and leading "this inebriate dream-life, in which like a
desolate spirit, it finds no rest, no settled composure,
though it can content itself in no other way; as a man who
is quite reduced in body and spirit finds his existence
altogether stupid and intolerable, and is driven to the
creation of a dream-world and a delirious bliss in opium."
Further, "As the Hindoo Spirit is a state of dreaming and
mental transiency--a self-oblivious dissolution--objects
also dissolve for it into unreal images and indefinitude."
This is why Indians have no History, "for history requires
Understanding--the power of looking at an object in an
independent objective light, and comprehending it in its
rational connection with other objects....(And) it is
because Hindus have no history in the form of annals
(*historia*) that they have no History in the form of
transactions (*res gestae*) no growth expanding into a
veritable political condition." It is as an embodiment of
such spirit in a state of dream that India "forms an
essential element in Universal History, as a land of
Desire," and as which it has finally consummated her role
by surrendering herself and her treasures to her English
lords. Is it not indeed the privilege of the spirit in
the waking state, as represented by the modern Hegel-
speaking Western consciousness, to be master of its
dreams, even if they be only his dreams?

More than seventy-five years were to elapse after
Hegel's lectures on the philosophy of history, where these
views are expressed, before Freud would publish his
Traumdeutung (1900), and another fifty years or so before
Heidegger's critique of the Western waking *Geist* and his
exhibition of it as the grandiloquent dream that it is, a
critique that was itself rendered possible by the explicit
self-exhibition of this as the Will to Power in the
thinking of Nietzsche. It was not until 1927 that, with
the publication of *Being and Time*, the notion of history
and the "power of seeing an object in an objective light,"

the very concepts of Time and of Being, were put into question by Heidegger. For, it is he who first distinguished between history and *Geschichte*, who said that unhistorical ages are not as such necessarily *ungeschichtlich* and that "history" is in a sense the standing destruction of the future and of the happening character of our relationship to the arrival of what still remains hidden, unthought and unsaid, in the beginning that launched us into our voyage through history. Is history a continuous movement toward absolute self-consciousness, as Hegel thought, or is it the *Irrtum* (the empire of confusion and error) that as Heidegger said, constitutes the *Wesensraum* of *Geschichte* itself. Not until James Joyce's *Finnegan's Wake* was this Western waking dream experienced as truly a dream and translated back into language appropriate to the dreaming state. Here, it may be added, the meeting with India is presented as the moment of awaking, not as the descent into a dream-world, as with Hegel. "It was a long, dark, all but unending night: now day, slow day. The lotus bells. It is our hour of risings. In that European end meets Ind."

Hegel, however, said something profoundly true, unbeknownst to himself, when he prognosticated, continuing his sentence on the English lordship over India, "for it is the necessary fate of Asiatic Empires to be subjected to Europeans; and China will, someday or other, be obliged to submit to this fate." For the spirit which woke up, or dreamt that it did, after Socrates in the history of Western thought, *has* conquered the world and incorporated it into its own big dream. This is world conquest, not in the political sense, nor even in the cultural sense (aren't we all today very cheerful and generous pluralists?) but in the sense of what Husserl called the *Europaisierung der Erde* and, following him, Heidegger. Nietzsche described this invisible spirit as "that uncanniest, *unheimlichste*, of all guests, Nihilism,

standing at the door of man's dwelling-place"; Husserl
thought of it, with unrelenting optimism, as the entelechy
inherent in the Greek origins of the Western philosophical
tradition and destined to eventual triumph. Some have
called it secularization, and others have spoken of it, in
more picturesque language, as the virus from the West, as
the whole world being sucked into the current of Christian
history. One manifestation of the modern age, Heidegger
said, is the flight of the gods, the withdrawal of
Divinity as such, adding that the greatest share in
bringing this about falls to Christianity. Arend Theodoor
van Leeuwen seems to agree, even to welcome this modern
phenomenon, not merely of the absence of Deity but of his
passing, so vividly depicted in Nietzsche's story of the
mad man. Heidegger has described this shadow creeping
over the world as the spread of technological thinking, as
the process of the complete Europeanization of the earth
and of man, attacking at the source everything that is of
an essential nature, threatening to bring about a drying
up of these sources. He has also called it, simply,
"world-civilization", which means today "the dominance of
the natural sciences, the dominance and primacy of
economics, politics, technology. Everything else is not
even superstructure any longer, but only an utterly
fragile side-structure. We stand in the midst of this
world-civilization," which is only a form of the world-
destiny of homelessness, not something which modern man
has himself made but a destiny into which he has rather
been sent forth, fated. In this sense at least the
non-Western world has become subject to, and a participant
in, what Heidegger has also called "the destiny, or
history, of Being," originating in the West but now
enveloping the entire earth. In so far as we in the East
are aware of this common destiny, not merely in terms of
the urgency to modernize but also as sharing in a common
"time of need," we cannot but listen to the Western voice

which speaks of the possibility of a "turn," a *Wende*, in
this destiny, if only we are willing to face up to the
task of learning to think Truth and Time, Being, World and
Man in ways other than those laid out by the Greek
founders of this destiny, and wake up at last from this
long Western dream of which we too have become a part,
wake up without forgetting to learn so much that this
dream has yet to teach us.

To return to Hegel and to his view, out-moded in its
formulation but not to be dismissed as just arrant
Hegelian non-sense even today, that the direction of
world-history moves from East to West, for Europe was to
Hegel the culmination of this history, as Asia was its
beginning. As for the future, he said, America is the
land to which it belongs, "where, in the ages that lie
before us, the burden of the World's history shall reveal
itself. The Light of Spirit arises in Asia, but it is in
the West, where the physical Sun sinks down, that there
arises the Sun of self-consciousness which diffuses a
nobler brilliance." In this daylight the Spirit is wide-
awake, having left behind, geographically, historically
and spiritually, the "immediate, unreflected consciousness
which characterises the East," the characteristically
Indian "Idealism of imagination, without distinct conceptions," where Absolute Being is presented "as in the
ecstatic state of a dreaming condition," where "the Spirit
wanders into the Dream-World, and the highest state is
annihilation," "a dreaming unity of Spirit and Nature,
which involves a monstrous bewilderment in regard to all
phenomena and relations." In philosophy as well as
religion thus, Asia represents a form of the Spirit which
has already played its role in history and therefore
belongs to a bygone age. It lives only as a vestige of
the past, for history according to Hegel is "the development of Spirit in *Time*, as Nature is the development of
the Idea in *Space*." Hegel arranges all the philosophies

and religions of the world in a progressive series
culminating in his own philosophy as the final stage in
the self-awareness of the Absolute Religion, Christianity,
and of all philosophies, as history comprehended, forming
together, to quote the great concluding sentence of the
Phenomenology, "at once the recollection and the Golgotha
of Absolute Spirit, the reality, the truth, the certainty
of its throne, without which it were lifeless, solitary,
and alone." In this progression, the religion of India is
one form of the determinate religions, which he calls the
religion of substance, and Indian philosophy likewise
represents the stage of intellectual substantiality and
inner abstraction.

William Ernest Hocking, otherwise so appreciative of
Hegel's "multitudes of penetrating observations" about the
East, saw the crucial weakness in this position, saw that
the East itself cannot be dismissed as a merely consumed
residue in the development of its own traditions of
thought. He recognized that the hermeneutic process of
self-understanding and self-interpretation through which a
religious and philosophical tradition like that of India
has developed continuously does not at a certain point in
time come to a sudden stop, becoming only a dead and
transcended moment in Western thinking. Pointing out "the
ineffectiveness of any attempt to deal with the Oriental
religions by placing them in *an evolutionary or dialectical order*, thus subjecting each in turn to the gentle
fate of being superceded by the next higher member of the
series," Hocking remarks,

> In this respect, I surmise that most Western
> students of Oriental religions are Hegelians at
> heart, tending to conceive the religions as
> members in a rational series whose terminus is
> necessarily one's own view....However genial
> Hegel's insight into the several religions, it
> remains true that the very notion of a serial
> order among the great religions is mistaken; that
> it is, in fact, *inconsistent with the dialectical
> principle itself*. For no people and no religion

ceases to think. If Chinese religion, for example, is defective, it will be Chinese experience
which will discover it, and the cure should come
in China, not in India. Why must the movement of
fundamental racial thought pass from region to
region, as if thought were no longer productive
in its old haunts? If Indian religion is defective, why must the more perfect stage emerge in
Tibet?....There is no advance without new energy
and new insight. But given these conditions, the
dialectical principle must assert itself, and
better *in situ* than in a new sphere where
continuity is lost.

Giving a more adequate formulation of the principle of
development, Hocking continues, "*From any position par-
tially false there is a nisus toward a truer position....*
Living thought and living religion never stand still. The
'dialectic' is incessant and everywhere. And this being
true, the next stage in any dialectical movement is the
natural property of the possessors of the previous
stage....no imperfect position can be fastened upon any
religion as its true definition." Hocking is still too
much of a Hegelian, however, to see here any problem in
the conceptions of "dialectic" and "development," and in
his views on the "logic" and the "structure" of world
history. Perhaps his ideas of the religious traditions of
mankind are too much dominated by the notion of "essence,"
of religions as entities each with its own specific
essence. But he was the first to see religious pluralism
in a new, more adequate perspective and prepared the way
for the bolder, more original and in many ways revolutionary approach of Wilfred Cantwell Smith in our own day.
Preceded only by Royce's account of the role and process
of interpretation in religious thinking, Hocking called
for "the way of Reconception" in the service of a world
faith--not a world religion--in which "the process of
uniting the religious mind of mankind" will be fulfilled
in the comprehension of an identical essence," thus
placing the hermeneutical problem at the very center of
the task of religious self-understanding. This is not the

place to examine in detail the contributions of Royce and
Hocking to philosophical hermeneutics from the perspective
of Heidegger's and Gadamer's thinking, which alone it
seems to me has succeeded in becoming aware of the metaphysical presuppositions or prejudgments implicitly
determining all Western thought and its culmination in
Hegel, including the conceptual concern with the "other,"
i.e., non-Christian traditions. As belonging to one of
these "other" faiths, however, I may be allowed to draw
attention to the following remarks of Hocking regarding
reconception and to question whether they do not exemplify
the continued operation of these same presuppositions.
Hocking says,

> In proportion as any religion gains in self-
> understanding through grasping its own essence,
> it grasps the essence of all religion, and gains
> in *power to interpret* its various forms. To in-
> terpret is the power to say more truly or in more
> understandable language what an idea or a usage
> "means"; to interpret is to give voice to what is
> relatively inarticulate and defenceless....
> Reconception conserves as much as possible of
> what is worth conserving in other faiths.

More explicitly, Hocking goes on to speak of "a certain
noblesse oblige in the relations among religions, of the
obligation to those less skilled in self-explication on
the part of those who have travelled far in the path of
self-understanding, of the chivalrous need to express for
them their meanings better than they themselves could
express them, of the joy of lifting a struggling thought
to a new level of self-understanding, of how much
"fairer--not to say more honourable--would it be to
attempt to anticipate for them what they mean." Without
pausing for the lengthy comment this calls for, let me add
that Hocking does indeed concede reconception to the other
religious traditions and admit the present "unreadiness of
Christianity" to claim triumph in the "competition to
understand and include, a rivalry as to which religion can
best express the meaning of the rest," despite its rela-

tive maturity and its superior "power of self-expression."
But this concession is only provisional, for the time
being only. As he says, "It is right, and indeed
necessary, for the good of men, that the non-Christian
religions should hold to their own, at least until they
find themselves in fact understood, translated, and
included in the growing power of a religion which in
achieving its own full potentiality achieves theirs also."
Are we not here back to Hegel, to his notion of a
potentiality that actualizes itself only by totally
comprehending and swallowing up the other, and to his
vision of hermeneutics as mastery of the other through the
concept, not a hermeneutic of self-understanding but, in
Hocking's words, of going through "the labour of understanding those (other) faiths," hermeneutic as a weapon
directed against the other, rather than as the very heart
of the happening of self-understanding. There is charity
here, it is true, but it is a charity of which the voice
is stifled by the metaphysics of *Geist*.

Except for Karl-Otto Apel in Germany, no one seems to
have attempted to bring Royce's very original and suggestive views on interpretation as a basic cognitive function
and on the concept of a community of interpretation into
relation with contemporary philosophical hermeneutics,
though he might well be described as the pioneer in this
novel mode of thought and the first to say, at least first
after Nietzsche, "Interpretation is, once for all, the
main business of philosophy," and to talk about a "metaphysics of interpretation." Without going into the
fascinating wealth of detail Royce offers us, I shall
mention here just two features of his thought which throw
us back again to Hegel. In the first place, Royce also
operates with the Hegelian notion of dialectic and
mediation, defined in terms of a triadic relation among
three minds, though he was enabled, by what he learned
from Pierce, to conceive it in an extremely generalized

sense. Secondly, Royce's metaphysics of interpretation is explicitly grounded in what he calls Absolute Voluntarism, specifically in that "attitude of the Will" in terms of which Royce interpreted loyalty, the teaching of St. Paul and the concept of charity. On both points Hegel's thought provides the basis, for spirit, according to him, is inherently Will, and Being in its fullness is Absolute Spirit, as the dialectical *Aufhebung* of the past and of the other its relentless instrument. To the will to interpret, or to charity understood in terms of will as the being of what is, the being of the other, far from being acknowledged in its otherness and as a voice trying to reach me with its truth, or in its identity with me in that which escapes the conceptual grasping of either of us, the being of the other can only be seen as "spirit in a state of dream" and as assimilable in that vast megalomanic dream into which reality itself is transformed when conceived as *Geist*.

As I understand it, Heidegger's thinking, with its putting into question of the "metaphysical" concepts of Being, Time, Reason and World, and with its critique of the modern metaphysics of the Will, represents the emergence of the *Western* consciousness in a state of dream into the waking awareness of itself for the first time since the rise in the West, to quote Nietzsche, of "a sublime metaphysical illusion" with Socrates, "the one turning point and vortex of so-called world-history," whose influence "down to the present moment and even into all future time, has spread over posterity like a shadow that keeps growing in the evening sun." The legacy that this dream has brought with it is our waking world of what is common to all, of mankind in the homelessness of "world-civilization" and in that constellation of the relationship between man and being which Heidegger has called the *Gestell*, the framework, which is the mode in which Truth as unhiddenness occurs in this age of

technology. Far from being the handiwork of the human
will, and therefore remediable by it, this mode of the
relationship between what is as such and man is part of
the same destiny by which Being discloses itself as Will,
while concealing its own truth in the hidden aspect of all
unhiddenness. What we need, in this time of planetary
need, is not "philosophy" as an expression of the conceptual mastery over things, but thinking as meditative
recollection and as a gesture of *Gelassenheit*, releasement, of being let into the letting-be in relation to
Being, as releasement toward things and openness to
mystery. These are cryptic utterances, I realize,
impenetrably gnomic and suggestive of a lapse into woolly
mysticism, and I shall not try here to explain them.
Instead, I shall just record my conviction that, in
respect of the ultimate concerns of thinking, a breakthrough has been achieved in Western speculative thought
during the last one hundred years of which the full impact
has yet to be experienced, and which promises not only new
hope for the ongoing process of philosophical and religious self-understanding in the non-Western world but
seems to me to be the only safeguard against the "invasion
from the East," against the abdication of thinking in
favour of the religious sensationalism of the present and
the apparent attenuation of trust in *philosophia* as the
pursuit of wisdom, in the West. Nietzsche's *Birth of
Tragedy*, Husserl's later work, Heidegger's *Being and Time*:
these are the landmarks here, pointing to the current work
of H. G. Gadamer and Eugen Fink, admonishing us to see how
much Hegel persists still in our thinking. For only when
we have seen this can we join together, in this time of
common need, to look for a hermeneutic that lets-be, a
hermeneutics that does not turn the past, or the other,
into a dream-image, an unreality, by the adoption of the
Aufhebung-principle of Hegel, but lets them be, real and
speaking in their own right.

Hegel has been the only Western philosopher of rank to
devote serious attention to Indian philosophical and
religious ideas and, despite the meager, often biased,
scholarly information at his disposal, to analyze and
examine them critically. Even though he did not share
Wilhelm von Humboldt's ardent admiration for the
Bhagavadgītā (Humboldt was thankful to God for letting him
live long enough to have a chance of reading it), anyone
who reads Hegel's very extensive review of Humboldt's
essay on it, cannot but be struck by the intensity of
purpose with which Hegel grappled with the difficulties of
understanding Indian ideas in terms of Western philosophical conceptuality and by the unsurpassed profundity
of his many insights. Apart from the foreignness of the
Indian world of ideas, Hegel's reproach against it was not
too different from his criticism of early Greek thought,
namely, that it represented the stage of abstraction and
of beauty rather than truth, a stage *not yet* determined
and *not yet* mediated by and in the dialectical movement of
absolute subjectivity. The Hegelian principle of *Aufhebung,* in the three-fold sense of *tollere, conservare,*
and *elevare,* dismisses the primordial and the pristine as
the abstract and the primitive, of value only as taken up
and absorbed into a higher stage of thought, needing
mediation and through that exhibiting its truth. The
first emergence of thought is for Hegel necessarily the
most abstract, the simplest and the emptiest, and the
happening of history consists in a movement from the less
developed to the more. Whether we begin with pure Being,
as in the Great *Logic,* or examine experience as the dialectical movement which consciousness exercises on itself,
as in the *Phenomenology,* or survey the march of history,
it is always the principle of *Aufhebung* which provides the
key to interpretation. Having defined history as the
development of Spirit in Time, Hegel goes on to admit that
the notion of the rise of a new life from the ashes of the

old is "a grand conception; one which the Oriental thinkers
attained." But this image of the Phoenix eternally
preparing for itself its funeral pile, consuming itself
upon it, but so that from its ashes is produced the new,
renovated, fresh life, this image, Hegel says, is symbolic
only of the life of *Nature* and is "only Asiatic; oriental
not occidental." *Spirit*, on the other hand, while consuming the envelope of its existence, does not merely pass
into another envelope, nor rise rejuvenescent from the
ashes of its previous form; it comes forth exalted,
glorified, a purer spirit, elevating itself into a higher
grade by working on the debris of the earlier. What is
Time, that the primordial must lose itself in the subsequent, and what is Truth, that it must ride on Time's
fictitious arrow and can shine forth only on the ruins of
a transcended past? What is thinking, that it does not
permit the past to retain some treasure in reserve, making
possible the arrival of the authentic future, and to Truth
the mystery of concealment in the very moment of
articulated disclosure?

Heidegger has taught us that interpretative thinking
conceived as an act of will, however adequate it may be to
acquiring mastery over entities or over facts and events
in the non-human realm, totally falsifies our awareness of
the human world and of the Being of all entities generally. To that the only appropriate mode of relationship
is that of letting-be (*Lassen*). For, the happening of
understanding, and of a tradition as its cumulative
result, is itself an ontological process, a continuous
language event and an event of truth, rather than a series
of operations performed by a subject upon something
objectively given; remembrance of what has been and upon
an anticipative reaching out to the future and openness to
it. This is what Heidegger means when he says that the
unsaid and the unthought of the earliest past, ever
inexhaustible, comes towards us as our future and as a

task for the future, rather than being annulled into the
present. This is what Gadamer means by his theory of the
wirkungsgeschichtliche Bewusstein, of the fusion of horizons and of the productivity of time, and this is the
sense of his insistence that understanding is not so much
a method as a standing within or entering into a happening
of tradition (*Uberlieferungsgeschehen*) in which the past
and present are constantly mediated, an experience which
we undergo rather than control. And here also lies the
extraordinarily illuminating power of his notion of the
self-propelled game, as a model for understanding, in
which he who understands is taken up, not as master of
himself, but as given over to the *Sache*, the matter which
seeks utterance in the inter-play between him and the
other. As participants in the game we are left without a
secure *Stellungnahme* outside of it, for we are already
incorporated into a happening of truth and come as it were
too late, as Gadamer puts it, when we want to know what we
should believe.

We live in a world in which the hitherto relatively
closed horizons of the different traditions of mankind are
opening out to each other and our divided histories are
being joined together, or are being rejoined, in strange,
unheard of ways (one recalls in Max Müller's glad
astonishment at discovering in the *Ṛgveda* a documentation
of the fact that Indians and Europeans are long-parted
brethren, belonging to the same Indo-Aryan family and are
meeting now after a divided history of four thousand
years). As yet, we have only had a hermeneutic of the
"other," i.e., of non-Western cultures and religions, and
we have philosophical hermeneutics, of which the concern
is self-understanding and in which the "will to interpret"
suffers its shipwreck. But so far we have no hermeneutic
of a global "we," appropriate to a world factually in
process of unification under the common destiny of the
Ge-Stell mentioned earlier, and aspiring to learn to speak

a common language and share in a heritage which is no
longer sharply partitioned. In the work of Wilfred Smith
we have the beginnings of a global hermeneutic awareness
of diverse religious traditions, an awareness made
possible by a rare renunciation of the voluntaristic
metaphysics of the will to interpret the other, a willingness to let the other be, only inviting him to engage in
the exciting and creative task of reappropriation that
lies ahead, for him and in respect of his own tradition,
endlessly open to the future and its promise. The non-
Western intellectual is brought to see that by joining in
this enterprise he may yet let his tradition deliver him
into a truth, new and fresh, and freer from the contin-
gencies of its historical context, by delivering to him
its treasures of the unsaid and unthought, the treasure of
the *zukünftige* that lies hidden, conserved, held in
reserve, in all living past. And beyond this, Smith
brings home to us, to Western and non-Western scholars
alike, that such reappropriation, guided by scholarly
discipline and close awareness of other traditions than
our own, is also the way in which we can contribute to the
emergence of common ways of speaking, as we move into the
future, and let a community of discourse come about as the
true realization of world-community, without all "other"
religious ways "being understood, translated, and
included," to use Hocking's words, in one's own.

The study of religion and philosophical thought stand
at the opposite ends of the spectrum of academic concern
with things human: the first, intensely personal, revol-
ving around the faith in the hearts of men and rooted in
man's love for man, as Smith has insisted; the other,
passionately impersonal, no less a form of love, and, as
Gadamer has observed, "in a profound and definitive sense
selfless." Neither of these by itself can bring into
being a community of discourse among men, but both
together, of necessity working separately but aware of

their function as creative, as *poiesis*, may yet initiate
the birth of a "we," no longer one in merely sharing a
common nightmare. Every religious tradition constitutes a
historically evolving body of interpretation, disclosing a
reality which it seeks to embody in language, and operating with concepts which it sometimes inquires into. The
Western philosophical tradition, devoted to inquiry into
these concepts of our ultimate concern, was until recently
confined within the horizons of its Greek origins, its
Christian unfoldment during the medieval and modern periods, and its pre-occupation with the sciences in recent
times. There are indications, however, that the spirit of
radical questioning that this tradition represents is not
only reasserting its vitality at the present time but is
also moving out beyond its traditional confines into a
more global awareness, no longer Greek in a restrictive
sense and beyond Orient and Occident, as Heidegger puts
it. I am convinced that such questioning, originating in
a listening to the voice of tradition, and the new ways of
thinking about man and about that from which he derives
his humanity, have an important part to play in enabling
us to realize, in Hölderlin's words, the dialogue that we
are, and the song that we may hope to become.

BEYOND BELIEVING AND KNOWING

*Über den alten Gegensatz der Vernunft und des
Glaubens, von Philosophie und positiver Religion
hat die Cultur die letzte Zeit so erhoben, dass
diese Entgegensetzung von Glauben und Wissen
einen ganz andern Sinn gewonnen hat und nun*
innerhalb Philosophie selbst verlegt worden ist.[1]

           ---G. W. F. Hegel

As a Western Indological scholar has remarked,
"Ancient India had no term exactly equivalent to our word
'law', in the same way that it had no word for 'religion'
or 'philosophy'."[2] Even at the present time, though we in
India do study philosophy and speak of religion, the
latter is not a subject of academic study. And, since we
have neither Book nor Church, there are no schools or
departments in universities devoted to the promotion of
studies corresponding to theology in the Christian world.
As one representing in some measure the continuing Indian
religious tradition, and therefore an outsider to the
problematic of the relation of philosophy and theology, I
can hardly contribute significantly to the principal
concern of this conference, of which, moreover, I have a
somewhat nebulous idea. I am grateful, nevertheless, for
this chance of speaking to you, even if it be only to
plead for a loosening of accustomed frameworks and taking
notice of other ways of seeing.

Translation of *"Jenseits von Glauben und Wissen,"* a paper
read at the Fourth International Symposium organized by
Alexander von Humbolt-Stiftung at Ludwigsburg, West Germany, October 12-17, 1976, originally published in *Trans-
zendenz und Immanenz,* edited by Dietrich Papenfuss and
Jürgen Sörig (Stuttgart: Kohlammer Verlag, 1977), 119-130.

Going beyond, the movement of self-surpassing, is as much constitutive of the human state as defining and setting up boundaries. It is this self-transcending movement, this reaching out and reaching down within, inherent in man, which defines him as *homo religiosus*, a bridge thrown across, from the realm of the visible to another shore. It is part of this movement to give itself a symbol or concept of that toward which it strains, its mode of being, its nature, its nearness or remoteness from us. At the same time, this movement seeks to form a conception of its own nature and mode. Is this appropriately describable as an act of believing or as a kind of knowing? Philosophical thought, itself a manifestation of this movement, has ceaselessly wrestled with this problem, aware of the inadequacy of each formulation, constantly moving beyond each, ever since the classic treatments of this question by Kant and Hegel. It is not my intention to examine here these views, or to ask how the problem itself came to be formulated subsequently in terms of believing and understanding (rather than knowing) and why it is theologians rather than philosophers who are at present concerned with this problem, despite the profound and far-reaching insights of a Scheler, a Jaspers and a Heidegger. I only draw attention to the challenge which contemporary theological reflection presents to philosophers to reconsider the problem, to rethink the concepts of believing and knowing and move beyond the charmed circle of traditional formulations of their relationship. A more significant challenge, presented by the relatively new discipline of comparative religion to both philosophers and theologians, will be considered here at some length later.

The term "beyond" in the title of this paper is also intended as a reminder of the fact that the terms belief and knowledge, and indeed this whole manner of posing the question, are proper to one particular group of religious

traditions and it is by no means certain that they are
adequate to the self-understanding of others. The theologian is concerned primarily with an explication of
Christian faith, but as required by his commitment to this
faith, he also has an interest in "other" religions, the
specific character of that interest being determined by
his particular theology of missions. In seeking to understand these other religious traditions he tends to interpret them in terms which have become normative in his own
and thus fails to see them for what they are in themselves. Even when theology is defined in a wider sense as
"a spiritual or religious attempt of 'believers' to explicate their faith,"[3] in Helmut Thielicke's words, the
theologian still projects upon non-Christian religions his
own way of understanding his tradition, still overlooks
the possibility that in other traditions the individual
may have other ways of being related to his tradition, and
to the truth it makes available to him, than that denoted
by the terms "believer" and "religion," other ways of
understanding the task of self-explication. A Hindu finds
it hard to identify himself by this name, given by others
to identify him, following necessities imposed by their
own conception of religion. Like the term "Hinduism", it
is not found in the vocabulary of his classic tradition
and has now been appropriated by him only under the pressure of historical circumstance, in imitation of Islamic
and Christian ways of regarding religious traditions and
one's belongingness to them, to use a favourite word of
Herder's. And what will a Buddhist, who knows neither a
theion nor a *logos*, do with the term "theology"? He seeks
refuge in the Buddha, the *Dhamma* and the *Sangha*, is a man
of faith in so far as he truly does so, but in what sense
is he a believer?

The two major traditions of Indian spirituality,
Vedanta and Buddhism, are as much philosophical as
religious traditions and are therefore neither purely

philosophical systems nor religions, as these terms are
understood in the West. They are both theologies in the
wider sense, for they are both rooted in the revealing
word, the one in the Veda, the other in the teaching of
the Buddha, and both are explications and interpretations
of a transcendent message. And neither of them is a
theology because each understands itself as a quest for a
truth which can satisfy and set to rest the disquiet of
reason, and because neither is based upon a dogmatically
laid down system of beliefs. Further, the truth, however
revealed, is not itself something to be believed merely,
or even known. It is not enough to acknowledge it as
such, pay worshipful homage to it, pledge loyalty to its
sway. It is a truth that is at the same time a call, a
demand placed on us, to realize it in our own personal
experience, within which alone it fulfills its character
of being the truth. The Buddhist may worship the Supreme
Wisdom and the Advaitin may bow down in prayer to the
Highest Truth, but in both cases this is only the
beginning of a process, to which a discipline of the
intellect is integral, and which culminates ideally in the
personal appropriation of that truth, in realizing or
actualizing it as one's own truth. So long as we insist
on interpreting religious traditions such as these in
terms of the believing-knowing dualism, they cannot be
understood in their own essence.

In the Indian tradition of Advaita Vedanta and
Buddhist philosophy, knowledge in the highest sense is
immediate, an experienced reality in which the duality of
knowing subject and known object lapses. The lower,
empirical, knowledge of entities in the world is mediated
by language, concepts and categories, though even here,
according to some schools, the conceptual activity of the
mind is more a hindrance than an indispensable means of
knowing. Empirical knowledge, though of a lower order, is
nevertheless knowledge, and what it provides is truth,

though of a lower order. In relation to the highest
truth, the lower may function as a ladder, a path and a
means of gaining access to it, and that is its potentially
religious value. But from the perspective of that truth
itself all else is untruth, all that passes for knowledge
in our ordinary life and all that goes under the name of
religion; it belongs to the realm of ignorance. *Homo
religiosus*, regarded individually or in terms of collective history, is "*ein Pfeil der Sehnsucht nach dem anderen
Ufer*,"[4] on his way to the truth, and all his ways of
symbolizing this truth, all his belief, all the concepts
by means of which he seeks to give to himself an account
of his relationship to reality, even the sense of the
sacred that accompanies him on this journey, his worship
and prayer, all these must fall by the wayside, as being
of this world, mental constructs, though of inestimable
value as leading on to a goal beyond themselves. Taken by
themselves, without relation to the goal, they are false
and empty of meaning; regarded in relation to that end and
its truth, they indeed have an essential pragmatic value
for religious, wayfaring man, but are untrue in the last
resort. Human religiousness, from this point of view, is
a pilgrimage, not the holding true of certain propositions
about the world and what transcends it, and not the
holding fast to certain ways of symbolizing man's longing
for the Infinite. As an *Unterwegssein*, it is necessarily
an *Irregang*, for on this journey idols must be set up and
idols must be broken, these same idols, our own, not those
of others. Without the faith that there is a goal to be
reached, without saying yes to the possibility that the
truth can be actualized, without the sense of something--
word, image, or person--sacred and without conceptual
constructs, we cannot take even the first steps on this
journey. Without the long travail of looking through and
beyond these symbolic, mythical and conceptual representations as constructs and seeing them as pointers on the

way, pointing, and inviting us, to move on, leaving them behind, without this there cannot be that awareness of moving closer to port which makes of a mere gazing at the far horizon into a voyage. And without the final perception of these symbols, including those called concepts, and of our very belongingness to a tradition, as idols to be discarded, down to the very last, there can be no arrival, no homecoming, no recognition that the goal was not somewhere else but where we always were, beyond all departure and arrival. Human religiousness culminates and finds its fulfillment in something that is beyond "religion," beyond belief and knowledge in the usual sense. Religion is indeed *aufgehoben* here and the "old opposition" of believing and knowing is overcome, but not in favour of mysticism, a concept which belongs properly to the prophetic religious traditions. A rethinking of these concepts, a moving beyond their restricted applicability is thus suggested, if violence is not to be done to other religious traditions.

As the noted American religious thinker Robert Bellah contends, "the confusion between belief and religion, which is found only in the religious traditions deeply influenced by Greek thought--Christianity and Islam--and is almost completely missing in China and India, involves a fundamental misapprehension of the nature of religion."[5] The concept of knowing too is rooted, like that of philosophy itself, in the Greek strand of Western thought and it is even harder for the Western scholar to realize that it may not correspond to the self-understanding of non-Western intellectual traditions. Hegel's extensive and repeated treatment of Asiatic religions, and of the Indian in particular, is the classic example of Western attempts to interpret these traditions as halfway houses in the march of the Spirit, as needing subordination to and incorporation within the Greek mode of knowing which is taken as paradigmatic, as Karl Löwith and Maurice Merleau-

Ponty have pointed out. Husserl also spoke of the *telos* towards universal acceptability inherent in the Greek gift of *theoria* to humanity and of the purely theoretical attitude from which philosophy has arisen in the West. He asked, rhetorically,

> whether the *telos* which was inborn in European humanity at the birth of Greek philosophy...is merely a factual, historical delusion, the accidental acquisition of merely one among many other civilizations and histories, or whether Greek humanity was not, rather the first breakthrough to what is essential to humanity as such, its *entelechy*...whether the spectacle of the Europeanization of all other civilizations bears witness to the rule of an absolute meaning, one which is proper to the sense, rather than to a historical non-sense, of the world.[6]

Nietzsche too saw in Socrates "the one turning point and vortex of so-called world-history,"[7] more than a half century before Husserl wrote the above words, but he spoke about "how the influence of Socrates, down to the present moment and even into all future time, has spread over posterity like a shadow in the evening sun." When he speaks here of "the profound *illusion*,...the sublime metaphysical illusion," and of "the disaster slumbering in the womb of theoretical culture," Nietzsche puts this Greek *entelechy* into question and makes the phenomenon of the Europeanization of the world appear in quite a different light. It is only when we experience the full impact of the opposition between these two viewpoints and grasp the wide-ranging implications of this opposition that we can appreciate the significance of Martin Heidegger's life-work. This is not the place to show in detail how this constitutes a massive, radical critique of pure reason, a bringing to light of the unexamined presup-positions of the Western heritage, how it requires us to think anew not only the concept of knowing but also to consider in what a different light the old contrast between knowing and believing is bound to appear now, for

in terms of that contrast a critique of knowing is at the
same time a critique of believing. The theoretical mode
of knowing is happily with us, like that other gift of the
West to the rest of the world, Christianity incognito, at
work in a secularized form, as the theologian Arend
Theodoor van Leeuwen has described it.[8] Both these gifts
have jointly contributed to the phenomenon of the Europeanization of the earth, "homelessness in the form of
world-civilization," as Heidegger called it.[9] I mention
here only in passing that the relevance of Heidegger's
thought, not to Christian theology, not to the enterprise
of philosophy as such, but to reflection in the context of
the study of world religions, is still to be realized
adequately, as also the relevance of Hans Georg Gadamer's
philosophical hermeneutics to our attitude and approach to
the study of other religious traditions. The work of both
has exhibited the possibility of a mode of experiencing,
of a relationship to what is, which is non-objectifying,
in which truth is disclosed and which is not yet a
knowing. These insights call for a rethinking of the
concept of believing, the other member of that pair
of opposites.

It is when we come to this new discipline, variously
called *Religionswissenschaft*, comparative religion,
history of religion or simply study of religion, that the
concepts of believing and knowing and their alleged
relationship are seen to be inappropriate to religious
traditions other than the prophetic group, as does indeed
the concept of religion itself. Even in this field, as
one reads some of the older literature, one has the
unnerving feeling that this whole academic enterprise
constitutes a massive attempt to reinterpret other
religious traditions in terms of the Christian tradition,
make them available and assimilable to the West, theologi-
cally or culturally, and incorporate them within the only
history there is, within Western history as world-history,

a continuation by other means, of the Hegelian imperialism
of the Spirit. Max Müller, with whom the Science of
Religion, as he called it, may be said to begin, a century
after the birth of Hegel, said, "The Science of Religion
may be the last of the sciences which man is destined to
elaborate; but when it is elaborated, it will change the
aspect of the world, and give new life to Christianity
itself."[10] Max Müller was a humanist scholar of towering
stature, with a passionate concern for man's commerce with
the Divine, and for whose pioneering work on the Veda
Indians will never cease to be grateful. He wrote to his
wife on December 9, 1867, "...I feel convinced,...that
this edition of mine and the translation of the *Veda* will
hereafter tell to a great extent on the fate of India....
It is the root of their religion, and to show them what
that root is is, I feel sure, the only way of uprooting,
all that has sprung from it during the last 3000 years."[11]
Another Oxford humanist Professor and author of the great
Sanskrit English Dictionary, Monier-Williams occupied the
Boden Chair for Sanskrit, a Chair which was established
for the special purpose of promoting the translation of
the Scriptures into Sanskrit, so as "to enable his
countrymen to proceed in the conversion of the natives of
India to the Christian religion."[12] The very first public
lecture he gave was on "The Study of Sanskrit in Relation
to Missionary Work in India."

The distinguished contemporary Indologist, historian
and uncompromising critic of Hinduism, Paul Hacker of
Münster, has in recent years worked out, in his additional
role as theologian of missions, an explicitly stated
theology of assimilation, appropriation and utilization
(*chrêsis* or *usus justus*, as the Church Fathers called it)
by the Christian of whatever elements of value there may
lie in non-Christian religions. As he explains,

> Utilization connotes, 1. that the assimilated
> elements are made subservient to an end different
> from the context from which they were taken,

2. that they can be taken over because some truth
is contained or hidden in them, 3. that they must
be reoriented in order that the truth might shine
forth unimpeded.[13]

Elsewhere he elucidates, quoting Gregor von Nyssa,

*Das gleiche besagt das bekannte Bild vom
Aigyptios ploutos oder von den spolia Aegyptorum:
die Schätze der Kirche, verwendet werden,
erfüllen sie ihren Sinn. Auf den Umgang mit
Texten angewandt, bedeutet das: Solange diese in
ihrem Kontext interpretiert werden, bleiben sie,
was sie sind: heidnisch, und eine christlich-
sachgemässe Interpretation muss gerade ihre
dämonische Zweideutigkeit und Unfruchtbarkeit ans
Licht bringen.*[14]

These words, like others addressed by Hacker to "softer"
theologians like Karl Rahner and Raymond Panikkar, are
addressed to fellow Catholics and I must apologize for
having overheard them. But I have heard them with great
admiration for the clarity with which a religious issue
has been stated and with amazement at the fact that
phenomenologists of religion have hardly taken notice of
this particular religious phenomenon--this age-old
phenomenon of transplantation and borrowing of elements
from one culture to another in the religious life of
mankind. A Hindu can only be grateful for such criticism
and even more so for this *Benutzung* for this double
mercy--far from depriving me of my treasure or making it
seem worthless so long as it remains mine, it enables me
to notice its preciousness all the better, as it stands
out from its context, to see it in a new light, when
transplanted in another context, and to realize with
greater vividness the value of the principle of *chrêsis*
for the ongoing and future destiny of "Hinduism" itself.
It is not for me to take a position regarding this
theological principle or any particular manner of
formulating it. But as a phenomenon it appears to me one
of the most striking things happening in the religious
life of the West, specially the United States, today. The

phenomenon may be given a theological interpretation (as
in the extensive literature on the problem of "other
religions"), or a humanistic, cultural interpretation (as
in the work of Mircea Eliade and others), or a philosophical one, as in the work of W. D. Hocking, Edwin Burtt
and other students of comparative philosophy. It may
exhibit itself at any of these levels; to a certain extent
even the rise of comparative religion is part of this
wider phenomenon. Is there something in the modern
Western concept of knowing, as Heidegger suggested, that
prevents it from letting the other be, which transforms it
into an object and thus takes possession of it, which
permits no inappropriable mystery in things, in persons,
in other cultural and religious traditions, no otherness
which is not at the knowing subject's disposal? Is there
something in the concept of belief, which is sustained by
the existence of an unbelieving other, out in the cold,
without the possibility of finding himself, lost?

There are other voices, however, speaking in other
tones, voices of scholars who are leading the discipline
of comparative religion to maturity. Here is Brede
Kristensen, phenomenologist of religion at Leiden until
1937:

> Let us never forget that there exists no other
> religious reality than the faith of the believer.
> If we really want to understand religion, we must
> refer exclusively to the believer's testimony.
> What we believe, from our point of view, about
> the nature or value of other religions, is a
> reliable testimony to our own faith, or to our
> own understanding of religious faith; but if our
> opinion about another religion differs from the
> opinion and evaluation of the believers, then we
> are no longer talking about their religion. We
> have turned aside from historical reality and are
> concerned only with ourselves.[15]

Here, though the language of belief is still naively used,
we have moved beyond belief as a proper name for Christian
faith, the other is acknowledged as a "believer" in his
own right and "knowing" has given place to "understanding."

The Dutch school of phenomenology of religion evolved to some extent under the influence of Dilthey and Husserl, but it cannot be said that it has taken seriously into account the critical ferment generated with the publication of Heidegger's *Sein und Zeit* nor the dynamism of self-criticism inherent in the naivety of the phenomenological starting point itself. Today, this phenomenological approach to the study of religion is still confronted with the task of appropriating the criticism and self-transformation to which phenomenology as a concept and as a method has been subject during the last quarter of a century.

The same may be said about the work of Joachim Wach, who emigrated to the United States in 1935. As a historian of the concept of understanding, he brought to bear upon *Religionswissenschaft*, of which the central concern according to him was the understanding of other religions, the discipline of hermeneutics as a *Geisteswissenschaft*. Wach himself had little appreciation of the new direction in which philosophical hermeneutics was moving in his own lifetime and it is regrettable that the very promising trend he initiated in the study of religion was allowed to lapse without bearing fruit. There are signs that with the recent translation of Gadamer's *Wahrheit und Methode* into English, sixteen years after its publication, coupled with the work of Paul Ricoeur, the relevance of the hermeneutical mode of thinking will become more apparent in America. Incidentally, Wach's basically theological concern was evident in his scholarly work in comparative religion. It exemplifies the not uncommon tendency of treating comparative religion as second, new ancilla to theology, as the Jewish scholar Zwi Werblowsky of Jerusalem has perceived and strongly criticized. Theological concerns must not obtrude here, as he pointed out; but, on the other hand, is the study of religion a matter solely of objective, scientific knowledge? Can there be such a thing as *Religionswissenschaft*, with an objectively given field of data and equipped with a method guaranteed to ensure valid knowledge?[16] Scholarly historical information must of course be gathered and organized, but does not the crucial and central task lie in understanding and interpretation, beyond that? It seems to me strange that this humanistic discipline, though free ideally from theological presuppositions and not confined to antiquarian scholarship, should still remain largely cut off from liberating contemporaneous developments in philosophical thought, as also from important trends, critical and visionary, in literature and literary theory. May it be that the very starting point, the conception of the study of religion as the study of "other religions" has resulted in an exaggerated concern with methodology, in an admirable openness to social science and anthropology, but in too little regard for the task of religious *thinking*, of finding an appropriate way of talking about *all* religious traditions and about the history of religion (in the singular) in their global togetherness? It is time that we realize that, as thinkers like W. C. Smith insist, the rise of this new discipline betokens the emergence of a novel approach to religion and promises to inaugurate a new era in the religious history of mankind; in other words, that it is governed by a religious interest no longer tied to specific theologies, and yet religious, pushing towards an integral, universal way of thinking about *homo religiosus* and about human history as in essence religious history.[17] Its aim is not to replace the plurality of the historical traditions by some kind of universal religion, but to acknowledge them and study them precisely in their plurality, in their interaction with one another, in their continued self-renewal, to play a helpful role in the response of each in the present crisis in its history.

One example of this new approach is the work of Mircea
Eliade, which is concerned largely with the cultural
appropriation by the West of elements of alien religiosity
by the study of myths and symbols, Yoga and Shamanism and
benefitting from the researches of cultural anthropology
and structuralism. This concern with the development of a
"planetary culture,"[18] as it has been called, seems to
answer to a real spiritual need in this age and is
generating a new form of religiousness, beyond belief and
beyond knowing in the scientific sense. There is a wide-
spread sense today that we stand at the edge of history,
"an der Zeitmauer," that we are entering a new phase in
the evolution of human consciousness, a post-modern, post-
traditional age, in which a simultaneity of all places and
times and the availability of all traditions to each has
become possible, where alternative realities have become
accessible. New ways of religiousness are being explored
and the need has arisen to find new ways of conceptualizing these manifestations, of moving beyond the knowing-
believing dichotomy. In so far, however, as this school
claims to arrive by the study of myth, ritual and symbols
at universal, objective, synchronic knowledge about human
religiousness, it seems to be pursuing a chimera. Even if
we take into account the phenomenon of transference from
one culture to another, it remains true that what a
symbol, myth or text means is the meaning it has for
people within a particular tradition, what role it has
played in their lives, what these men have done to or with
it, how it has shaped their history and governed their
perception of truth. For, even in the midst of *Welt-
zivilisation,* planetization, and a sense of the end of
history, the ancient religious traditions, in a world that
has changed, continue to flourish and interact, and others
step into history for the first time. This is a time of a
new kind of crisis for all of them, to be sure, but it by
no means denies to any of them a future, a future which

will be shaped, in some measure at least, by *their* past
and by the way they perceive their present in the light of
that past. Each of them has unexhausted resources within
it to enable it to move forward, and each is now, more
self-consciously than ever before, in a position to
strengthen itself by having a share in the resources of
all the others.

The cumulative religious tradition of India, comparable at the present time to a temple in ruins, has been in
the past an open temple. It was once touched by Greek
power and beauty, and by the traditions of neighbouring
China; Islam and Christianity have massively contributed
to it and Buddhist religious thought has been at the very
heart of its self-awareness. His present crisis can also
be the moment of renewal for the Hindu, thanks to his
wounded history itself, for now as never before, he can
free himself from the dead hand of the past. Now he can
joyfully let his religious imagination be enlarged and
vivified by the heritage of the Greeks, by the vision of
Christianity, and the message of Islam, and he can freely
seek to appropriate through creative reinterpretation the
tradition of which he is both a product and a trustee. He
can accomplish this, but only to the extent that he can
see himself and his tradition in the wider inter-religious
context of world-history. Does he have the fortitude, the
courage and the faith to live creatively, not just reac-
tively, in this new world, not of his own making, and join
in the common quest for a home here, and in the human
pursuit of that which is beyond time?

No one in our time has seen the implications of this
more clearly, is wrestling with them as problems for
creative religious thinking, more energetically, than
Wilfred Cantwell Smith, until recently at Harvard and now
at Dalhousie University in Canada. As a historian of
Islam, he is keenly aware of the historical dimension of
religion and of the fact that the religious history of

mankind, divided so long into several histories, is today
joined in a novel kind of self-awareness. Disciplined
historical information about the diverse religious
traditions is becoming more available and such knowledge
is altering the self-awareness of each tradition. In the
second place, there is a growing appreciation that to
people belonging to these different traditions, their
tradition has been the light by which they have symbolized
the transcendent, glimpsed the truth and experienced the
touch of the Holy. To understand the faith of other men
is to discern what their tradition has meant to them. To
see this means to be able, like them, to use their
religious tradition to enable us to see life through their
eyes. Like learning a foreign language, this can be done
and, as with language, it gives us access to a new world.
This in turn alters our understanding of our own faith,
puts it in a global perspective and thus enables us really
to understand it for the first time, though never finally.
As Smith has said, "An attempt to study Islam (for
example) in itself is inadequate: what in fact one is
studying is the Islamic strand in the history of man's
religiousness,"[19] including that of the student's own
tradition. Every religious tradition can now be seen as
developing within the context of an encompassing, evolving
totality. And in this emergent global awareness, which is
also a novel awareness of one's own faith as Christian or
Hindu, it becomes possible and imperative to re-examine
systematically the central concepts in terms of which each
of us has understood his own faith so far, including the
concept of religion as a reified entity. Smith himself
has been devoting his energies to an analysis and reconception of "religion" and "belief", somewhat as Heidegger
has done in the case of "philosophy" and "knowledge". In
his critical stance towards the notion of method and of
the goal of objective knowledge in this particular
Geisteswissenschaft, he joins hands with Gadamer, as

indeed in his entire hermeneutical concern, without
borrowing from outside. In his widened conception of
faith, as different from belief (again somewhat like
Heidegger's broadened conception of thinking as different
from philosophizing), the intellectual pursuit of truth is
also seen as an expression of faith, rather than being
excluded from it. What we have here is not theology and
not philosophy, but a new kind of thinking demanded by the
present and coming religious consciousness of humanity, so
that one day we may learn to speak as participants in the
shared history of a religiously pluralistic world rather
than opponents in a divided one. Some scholars have been
critical of Smith for giving up too much for a committed
Christian; others for being too hesitant as a thinker.
They forget that such renunciation, far from meaning a
loss, is always a multifold gain, and that in thinking it
is the breakthrough that counts, the sighting of a path,
the opening up of a vista. His sensitivity for the *Sache*
of his thinking and his sense of responsibility for his
calling as a thinker is too strong to ever let him forget
that, as he has said, one must tread softly here, for one
is treading on men's dreams. That these dreams sometimes
turn into nightmares, often into grotesque life-formations,
in which piety becomes paranoia and everything changes
into its unholy opposite, that is only the negative side
of this very human pursuit of transcendence. What other
safeguard is there against this than the single individual's unrelenting watchfulness over the ways of his own
mind and heart?

NOTES

1. *"Glauben und Wissen"* in *Gesammelte Werke* (Hamburg:
Meiner, 1968), 4:315.
2. Daniel H.H. Ingalls, "Authority and Law in Ancient
India," *Journal of the American Oriental Society*,
supplementary volume 17 (1954): 34.

3. "Theology" in *Encyclopedia Britannica* (Chicago, 1975), Macropaedia 18, p. 274.

4. Nietzsche, *Also Sprach Zarathustra, "Zarathustras Vorrede,"* 4.

5. *Beyond Belief* (New York: Harper & Row, 1970), p. 220.

6. *Die Krisis der europäischen Wissenschaften* (The Hague: Nijhoff, 1954), Part 1, 6.

7. *Die Geburt der Tragödie,* 15.

8. *Christianity in World History* (New York: Scribners, 1964), 18.

9. *"Dankansprache,"* in *Ansprachen zum 80. Geburtstag-- Martin Heidegger, 26 September 1969* (Messkirch, 1969), 35.

10. *Chips from a German Workshop I* (London, 1867), xix.

11. *The Life and Letters of the Rt. Hon. Friedrich Max Müller* (2 vols.), edited by his wife (London, 1902), 1:346.

12. M. Monier-Williams, *A Sanskrit-English Dictionary* (Oxford, 1889), ixf.

13. "The Christian Attitude Toward Non-Christian Religions" *Zeitschrift für Missionswissenschaft und Religionswissenschaft* 55, 2 (1971): 95f.

14. *"Interpretation und 'Benutzung,'" Zeitschrift für Missionswissenschaft und Religionswissenschaft* 51, 3 (1957): 262.

15. *Religionshistorik studium* (Oslo, 1954), 27, cited in Eric J. Sharpe, *Comparative Religion: A History* (London: Duckworth, 1975), 228. See also Brede Kristensen, *The Meaning of Religion* (The Hague: Nijhoff, 1960), Chapter 1. See also Brede Kristensen, *The Meaning of Religion* (The Hague: Nijhoff, 1960), ch. 1.

16. Cp. Eric J. Sharpe, ibid., 275f.

17. See especially Wilfred Cantwell Smith, *The Meaning and End of Religion: A New Approach to the Religious Traditions of Mankind* (New York: Macmillan, 1963) and *Religious Diversity: Essays by Wilfred Cantwell Smith,* edited by Willard C. Oxtoby (New York: Harper & Row, 1976).

18. Cp. Mircea Eliade, *The Quest: History and Meaning in Religion* (Chicago, 1969), 69.

19. "Mankind's Religiously Divided History Approaches Self-Consciousness," Harvard Divinity Bulletin 29, 1 (1964): 11; *Religious Diversity* (New York: Harper & Row, 1975), 108.

HEIDEGGER AND VEDANTA: REFLECTIONS
ON A QUESTIONABLE THEME

What is questionable can sometimes be worthy of
thought, and what is unthinkable can sometimes be glimpsed
as that which thinking is about. Both Heidegger and
Vedanta thought amply illustrate this. No other justification can be offered for the following very questionable
enterprise of bringing together two disparate ways of
thinking, so wide apart in time and in their entire context. The attempt can have unquestioned validity only for
those who believe, like Nicolai Hartmann and many contemporary comparativists, that there are "eternal problems"
in philosophy, everywhere and at all times the same, or,
with Paul Deussen, that it is the same voice of the Eternal Truth that is heard by thinking spirits everywhere.[1]

Perhaps, however, the task of thinking, in the comparative sphere, is not limited to the search for what is
common to the thought-content (the thoughts, the *Gedanke*,
the answers given) of two different philosophical traditions, or the construction of new concepts overarching
them, nor to the quest of motifs in another tradition that
may supplement a deficiency in one's own and so "enrich"
it. Perhaps there is, beyond this, the more exciting, in
the end even more rewarding, task of trying to see and lay
open the hidden truth of the paths taken by thinking (the
Denken, the movement of thinking, the questions asked) in
each, and letting questions arise in the process and stay
with us, without seeking to come up with precipitate
answers. This involves a movement of thought that is less
like an arrow in flight toward its target than a roving

Originally published in *International Philosophical
Quarterly*, 18 (1978): 121-149. Sanskrit words appear as
printed in the original publication.

and a rambling, a movement to and fro, between two different realms of discourse and vision, an exploration of
two different topologies. There are no predetermined
rules for a game of this kind, only the playing of the
game can generate the rules, if at all. So much by way of
apology for the following fragmentary, somewhat
Heideggerian, remarks on this questionable theme.

I

Deussen quotes the following passage from Samkara's
Commentary on the *Brahmasutra* (I, iii, 33) as "characteristic for Samkara's period as well as for his
theological conception":

> For also, what is for us imperceptible was for
> the ancients perceptible; thus it is recorded,
> that Vyasa (the author of the *Mahabharatam*) and
> others used to meet the Gods and (*Rishis*) face to
> face. But if some would assert that, as for
> those now living so for the ancients also it was
> impossible to meet with gods and the like, they
> would deny the variety of the world; they might
> also maintain that, as at present, so also in
> other times, there was no world-swaying prince
> (*sarvabhaumah kshatriyah*) and thus they would not
> acknowledge the injunctions referring to the
> consecration of kings; they might further assume
> that, as at present, so also in other times, the
> duties of castes and *Asramas* had no stable rules,
> and thus treat as vain the canon of law which
> provides rules for them. We must therefore
> believe that the ancients, in consequence of
> pre-eminent merits, held visible converse with
> Gods and (*Rishis*). The *Smriti* also says
> (*Yogasutra* 2, 44): "through study (is gained)
> union with the beloved godhead." And when it
> further teaches, that Yoga bestows as reward the
> mastery of nature, consisting (in the freedom
> from embodied being and its laws, and thereby) in
> the ability to become as small as an atom and the
> like, this is not to be rejected out of hand by a
> mere dictatorial sentence.[2]

Samkara goes on to quote the *Sruti* (*Svetasvatara Upanisad*
II, 12) proclaiming the greatness of Yoga, and adds that

we do not have "the right to measure by our capabilities
the capability of the *Rishis* who see the mantras and
Brahmana (i.e, the Veda)." Samkara remarks in conclusion,

> From all this it appears that the *itihasas* and
> *puranas* have an adequate basis. And the
> conceptions of ordinary life also must not be
> declared to be unfounded, if it is at all
> possible to accept them. The general result is
> that we have the right to conceive the gods as
> possessing personal existence, on the ground of
> *mantras, arthavadas, itihasas, puranas,* and
> ordinary prevailing ideas.[3]

Here, the gods are absent but they are not denied;
they have withdrawn from man's sight but still form a
presence on the horizon. A world has passed, but its
links with the present are not broken. The present,
though impoverished, is still seen, understood and interpreted in the light of a nobler past and as continuous
with it. Samkara would not perhaps have said, with
Heraclitus, that "Here too there are gods," but would have
found little to quarrel with Catullus when he said of the
golden age: then indeed did the gods come down and visit
with men. Life, in this Upanisadic tradition, was still
experienced as touched by the Divine, and the dimension of
the holy provided the context for all inquiry into reality
and into the nature and destiny of man, and for the pursuit of freedom and immortality. The quest for truth was
still a quest for the truth of life, for the living truth,
and its articulation into a coherent body of argued and
examined statements; it was not just a matter of detached
theoretical contemplation. It was a profoundly religious
quest, and yet a passionately intellectual one.

The eighth century in India, when Samkara probably
lived and wrote, was the century that experienced the
impact of the Buddhist thinker Dharmakirti, of Kumarila
and Prabhakara, thinkers of the Purva Mimamsa school, of
Mandana Misra, the lone-wolf in the history of Advaita
Vedanta, as he has been aptly described, and a century

which was heir to the imposing and strikingly original
work of the Speculative Grammarians. But the India of
this century, and of many more centuries to come, was not
yet under the shadow of what Nietzsche called "the spirit
of Socratism," and its thinking was not primarily an
operation with concepts about a reality understood solely
in terms of being, but had something of the quality of
meditation, reflection, and remembrance, even in the midst
of the lively give and take of argument and debate so
characteristic of the Indian philosophical scene. What is
to be heard, thought about, and meditated upon is not a
bare ontological principle or a metaphysical ultimate,
ground, or *arche*, but a reality experienceable and
experienced as sacred. And the hearing, the reflecting
and arguing, the meditating, the learning and teaching,
the composition of commentaries and independent critical
or creative works, all these activities are carried on
within the dimension of the holy and the ambience of
the Divine.[4]

The medium is not irrelevant to the message and is
often part of it. But concern for the "philosophy" of the
Upanisads and of the Vedanta, for their content, has stood
in the way of sufficient attention being paid to the
medium: the literary structure and style; the poetry and
not just the prose of these writings; the rhetoric and
what appear to be minor embellishments; the magico-mythic
elements still clinging to an endeavor where they do not
seem rightfully to belong (for example, the role of the
sacred syllable *Om*); above all, the verses of obeisance
and praise to be found at the beginning and conclusion of
most Vedanta works.[5] It is not just a matter of conven-
tion and good form when Gaudapada concludes his *Karika*
with a salutation to "the state of non-multiplicity" or
when Samkara begins and concludes his commentary on the
same work with an obeisance to "that Brahman which
destroys all fear in those who take shelter in It," and

when, at the commencement of *Upadesasahasri* XVIII, he bows
down "to that Eternal Consciousness, the Self of the
modifications of the intellect, in which they merge and
from which they arise"; or when Suresvara, in the opening
verse of the *Naiskarmyasiddhi*, offers obeisance to "that
Hari, the witness of the intellect, dispeller of darkness." And when, towards the end of this work, he speaks
of the Vedanta as a "science flowing out from the holy
foot of Visnu," this is no figure of speech only.

Nor is the idea, and historically the fact, of a
world-renouncer (*sannyasin*) and a wandering monk as the
only one competent to pursue the inquiry--not just any
"secular" scholar--into this sacred reality, a mere
sociological curiosity. For Vedanta, thinking is not
simply an expression of that universal urge so crisply
stated by Aristotle: all men by nature desire to know
(*eidenai*); the urge which becomes, when joined with the
pathos of wonderment (*thaumazein*), the *arche* of all
philosophy, as Plato said. Nor is it identifiable with
that *episteme theoretike* which, in Aristotle's words,
inquires after the first principles and causes of being or
with that pursuit which he described as "that which is
sought both of old and now and forever and forever missed
is, what is being (*ti to on*)?"[6] In the Upanisadic tradition, too, there is a seeking, to which the intellectual
quest is integral, but there is also a finding, which does
not consist in merely putting at rest the *pathos* of
thaumazein or in the discovery of its inexhaustible power
to nourish unceasing inquiry, but concerns the whole man
and the transformation and fulfillment of his human state.
And both, the seeking and the finding, presuppose the
experienced dimension of the holy and the darkly seen
presence of truth as sacred and saving.

II

Turning now to Heidegger, we find ourselves in a
completely different life-world; it is the world of our
present-day experience, life as we all experience it,
irrespective of how we individually choose to respond to
it. The world in which and for which Heidegger writes is
a world that has blossomed under the shadow of the Greek
theoretical spirit; the world which Nietzsche meant when
he spoke of "how the influence of Socrates, down to the
present moment and even unto all future time, has spread
over posterity like a shadow that keeps growing in the
evening sun"; a world under the domination of that "profound illusion," again in Nietzsche's words, which lies in
"the unshakable faith that thought, using the thread of
logic, can penetrate the deepest abysses of being, and
that thought is capable not only of knowing being but even
of *correcting* it."[7] It is, further, a world which has
been determined by the spread of Christianity and its
subsequent secularization, so that, in the words of Arend
Theodoor van Leeuwen, "in the spread of modern Western
civilization throughout the world something of the spirit
of 'Christianity incognito' is at work."[8] It is a world
shaped by the Enlightenment and by the spirit of technology, a world disenchanted and desacralized, as Max
Weber saw. As Heidegger has also described it, a
characteristic feature of the modern world is the flight
of the gods (*Entgötterung*):

> This expression does not mean the mere setting
> aside of the gods, a crude atheism. The disap-
> pearance of the gods is a two-sided process.
> First, the world image is Christianized, in so
> far as the ground of the world is set up as the
> infinite, the unconditioned, the absolute; on the
> other hand, Christendom gives a new interpreta-
> tion to its Christian character by transforming
> it into a world-view, thus adapting itself to
> modernity. Desacralization (*Entgötterung*) is the
> state of indecision regarding God and the gods.
> Christendom has the largest share in the

emergence of this state. But desacralization
does not exclude religiosity; indeed, it is
through it primarily that the relationship with
the gods is transformed into religious experience
(*Erlebnis*) as a subjective process. Once it
comes to this, then the gods have indeed fled.
The consequent emptiness is filled up by the
historical and psychological investigation of
myth, as a substitute.[9]

The question of Being, as Heidegger poses it, is
marked by a radical putting into question of all that has
led up to this present state, of the entire Greek-
Christian tradition of thought which he sums up under the
word "metaphysics." Equally radical is his attempt to so
transform "the question of Being" itself, from its
original formulation by the Greek thinkers, through the
thinkers of medieval Europe, down to his own initial
manner of posing it that this questioning itself becomes a
path of preparing for a possible future in which the
dimension of the holy may once again give meaning to our
world, no longer forsaken by the gods, and man heal
himself through a thinking which has freed itself at last
from its tutelage to the Greek paradigm.

The world-historical context in which Heidegger raises
the question of Being is one which he has described as
"the darkening of the world, the flight of the gods, the
devastation of the earth, the transformation of men into a
mass, the hatred and suspicion of everything creative."[10]
The essence of this darkening of the world is the absence
of God, as Holderlin experienced it, in this destitute
time, to which we ourselves still belong. Heidegger's
explanation of the neediness of this time is worth quoting
in full:

For Holderlin's historical experience, the
appearance and sacrificial death of Christ mark
the beginning of the end of the day of the gods.
Night is falling. Ever since the "united
three"--Herakles, Dionysos, and Christ--have left
the world, the evening of the world's age has
been declining towards its night. The world's
night is spreading its darkness. The era is

defined by the god's failure to arrive, by the
"default of God." But the default of God which
Holderlin experienced does not deny that the
Christian relationship with God lives on in
individuals and in the churches; still less does
it assess this relationship negatively. The
default of God means that no god any longer
gathers men and things unto himself, visibly and
unequivocally, and by such gathering disposes the
world's history and man's sojourn in it. The
default of God forebodes something even grimmer,
however. Not only have the gods and the god
fled, but the divine radiance has become
extinguished in the world's history. The time of
the world's night is the destitute time, because
it becomes ever more destitute. It has already
grown so destitute, it can no longer discern the
default of God as a default.[11]

The question of Being, as it unfolds in Heidegger's
thinking, is directly relevant to this destitution of the
present age, "for which the ground fails to come, hangs in
the abyss"; it is a reaching down into the abyss,
experiencing and enduring it, so that a "turning of the
age" and the return of the gods may be prepared for
through a rethinking of Being.

With all his originality and brilliance, Samkara
writes as at one with his tradition, a tradition mediated,
it is true, by the passing of the Vedic age and by a long
period of Buddhist intellectual and religious dominance,
but yet unbroken. Heidegger, on the contrary, starts off,
with Nietzsche as precursor, as a radical thinker in whom
the crises of thought and sensibility in the sciences and
philosophy, in theology and in literature, are gathered to
a focus. Samkara too was not just a traditionalist intent
on restoring the Vedic tradition but was a thinker moved
by the experience of his age as destitute, pervaded by an
absence and hanging in the abyss. The rise and development of the Buddhist schools (as of some others) in the
preceding centuries was only a symptom of this, bringing
to the surface a corrosion in the very substance of
things, the abyss that was opening up in the very core of

what is and summed up in the formula, "Everything is
without a self," and in the elevation of the subjective
sphere as the ultimate frame of reference. It is from
within this awareness that Samkara understood his work and
started on his way of thought, seeking to exhibit how it
was still possible and supremely needful to think of life
as grounded in Being (*atman*), to show how experience is
unmeaning and an unmitigated pain unless thought of as
grounded in a "self," revelatory of it and therefore alive
with "the radiance of the divine" (in Heidegger's sense).
Samkara said,

> This tree of *samsara*, the round of worldly exis-
> tence, which sprouts from action and constitutes
> the field of confusion and error, must be torn
> out from its very roots. Alone in pulling it out
> lies the fulfillment of life's purpose.[12]

A statement like this can easily be misunderstood as a
classic example of a life-denying philosophy. In reality,
what it denies is not life but the death-in-life that
consists in taking things as empty of a self, without a
ground in Being and yet holding us in their grip through
the illusion of being all that there is, exercising this
magic spell over us. The purpose of life is fulfilled in
exorcising this spell and realizing that the spell arises
from our disregard of the truth, the self, veiled under
things, and is itself a reflection of our identity with
this self or Being.

All great thinkers respond creatively to "the time of
need," and so did Samkara, massively, passionately and
effectively, to the nihilism of his time, seeking to avoid
the extremes of conceiving Being objectivistically, as an
object of representation, and total subjectivism. But he
did so in an age of divided history--of cultures, peoples,
whole civilizations--and he thought from within the confines of a specific culture, and spoke to men sharing a
common tradition, still felt as binding, with common ways
of experiencing life and of speaking and inquiring about

it. Heidegger's thinking, on the contrary, is a response,
in full historical self-awareness, to the phenomenon of
what he calls "world-civilization," to its correlate, the
process of "the Europeanization of the Earth," and to its
consequence, homelessness. As Heidegger puts it,
"Homelessness has become a world destiny in the form of
world-civilization."[13]

This homelessness has come about--has long been coming
about, enveloping the future in this inexorable process,
as Nietzsche perceived--as a consequence ultimately of the
originally Greek comprehension of Being, of the way Being
disclosed itself to the Greeks. More accurately perhaps,
it is a consequence of the thinking generated by this disclosure (thinking as "philosophy," as metaphysics) and
what remained unthought in the Greek understanding of
Being. This comprehension, never made explicit, remained
dominant in Western thought until Nietzsche's awareness of
it as a prejudice, though he never succeeded in adequately
formulating this awareness. It also determined the character and nature of this thinking itself, until Nietzsche
subjected it to radical questioning, again without clearly
seeing the way to a satisfactory formulation of his
insight. It is precisely this that Heidegger seeks to
accomplish, bringing Nietzsche's insight "to a full
unfolding,"[14] inquiring about the predetermined perspective on which the Greek understanding of Being depended
and trying to see how the dreary homelessness of our mode
of being in the world today has come to pass. It is thus
that Heidegger is able to bring Western thought, for the
first time in history, to an awareness of its specific
limits, as something historically conditioned and "factitious," as based on specific presuppositions which have
constituted its unthought, unverbalized foundation. He
has thus brought it to a realization of its own parochial
character as Western thought, that is, as "philosophy" as
distinct from other possibilities and modes of thinking,
adumbrated or realized elsewhere, elsewhen.

III

But how has this homelessness, this transformation of home into wilderness, how has this harvest of what seems like death, become a world destiny in the form of world-civilization? Why must the seeds sown once in Greece generate a desert bound to envelope the whole world of man? Much of Heidegger's thinking since the late thirties has been devoted to showing how Nihilism is not just an isolated phenomenon in the history of the West, nor even the central feature, but that it is the very law of this history, its "logic."[15] How this Western history has assumed in modern times more and more a world-historical character is a question that has been variously answered by Hegel, Marx, Nietzsche, and Christian theologians. Is it because of an inherent entelechy in the Greek idea of reason (the fountainhead of all philosophy and science) towards universal and glad appropriation, as Husserl thought, that a geographically localized history has become planetary? According to Heidegger, science and technology, themselves rooted in "philosophy" and in "metaphysics" as characteristically and uniquely Greek forms of thought, are universally triumphant because they are unrivalled instruments of power over that which is, over every being or entity (*to on, das Seiende*), as presented in the light of the conception of Being implicit in the Western metaphysical tradition. It is when beings are seen in this light that they acquire their character as sheer entities to be measured and manoeuvred. The "Europeanization of the Earth" is in reality the irresistible triumph of this light, through which things become entities and then (in the modern era of subjectivism) objects.

But a prerequisite for the irresistible power of this light is that it should itself remain invisible, that what has remained unthought in the Greek version of Being, its presupposition, should remain unthought. It is to the task of penetrating to this "unthought," of thinking it, that Heidegger addresses himself, and exhibits in his thinking how this power of "being" can be broken and abated, how a turn in the world destiny of universal homelessness can be brought about. The world has become one only today, in the sense of being universally under the sway of the Greek mode of thinking as the thinking of Being, in terms of Being and as exhibiting everything under the aspect of Being. In seeking to think the unthought in all thinking of Being, Heidegger is the first world-historical, planetary thinker, a thinker who has attempted at the same time to rethink the nature of thinking itself as called for by his discovery of the truth, of that primordial dimension or region from which Being itself derives its nature, a region no longer Greek or parochial.[16]

Nietzsche saw the spectral presence of Nihilism, that uncanniest of guests, standing at mankind's door. Heidegger has succeeded in clearly seeing his visage, identifying and touching in thought this threatening shadow, tracking him down as to his provenance and pinpointing the exact character of the threat he poses for the world. A danger hangs over the world and over man in it; its presence stalks the world. It is not the loss of religion in general or the brokenness of a particular faith which could be healed by taking the road East; it is not the Atom Bomb and the vividly present possibility of total annihilation for mankind; it is not even modern technology and its effects on human personality and culture. The danger comes from what Heidegger has called the "framework (*Ge-stell*)," the peculiar constellation of man and Being that lies hidden, unthought, in technology as its characteristic mode of concealment.

But, "where there is danger, there grows also what saves," Heidegger points out, quoting Holderlin. Within

that itself which has generated this danger, and is its
unrecalled foundation, there lies the saving resource,
forgotten, unthought and therefore preserved and held in
reserve. That same Western metaphysical tradition which
has, inevitably, grown into a world-wide destiny contains,
when we reach down into its ground, the remedy which alone
can bring about a turn in this destiny. The cure must
come from the source of the disease, if it is to be effective, because the disease itself is a destiny flowing from
what has not been brought within the reach of thinking
contained in this source itself, lying in it as a guarded
treasure. It is this unthought of the Western tradition,
lying beyond the Greek, out of which alone a planetary
thinking adequate to the phenomenon of "world-
civilization" can emerge. As Heidegger has said,

> The present day planetary-interstellar world
> situation is, in its essential origin that can
> never be lost, through and through European-
> Western-Greek....What alters, is capable of doing
> so only out of that which still remains saved of
> its great origins. Accordingly the present-day
> world situation can receive an essential
> alteration, or at least a preparation for it,
> only from that origin which has become fatefully
> determinative of our age.[17]

The thinking of the unthought of this imperishable
Western beginning, however, is also the liberation of
thought from its parochial mould and its meeting with the
unthought of the other few, really great beginnings in
human history. In no case can it be just a return to
those beginnings, but only the gathering of resources for
a novel beginning in the realm of thinking, for which
perhaps, as Heidegger hopes, the initiative and the
preparation can come from Europe, "this land of evening
out of which the dawn of a new morning, of another world
destiny can come."[18] Heidegger's thinking, as he himself
conceives it, is a waiting and a preparation for the
arrival of what was glimpsed once as promise, but which
came bearing a harsh visage, concealing itself behind it

completely, and which can come again: the holy, the
divine, God, without the "metaphysical" mask. Without
living commerce with the Immortals, man has become incapable of truly experiencing himself as mortal, and the
quest for immortality has become unmeaning. For "mortality," as conceived in terms of the metaphysical conceptions of Being and time, is only a sham and an evasion of
the possibility of that awesome experience.

Heidegger's thinking has little to do with "cultural
synthesis" or with the notion of a "planetary culture," or
with the idea of a "universal philosophy" for the man of
today, gathering together the complementary insights of
the philosophies of the West and the East. His thinking
is post-philosophical, in the sense of being no longer
"metaphysical" and no longer operating on the presuppositions implicitly at work in all "philosophy." Yet it
is finite, in the sense that it does not claim to make an
absolute beginning but can emerge only as mediated by the
course of the Western metaphysical tradition and its
thinking of Being, as still linked to that which it seeks
to overcome. It is, in a sense, the carrying forward
through revolutionary transformation of the tradition of
Western thought, beginning all over again, so to speak, an
enterprise that remains imperishably, essentially Greek
and Western; no longer "philosophy," yet, as thinking and
asking, still concerned with questions that could be
formulated only as mediated by the Greek-Christian course
of Western philosophy, with unconcealment (*aletheia*),
opening (*Lichtung*) and presence (*Anwesenheit*).

Heidegger mentions Indian Philosophy (and Chinese) a
couple of times in his writings, but only to point out
that it is not "philosophy," a term which ought to be
reserved for the uniquely Greek form, mode, and concern of
thought. As compared with several pointed references to
"East Asian thinking," he refers in a positive sense only
once, and that, too, almost casually, to anything in

Indian thought. This happens in the course of a discussion between him and Eugen Fink on Fragment 26 of
Heraclitus, regarding the nature of sleep, where Heidegger
remarks, "For Indians the state of sleep is the highest
life," a remark dismissed by Fink with the words, "That
may well have been the Indian experience."[19]

This unconcern is somewhat surprising in view of the
attention given by Herder, the German Romantics,
Schelling, Hegel, Schopenhauer, and Nietzsche to Indian
philosophy, surprising in view of the fact that Deussen,
who was a friend of Nietzsche, had brought, through his
consummate scholarly work and enthusiastic appreciation,
the philosophy of the Upanisads and the system of the
Vedanta to the notice of the German academic world,
assigning as he also did a position of importance to
Indian philosophy in his *Allgemeine Geschichte der
Philosophie*. It is not likely that Heidegger had no
knowledge of these developments, or of the interest of his
colleagues and contemporaries Rudolf Otto, Max Scheler,
Georg Misch (Dilthey's pupil), and Karl Jaspers in Indian
thought. It is clear that he deliberately steers clear of
the tradition of Indian thought. His interest in "East
Asiatic" ways of thinking (not so much in its content) is
understandable, for here as in Meister Eckhart he finds
the possibility of a nonconceptual, non-metaphysical way
of thinking and speaking in some sense realized, and so of
value to his own quest and to the matter (*Sache*) of his
own thinking. But Heidegger is critical of the Neo-
Kantian presuppositions with which his older contemporaries approached Indian thought; nor does he share
Hegel's diametrically opposite concern for appropriating,
subsuming, and cancelling all non-Western modes of
thought, like all earlier stages of Western thought
itself, into the total self-possession of the Spirit in
the form of the Absolute Spirit. Therefore, in spite of
being as mindful of the historicity of thinking as Hegel

was, Heidegger is under no compulsion to incorporate
non-Western achievements of thought in his thinking and
exhibit them as consummated and superseded in it. Concerning himself with the opaque foundations of the Western
thinking of Being in a ceaselessly backward movement of
thought, rather than with the ever-progressive movement of
the spirit toward complete self-transparency like Hegel,
Heidegger leaves these traditions aside, lets them be, as
repositories of a treasure which may be relevant, at some
future time, to that planetary thinking for which he
claims to do no more than prepare at this critical time of
the in-break of world-civilization in our midst.

Deussen said in his *Allgemeine Geschichte der
Philosophie*,

> One purpose will surely be served when the Indian
> world-view becomes known. It will make us aware
> that we, with our entire religious and philo-
> sophical thought, are caught in a colossal one-
> sidedness, and that there can be found yet a
> quite different way of grasping things than the
> one which Hegel has construed as the only
> possible and rational way.[20]

No less than Deussen and many others who have been
saying this since, and far more acutely, Heidegger is
aware of this "one-sidedness." But Heidegger is extremely
suspicious of the concept of "world-view" and his way,
therefore, has been that of becoming aware, through
radical, persistent questioning and tracking down, of the
origin and nature of this one-sidedness rather than of
hastening to a premature answer like that of Deussen, an
answer that is still rooted in his unexamined Schopenhauerian and Kantian presuppositions. Here, the Indian
Weltanschauung remains an alternative image for mere
aesthetic contemplation and it is an image which is in
itself largely a projection of these presuppositions. As
against Deussen's, the Heideggerian question is: Must not
there be a different way of grasping things than the one
which was launched by the Greeks, a way that needs to be

fashioned yet by becoming aware of the implicit and
unquestioned foundations on which they built? And must it
not be, not an *alternate* way which can be substituted for
the Greek, but rather a *foundational* way which can provide
the Greek and the Western enterprise with the foundation
of a more primordial awareness and thus break its
appearance of absoluteness and independence? For there is
no choice between two alternatives today. The Greek way
has become world destiny. This is our world, and the only
choice left is whether through another manner of thinking
than the "metaphysical" we can enter into the region, yet
to be recognized and articulated in language but not
beyond reach, as the invisible basis of that world--the
region of what Heidegger has called the event of
appropriation (*Ereignis*). The quest of thought here is not
personal, the achievement by the single individual of his
ultimate human purpose through insight into reality, but
world-historical, as "philosophy" is world-historical--the
quest of a common world of shared meaning and ways of
speaking. It is thus not evident how the Indian tradition
can help in this enterprise, as it is becoming evident,
partly in consequence of Heidegger's thinking, that the
Indian enterprise of self-understanding in respect of its
tradition is by no means always helped by being translated
in terms of Western conceptuality. This, too, may be a
reason for Heidegger's lack of Schopenhauerian warmth for
Indian philosophy.

And there is another, more crucial, point worth
mentioning perhaps in this regard. Heidegger's quest for
the "sense of Being" is at the same time a quest for the
right or appropriate language in which to talk about it,
in which the region from which Being itself gets its sense
can find utterance. This region, as it finally comes into
view in Heidegger's thinking is "that realm of the event
of appropriation, vibrating within itself, through which
man and Being reach each other in their nature, achieve

their real nature by losing those qualities with which
metaphysics has endowed them."[21] Thinking this "self-
vibrating realm" is building with language "a self-
suspended structure" expressive of this realm, inaccessible in the language of metaphysics. Here, "language is
the most delicate and thus the most vulnerable vibration
holding everything within the suspended structure of the
appropriation."[22]

Heidegger's search for the appropriate language with
which to build in this realm, that is to think it, leads
him progressively away from metaphysical, conceptualizing
ways of speaking and makes him even wonder whether Western
languages, just because they are superbly suited for
metaphysical thinking, can ever lend themselves to non-
representational utterance. For the thinking of Being the
Greek language is paradigmatic, for it alone, Heidegger
says, is *logos*; "what is said in it *is* at the same time in
an excellent way what it is called....What it presents
(through its *legein*) is what lies immediately before us.
Through the audible Greek word we are directly in the
presence of the thing itself."[23] Because to the Greeks
the nature of language is revealed as the *logos*, Greek is
the language uniquely fitted for that "expressly adopted
and unfolding correspondence which corresponds to the
address of the Being of what is" which is philosophy, as
Heidegger describes it, and for that very reason inadequate to the attempt at a thinking responsiveness to that
other domain beyond the Being of what is, the domain of
the truth of Being, from which Being itself derives.
Since we can neither ever again return to this nature of
language, nor simply take it over, Heidegger says, we must
enter into a dialogue with the Greek experience of
language as *logos*.

As Indo-European, Sanskrit also is in some measure
"metaphysical," as distinct from the languages of the Far
East, with the notions of Being embedded in it, gramma-

tically and conceptually. It is metaphysical in being representational, concept-generating and in being productive of ontological speculation about Being as the ground of all that is, and so giving the appearance of setting up a reality other and higher than this world, in the sense attacked by Nietzsche. Since *this* possibility of thinking has been fulfilled in its amplest and purest form in the Greek tradition, Heidegger is not interested in how Sanskrit speaks (in the sense in which, according to Heidegger, it is language that speaks, not man), nor in the tradition that has evolved out of it.[24] The extreme opposite of both Greek and Sanskrit, in their characteristic mode of disclosure, the Far Eastern languages hold greater promise for the thinking that reaches out to a non-representational mode of utterance. Thus, the very reasons for the delighted surprise and excitement with which the discovery of Sanskrit was hailed by European linguists, along with the thought forms in Indian philosophy by scholars such as Garbe and Deussen, are reasons for Heidegger's relative indifference to the Indian tradition.

IV

In this tradition, *Brahman* plays the same role as *Logos* in the Greek and *Tao* in the Chinese, corresponding to the notions of *verbum*, *oratio*, and *ratio* respectively, as Johannes Lohmann has pointed out.[25] But whereas with the Greeks, by virtue of the very *logos* character of the language, attention was directed away from the light of the *logos* to what it illumined, that is, the world of entities, of what is, in the Indian case language itself entered, so to speak, into the reality it disclosed, shining forth itself also, while illumining and opening up the domain of meanings. The original Vedic sense of

Brahman as poetic, creative and sacred utterance (as Paul
Thieme has shown), sliding subsequently into the sense of
the reality finding such utterance, the source of all
utterance and itself beyond human speaking, manifested
itself in the conception of *Vak* or speech as the
primordial reality, in the extraordinary attention given
to grammar (the invention of this discipline itself),
finally in the emergence of the school of speculative
grammar which culminated in the great *Vakyapadiya* of
Bhartrhari and the philosophy of Word-monism.

In the Upanisads themselves and in the schools of
Advaita Vedanta which arose after Bhartrhari this
awareness of language, either as Word principle or as
Sruti, is never absent. Samkara's insistence on the
inseparability of the liberating Brahman-knowledge and the
Vedic word about this knowledge and on the immediacy of
the relationship between the two is as good an example of
this as any. That the word of the *Sruti* itself falls away
and is left behind in the experience of what it has disclosed is no argument against the above, for all saying,
as such, is a showing, a mode of disclosure, and the
former is not just a tool for the latter but itself a
reality inseparable from it, as Heidegger has insisted.
The designation of the Veda, of even all primordial
utterance sometimes, as the Sabda Brahman--an aspect of
Brahman or as the "lower" Brahman--and of the Word-
principle as Brahman itself is not uncommon in Vedanta
literature and expresses this whole way of thinking. When
this is forgotten and language is understood as having a
solely instrumental reality, Vedanta thought is easily
treated as a kind of "theology".

It is not surprising that Professor Lohmann should
take recourse to the concept of "magic" whenever he
touches upon the beginnings of Indian thought. For "magic"
is only the name of a category employed to indicate what a
blind spot prevents one from seeing, what Lohmann's

idealization of the Greek prevents him from thinking.
Greek culture *is* paradigmatic, and perhaps we in India can
do with even more emphatic reminders of this fact. But in
the perspective of Heidegger's quest for what is "never
Greek any more" and for "planetary thinking," in this age
of world-civilization and man's homelessness, there is
little meaning in such idealization. The presence of the
Greek as world destiny is a hard reality to be faced and
interrogated, now and for a long time to come, by thinking
men everywhere. It requires a rethinking of the meaning,
and the negative value, assigned by metaphysical thinking
to the notions of the irrational, the magical, the mythic,
the symbolic, the merely poetic and fanciful and so forth.
It is a demand to rethink the relation between the contrasting spheres of "religion" and "philosophy," and the
contrast itself, generated in Western thought by the
coming together of the Greek and the Christian as major
components in this metaphysical tradition, to rethink the
concept of "mysticism" as a type of religious or
philosophical view or position.

The value of a thinker such as Nietzsche, even more so
Heidegger, lies in this that they invite us to such
"revaluation" and rethinking of concepts, categories and
thought-forms, not in the solutions they supposedly offer
to certain perennial philosophical "problems," nor in the
philosophical doctrine or system they may be thought to
teach or propound. Comparative philosophy so far has
proceeded largely on the basis of an uncritical employment
of these "metaphysical" concepts, assumed as obviously and
eternally valid, in the understanding of "philosophies"
such as those of India.[26] But something remarkable will
be seen to happen when we take seriously Heidegger's talk
of "the end of philosophy" and his "overcoming of
metaphysics" (understanding these phrases in *his* sense,
not just projecting an imaginary meaning into them, out of
context): freedom from this metaphysical bias, the

loosening of the hold of the "concept" on thinking, the liberation from prejudices functioning as norms and as standards of comparison, the openness to "the matter of thinking," wherever going on, East or West. For example, if "philosophy" is a synonym for the mode of thinking arising from the Greek venture and if there is no such thing as Indian or Chinese philosophy, as Heidegger insists, what happens to the concept of "comparative philosophy" itself? If the term philosophy is taken in this strict sense, as a proper noun, there is nothing to compare; if we still insist on comparing, it can only be for the sake of judging the non-Western, in the manner of Hegel, with the Greek-Western as the norm. But if we bring ourselves to share Heidegger's insight in this matter, we may also see the nullity of the contrast between "religion" and "philosophy" in the Western tradition (for, with the end of "philosophy," the opposite number of the pair also meets its "end"), and thus becomes open to the *Sache des Denkens* in those other ventures at thinking.

Comparative philosophy, if we still retain the name, would then be a name for the task, infinitely open, of setting free, bringing into view and articulating in contemporary ways of speaking, in new ways of speaking, the matter of thinking which, in what has actually been realized in thought, still remains unsaid and so unthought, in the traditions of the East. Otherwise, comparative philosophy will amount to no more than an unthinking attempt at perpetuating Western "philosophy" by translating Eastern thinking into the language of Western metaphysics, taken as the universally valid paradigm. And this is bad, not because it is Western but because it hides an unthought opacity that stands in the way of adequately reaching out to the other, for it either prompts to an assimilation of the other or leads to a perpetuation of its otherness.

As Heidegger speaks of it, the end of philosophy as metaphysical thinking does not mean its termination but rather its consummation, the fact that it has reached "the place in which the whole of philosophy's history is gathered in its most extreme possibility."[27] It exhibits itself as "the triumph of the manipulable arrangement of a scientific-technological world and of the social order proper to this world. The end of philosophy means: the beginning of the world civilization based upon Western European thinking."[28] Are we to think of comparative philosophy as a continuation of this consummation or completion, a contribution to it required by the emergence of world-civilization and in its service? Or should we rather not think of it in terms of "the task of thinking" which, according to Heidegger, still remains reserved for thinking at the end of philosophy, a *first* possibility which was contained in its beginning but which it could not acknowledge or realize? Whether we choose the first or the second alternative depends upon whether or not we see this world-civilization as "the world destiny of homelessness," question it (not deny it, or want to substitute something else for it), and are willing to question the thought of Being as Ground which heralded its moment of birth.

For any one in search of "philosophemes" common to Heidegger and Vedanta, or of similar-looking ideas in them, there is a great deal to be found regarding man's nature, the world, and man's relationship to it, the unity of Being, the identity between man and Being. Each of these topics can provide the starting point of an examination in depth of the similarity and the differences between the two, and beyond these, to meditation on these central concerns of thought. There is, above all, the idea of Being (Brahman-Atman) as the ground of all, that appears to offer an interesting point for comparison and contrast, for this is the basic concept of the metaphysical tradition and in Vedanta thought it is even more emphatically crucial. This is what made the arch-anti-Platonist Nietzsche describe the Vedanta as "the classical expression of the mode of thinking most alien to me," in his letter of 16 March 1883 to Deussen. Following Nietzsche, Heidegger also is engaged in the attempt to root out the very idea of a transcendent ground of things which seems most characteristic of Vedanta thought.

As one looks more closely, however, matters become more intriguing and complicated, calling for a fuller investigation than can be undertaken here. The second sutra of Badarayana's *Sariraka-mimamsa-sutra* both sums up a long tradition and presents a task for centuries to follow when it declares: Brahman is that from which, by and into which, all this arises, is sustained and returns. Is this Anaximander all over again? Is it Aristotle? If Brahman is identified with the Greek notion of Being (not to speak of its scholastic variants), conceived as ground, then Heidegger's whole effort is to demolish this idea, for his entire thinking is a critique of just this single concept. Can Brahman be so identified? If not, then the "all this" of the Upanisads cannot just be identified with the "entity" of Heidegger or with the *to on* of the Greeks, for here the "this" is not thought of solely under the aspect of its being-ness. As for the notion of "ground," here again, despite the seeming similarity, different things were going on in the two traditions, with very different consequences. But into this fascinating problem, perhaps basic to the comparative enterprise, we cannot enter here.[29] Instead, let us discuss in what follows, though again only briefly, two questions of a more general character: Is Heidegger an ontologist, and is Vedanta an ontology? Is Heidegger a mystic and is Vedanta a mystical philosophy, is Samkara a mystic? What makes these questions specially interesting is the fact that none of them can be answered with a simple "yes" or "no," that *as* questions they are themselves questionable.

V

Although taking the question of the "sense" of Being as his starting point, Heidegger is certainly not an ontologist, either in the traditional meaning of the term or in some new sense. The point hardly needs laboring, since he has expressed himself with all clarity on this matter in his later writings. He does not take ontology for granted as the first philosophy or as *metaphysica generalis* and then go on to make some original contribution to it, or provide a novel analysis of the "meaning" of Being but, on the contrary, subjects the very idea of ontology to the most radical questioning. For the first time in the history of Western thought, he exhibits the derivative, contingent, specifically Greek character of this whole notion, this whole manner of conceiving the matter of thought and of thought's response to the matter by which it is addressed. The Being of what-is emerged as the unique matter of thinking at the beginning of Western thought and this, Heidegger points out, is itself the beginning of the West, the hidden source of its destiny.[30] This great beginning of Western philosophy did not arise out of nothing but emerged in the process of overcoming "its extreme opposite, the mythical in general and the Asiatic in particular."[31] Heidegger's quest is for the source from which this thought of Being, indeed from which Being itself, emerged as the first and last for thinking, and a quest for that which remained unthought in this thinking, variously called by him Appropriation (*Ereignis*), Clearing (*Lichtung*) and Truth (*Aletheia*), or unhiddenness. And yet Heidegger is a thinker of Being from beginning to end, gnawing away at this marrow-bone (as Hamann said of his own concern with *Logos*) until he is able to dispel the darkness over this depth (luckier than Hamann perhaps, to have found the key to this abyss).[32]

Throughout his work there is a strange, bewildering nebulousness or lack of precision in the use of the word "Being," apparent in the adoption of such expressions as "the truth of Being," "Being itself," and of variants such as "*Seyn*" and "Being" struck out with a cross mark, so that one can always pick out passages from different periods of his writing to prove that, after all, it is "Being" Heidegger is really talking about without being quite clear as to what he is trying to say. This would be a mistake, for this nebulousness is not confusion but part of the stringency or rigor (which is something quite different from "exactness," as Heidegger points out) necessitated by this path of thinking itself. It must be remembered, further, that for Heidegger thinking is a movement and a wayfaring, in which what is thought about itself undergoes continuous transformation, as thinking fashions its path and moves forward, that is, away from the matter as conceived at the starting point, and from the manner of thinking it, towards a destination of which it has no foreknowledge. Seeking for what can have no name until it is seen, Heidegger uses the word "Being" as a provisional first name for the greater part of his path of thinking, until the long drawn out act of renunciation is completed.

The starting point is the Greek thought of Being, but the path is one of continuous overcoming of this thought, until thinking is itself set free from its bondage to this thought and from the determination of its own nature by it. Heidegger is a thinker of Being, yet not an ontologist; he is a thinker of Being who has caught a glimpse of the truth covered over by the thought of Being. Heidegger said in 1935, "In the seemingly unimportant distinction between being and thinking we must discern the fundamental position of the Western spirit, against which our central attack is directed."[33] From the perspective of the successful carrying through of this attack in the

following three decades, we can say that thinking is not,
in its true nature, the sort of activity which can be
about Being, with Being confronting it as its *Sache* or
matter, but must be *of* Being; that Being is not the sort
of thing which, eternally there, self-established and
shining in its own light, beckons thought to grasp it in
its three-pronged onto-theo-logical movement; that both
Being and thinking (man) belong together in a deeper unity
(inaccessible to any form of dialectic), from which they
both derive their nature and which exhibits itself, while
yet concealing itself, as the proper matter of thinking
that is no more a grasping, no longer a striving to form a
system of concepts for what is beyond all conceptualizing.

VI

Neither the Upanisads nor Samkara can be said to be
concerned with a theoretical inquiry (*episteme theoretike*)
into being as being (*on he on*) or into the *ontos on* and
their question is not identical with the Greek "What is
Being (*ti to on*)?" nor with Heidegger's questioning of the
ambiguities and the unthought presuppositions of that
question. Brahman, that one being (*sat*) which the wise
speak of in many ways, is not identical with the *to on* of
Aristotle, "spoken of in many ways"; and the Brahman-vidya
is not a *legein* of Brahman (so that it is as inappropriate
to speak, with Paul Hacker, of Atomology as it would be to
describe Vedanta as a Brahmology). It is not the conceptual knowledge of Being, though wisdom about Being
(*sad-vidya*) or about Brahman as Being, is part of it.
Brahman is *sat* (Being), the ground of all that is,
including my own being, which is of the nature of sheer,
pure *chit* (awareness, of which "knowing" is itself a
derivative mode) and potentially capable of rising above
all otherness and, therefore, pure bliss. Thus Brahman is

Being, but not in the sense in which it is other than what
it is Being for or to, not in the sense of what knowing,
thinking and speaking are about, other than them, as a
reality confronting them, but inclusive of these as themselves modes of Being. It is *sat, chit* and *ananda* in one
and as one, and my being is one with it. We can, if we
choose--and as metaphysics does--consider things
(including my self) solely and exclusively under the
aspect of their being (is-ness), only taking notice of the
fact that they *are*. But this would be something like
Blake's "Single vision and Newton's sleep," for no being,
as simple is-ness, is exclusive of the fact of being lit
up, of lighting up, of being gathered into a unity with
what it lights up and with where this lighting up occurs--
in me, who am in essence (as *atman*) just this lighting up
itself and so identical with that is-ness. So regarded,
however, is-ness (Being) becomes an aspect, though
integral and essential, of something more "comprehensive"
than it, thinkable separately and by itself, even as an
aspect, only by an illegitimate abstraction. Brahman,
therefore, is beyond Being and Non-being; "it cannot be
spoken of either as being or as not being," as the
Bhagavadgita has it.

It has been rightly pointed out by Paul Hacker that
Samkara was wary and hesitant, for this reason, of
dwelling too much on Brahman as Being, unlike his
followers, but focused instead on Brahman as awareness
(*chit*) and preferred hence an Atman-oriented approach to
ultimate truth.[34] Being, taken by itself, carries a
suggestion of objectivity, as being for another than it,
for which reason K.C. Bhattacharyya also relegates
metaphysics to the "philosophy of the Object." The self
should first be realized as existing, but only as a
stepping-stone to the self-revelation of its essence, to
which the ideas of being and not-being are not applicable,
as Samkara says.[35] In so far as Brahman, in itself devoid

of all distinctions, is the basis (from our human perspective) of all diversification and the seed of all activity, it can be spoken of as existing; or, because only by thinking of it as being can we be prompted to realize it.[36] But, being beyond the reach of the senses, it cannot be an object of consciousness accompanied with the idea of either existence or non-existence, as we have it in ordinary experience. Further, Brahman does not belong to any class or genus, and therefore cannot be denoted by the word *sat*, for we cannot speak about anything that exists in the empirical mode without referring it to a class.[37] And if *sat* were itself regarded as only a class name, it would be no more than the "Being of or in beings" and cannot be the prior ground of all that is.[38] Brahman has a unitary nature and we cannot define it as merely "that which is (*sat*)," or as merely consciousness or thought (*bodha*) or as being made up of the two together; "for he who would maintain that Brahman is characterized by thought different from existence, and at the same time by existence different from thought, would virtually maintain that there is a plurality in Brahman."[39]

The *locus classicus* of the more ontologically oriented treatment of Brahman as Being (*Sad-Brahman*) is chapter VI of the *Chandogya Upanisad* and later Advaita thinkers have attached relatively greater importance to the notion of Brahman as *ens primum* (*Satta*), as Paul Hacker points out. But it is in the *Brahmasiddhi* of Mandana Misra that we find a view of Brahman as the universal Being that is presented in and animates all experience. Mandana himself was probably influenced in his ontological interpretation of Brahman by the speculative grammarian Bhartrhari, according to whom Brahman is the Highest Universal (*Mahasamanya*) the Great Being (*Mahasatta*) which expresses itself in all words. For Samkara, however, such a view would be intolerable because it objectifies Brahman by making it an object of knowing. As he says,

> The purport of this science is not to represent
> Brahman definitely as this or that object, its
> purpose is rather to show that Brahman as the
> eternal inward self is never an object, and
> thereby to remove the distinction of objects
> known, knowers, acts of knowledge, etc,, which is
> fictitiously created by Nescience.[40]

We thus see that "ontology" hardly provides a basis
for comparison between Samkara and Western thinkers like
Parmenides, Eckhart, or Aquinas. Deussen made use, though
sporadically, of Greek ontological concepts to illumine
Samkara's thought. More systematic attempts have been
made to compare Samkara with Eckhart by Rudolf Otto and
with Thomas Aquinas by Richard De Smet and Paul Hacker.
But in so far as the final point of reference in these
latter comparisons also perforce remains the Greek notion
of Being, they cannot be regarded as shedding light on
what *Brahma-vidya* is about or what *Atman-bodha* stands for.
In this respect, at least, a consideration of Advaita
Vedanta in a Heideggerian perspective perhaps offers a
better chance, for the thinking of Heidegger and Samkara
may be found to have a touching point somewhere in that
"region of all regions," beyond the thought of Being and
Non-being, in which it has its sojourn. About these two
thinkers also it may with some truth be said that they
"dwell near to one another" though standing "on mountains
farthest apart."[41]

VII

Is Heidegger a mystic? It is true that he refers to
Meister Eckhart and Angelus Silesius, mentions Tao, speaks
of Way and Topos and Leap, talks of the identity of man
and Being in a primordial belonging-togetherness, of the
abruptness of an unbridged entry into the region of the
Ereignis. There is enough evidence to show that Heidegger
has been deeply interested, from his early writings, in

medieval mysticism in general and Eckhart in particular
and in his later writings he borrows freely from the
vocabulary of Eckhart. As John D. Caputo has shown,
Eckhartian concepts such as those of *Abgeschiedenheit*
(detachment) and *Gelassenheit* (abandonment, releasement)
have substantially contributed to this thinking.[42] Yet,
it must be kept in mind that all this happens in the
context of *thinking* and in its service. Heidegger appropriates what he finds to be genuine thinking contained in
the works of the mystics, takes them as gestures of
thought, as happenings on the path of thinking, never in
the sense of finding access to a realm and an experience
which lie beyond the reach of thinking, never as the
necessary or even possible abrogation of thought. As he
points out even in his early Duns Scotus book, the notion
of mysticism in the sense of an irrationalistic *Erleben*
(immediate inner experience) rests on an extreme rational-
ization of philosophy, on the conception of philosophy as
a rationalistic structure divorced from life.[43] Almost a
quarter of a century later, Heidegger makes the same point
when he asserts that mysticism is the mere counterpart of
metaphysics, into which people take flight when, still
wholly caught in their slavery to metaphysical thinking,
they are struck by the hiddenness in all revealment and
lapse into unthinking helplessness.[44] When we abandon the
presuppositions of such thinking and the traditional
conception of *Lichtmetaphysik*, however, we can acknowledge
this mystery of concealment as manifest, *as* concealment,
in all disclosure, and can think it as such. "Mysticism"
then loses all meaning and becomes both unnecessary and
impossible. It should also not be forgotten that,
according to Heidegger, pointing to and intimating something are gestures of thinking, not of the resignation of
thought. As he says,

> What makes itself known only in such a way that
> it becomes apparent in its self-concealment, to
> that we can respond also only by alluding to it,

> indicating it....This simple pointing is one of
> the distinctive marks of thinking.

Such pointing in words is not a relegation of the *Sache*
(the matter) to the realm of the ineffable and the unknown
but a way of being related to it in thought, the seeing of
what is pointed out. Thinking is a seeing of what comes
into view and so a form of experiencing, the profoundest
modality of experience in fact. The traditional,
metaphysical contrast between entities known by reason
(thought conceived as *ratio*) and what is experienceable
breaks down.

Thus, Heidegger speaks of the *experience* of thinking,
of thinking as itself an experience, appropriating within
thinking the precious element of immediacy in all mysticism. Little attention has been paid to this extraordinary role of "experience" in Heidegger's writings. He
speaks of the experiencing of Being, of the hiddenmost
history of Being, of the basic experience of nothingness,
of "undergoing an experience with language."[46] According
to Heidegger, thinking is thus in a profound sense
experiencing. "To experience," Heidegger says, "means
eundo assequi to obtain something along the way, to attain
something by going on a way....To experience is to go
along a way."[47] And thinking is the pre-eminent mode of
going along a way for man. Further, what one undergoes on
the path of thinking is not just "intellectual insight"
but experience in the most transforming sense. As
Heidegger describes it,

> To undergo an experience with something--be it a
> thing, a person, or a god--means that this
> something befalls us, strikes us, comes over us,
> overwhelms and transforms us. When we talk of
> "undergoing" an experience, we mean specifically
> that the experience is not of our own making; to
> undergo here means that we endure it, suffer it,
> receive it as it strikes us and submit to it. It
> is this something itself that comes about, comes
> to pass, happens.[48]

> To experience something means to attain it
> alongthe way, by going on a way. To undergo an
> experience with something means that this
> something, which we reach along the way in order
> to attain it, itself pertains to us, meets and
> makes its appeal to us, in that it transforms us
> into itself.[49]

If we ponder these remarks and undergo, with
Heidegger, an experience with thinking, we may come to see
that there is something wrong with the current and
unquestioning characterization of Eastern thought as
"mystical," especially by scholars of religion, and thus
with the perpetuation of *Erleben* as the alternative to
"mere" thought. Such an attempted perpetuation may be
understandable in theologians like Rudolf Otto, with their
quest for the "inner relationship of types of human
experience and spiritual life,"[50] carried on in unexamined
acceptance of "metaphysics" as the normative mode of
thought. We can see what is wrong here if we understand
why Heidegger, "having experienced theology in its own
roots, both the theology of the Christian faith and that
of philosophy, prefers to remain silent about God in the
realm of thinking,"[51] and if we recall his remark in *Being
and Time* about "those residues of Christian theology
within the problematics of philosophy which have not as
yet been radically extruded."[52] It is this extrusion
which has enabled Heidegger to reclaim for thinking its
proper plenitude, to set it free to reach out limitlessly
to its *Sache*, and widen its sphere to an unbounded
horizon. Such liberation of thinking can enable us to
look out for the thinking going on in other religious and
philosophical traditions. "Mysticism," too, is one such
residue that has fused in recent religious thought with
subjectivism, the form which metaphysics has assumed since
Descartes, according to Heidegger, resulting in the
present day pursuit of *Erlebnis* and the quest for types,
patterns, and structures of inner experience or of its
correlate, the world of objectivity as disclosed in such
experience.[53]

VIII

From the perspective opened up by Heidegger's thinking
we may seek in the Upanisads and in the tradition of
Vedanta thought for "the thinking experience" of Uddalaka
and Yajnavalkya, of Samkara and his successors. For what
is central, at least in the Advaita tradition of Vedanta
philosophy, is the "way of knowledge," the way of insight
through meditative thought, the way of "the experience of
thought." Here, as in Heidegger, such realization of
truth in and through thinking comprises a two-fold
movement, the movement of "hearing" and the movement of
questioning, with the former as basic and first, as in
Heidegger. It culminates in a "seeing," which is not the
act of a subject directed toward objective being, either
in the Greek sense of *theoria* or in the modern subjectivistic sense, but as the shining forth of the *Sache*
itself, in the sense of being appropriated by it and owned
into an identity with it, prior and primordial, as in
Heidegger. Finally, this whole process in which truth is
realized in thinking experience occurs within the dimension of the holy, as Heidegger thinks it, as a sacred
happening, within an experience of Being "which is still
capable of a god," which is not yet "too late for the gods
and too early for Being."

This comparison is not intended to establish any
thesis about the similarity of two entities, the structure
of Heidegger's thought (thus transforming it into a
"philosophy") and Advaita Vedanta as a thought-form (thus
devaluing its essentially religious character), but to
imply that it is thinking that is happening in the latter,
not just the rational justification of a set of assertions
in the *Sruti*, in acknowledgement of it as an "authority,"
nor just the construction of an intellectually satisfying
system of speculative philosophy, but a thinking which is
experienced *as* thinking of ultimate concern. But this

thinking is neither "no-more-metaphysical" nor "not-yet-
metaphysical" (in the sense Heidegger speaks of these in
Heraklit); it has not been mediated by medieval Christianity, nor by the new awareness introduced into modern
Western thought by the rise of historicism. It is not
haunted by the reflective sense of the finitude of
thinking as such, as Heidegger naturally is, in reaction
against Plato and Hegel and the entire metaphysical
tradition. As thinking, it moves straight ahead toward
its *Sache* not thematically mindful of its own character as
a "thrown project," but seeking the impossible, fullness
of light, all light, without shadows and dark corners,
seeking the total elimination of pain and fear, of the
ensnarement by things and all forms of objectivity and
otherness in life, seeking the annulment of mortality.

But this naivety, if it must be called such, is
minimal in the Vedanta tradition. For we have indeed here
a vivid and energetic awareness of the possibility, ever
present for thinking, of grasping, in Hegel's words, only
"clouds of error instead of the Heaven of truth."[54] This
is exhibited in the very extensive treatment of the
problem of knowledge--its nature, sources and criteria of
validity--and the nature of error in Vedanta, as in all
schools of Indian thought. Guarded by the equally primal
awareness of the voice of the Upanisadic word, undis-
tracted from listening to it, Vedanta thinking could move
on, however, without that fear of erring which, in Hegel's
words again, is already the error itself. Is it not
precisely in this straining towards the impossible, the
Absolute, that the very passion, the ecstasy, and the
moving power of all great thinking lie, in this incessant,
relentless pushing beyond its ever incomplete accomplishment, in this unceasing self-transcendence, in this movement of unending self-overcoming which Nietzsche has so
penetratingly seen and described, and which attains a
straining and a stretching to the utmost in the thinking

of Heidegger, just because he is aware as no other thinker
of the West of thought's finitude and in spite of his
disclaimer that his thinking has no wisdom to deliver and
is not put forward as a *Heilsweg*, a promise of salvation?
What greater healing can there be than the thinking
experience by man of being at one with that from which, in
his all too human state, he experiences division and of
being freed from the tyranny of that thing out there, and
this, here inside his mind, confronting him as an other
to himself?

It is true that we find in the founders of systematic
Advaita thought, Gaudapada and Samkara, a great deal of
insistence on setting aside, suspending and even nihilating the activity of the mind, so that we may have a
vision of the true self and of what truly is, without
being obstructed and tricked by this seed-bed of all
seeming. A number of considerations, impossible to enter
into here, account for this: the starting point with the
self (rather than with the Being of beings, in the Greek
sense), the prevailing conceptions about the mental
faculty and the concern for distinguishing it from the
self (which is the self or "being" of the mind itself),
the discovery of the constructive, projective and representational functions of the mind as sources of error in
our understanding of the world and ourselves by the Buddhist thinkers, and, above all the uncompromising resistance to the two "nihilistic" and "semi-nihilistic" ways
of thinking dominant at the time (though as possibilities
ever present threats to the Advaita mode of thinking),
namely, the Madhyamika and the Vaisesika philosophies.

According to the first, thinking is the positing of an
"it is" where there is in reality no entitative Being;
according to the latter, thinking moves within and knows
only the realm of entities and is intrinsically categorial
in its procedure. In its concern to preserve the primal
reality undiminished by the least vestige of opacity

(somewhat in the Sartrian sense), the former replaces
Being by Nothingness, giving to thinking the preliminary
and solely negative role of a dialectical cancellation of
its own thetic, positing activity. The latter takes
cognizance only of beings, of Being only as a class
concept and of Non-being as the absence of a being. Each
denies Being as the ultimate "that from which"; each
conceives thinking in accordance with its view of the
Sache of thinking.

Advaita thinking lives in the tension between these
two stances, refusing to go the way of systematic denial
but acknowledging the illusions to which thought is ever
exposed, and refusing also to accept the position that
there is nothing for thinking to be addressed by except
entities and that there is no other mode of thinking than
the ontic-categorial. This is the Upanisadic way of "yea-
saying," of saying yes to the realm of entities (for they
are "beings in Being," upheld in and by Being, are
grounded in a self; the "is" in any entity cannot be
denied, for it is none other than the "is" that I myself
am); of saying yes to the negativity infecting all mortal
experience (for I, ever in the midst of entities, am
"always already forfeited to them," am duped by them—
"*genarrt durch das Seiende, dem Sein so entfremdet,*" as
Heidegger puts it—am caught in the play of seeming, in
this mirror-game of reflecting and being reflected in
beings, confused between the realm of beings and the self
of which and for which they are beings); of saying yes to
that other dimension, beyond beings and yet in them, the
dimension from which all is-ness derives, which is the
primordial openness and truth and which is also the
dimension of the holy, that "*Wesensraum*" of Divinity from
which the real shines forth as the god, as God; of
affirming that gesture of thinking which lies in saying,
"It is." Does not the *Katha Upanisad* (VI, 12 and 13) say,
"Not by speech, not by mind, not by sight can he be

apprehended. How can he be apprehended except by him who
says, 'He is'?" Intellection "dissolves" in such thinking
of the self, Samkara points out in his comment on this
verse, but only as pregnant with a notion of existence
(satpratyayagarbhaiva viliyate).

The thinkers of the Upanisadic-Buddhist-Advaita
tradition were acutely, intensely, and vividly alive to
the havoc wrought by representational thinking because
they lived in awareness of a dimension other than the
workaday world in which such thinking is valid, perhaps
inevitable as well as necessary. This sensitivity was all
the more heightened by the fact that this "other" dimension was not thought of as wholly transcendent but as the
truth of this workaday existence itself. However, the
doctrine of two truths, or two levels of reality, as
developed by Nagarjuna and Samkara in different ways and
to different ends, is not quite the same as the distinction between the grasping, conceptual, and representational thinking generated in the metaphysical-
philosophical tradition of the West and the notion of non-
representational, meditative, reminiscent, topological,
and preparatory thinking as we have it in Heidegger.
Also, Heidegger's distinction should not itself be understood in a "metphysical" sense, or as a philosophical
thesis about the nature of thinking, for it is itself part
of a movement of thought that seeks to overcome and get
behind, so to speak, the Greek metaphysical thought of
Being, so that someday "the farewell from all 'It is'" may
come to pass,[55] so that there may be a turn in the world
destiny of homelessness.

The Brahman-Atman of the Upanisads is not the same as
the Being of Western thought; they are different starting
points, each uniquely itself, for thinking in the two
traditions, and they are untranslatable one by the other,
for we do not yet have a name for what may be identical in
them (though perhaps "Brahman" has the advantage of

including in itself, but not being exhausted by, the
notion of Being!). The history of Being, its mittence
(*Geschick*) is the hidden history of the West, now over-
spreading the world and culminating in the all-consuming
"Europeanization of the earth," in world-civilization and
the loss of world as home for man. Brahman-Atman, too is
Geschick and yet, not in the sense of historical destiny;
perhaps a *Geschick* still, indeed in a more real sense so,
when we have once achieved the "releasement toward things
and openness to the mystery" of which Heidegger speaks in
his address on *Gelassenheit*?[56]

Vedantic thought or Vedantism, in so far as it is a
way of thinking and is not simply a name for what has at
any time been actually thought in it (in respect of content, structure, and style), has been and will remain,
like all genuine, original thinking, a thinking of the
unthought in what has been thought, to speak in
Heidegger's language, and a perpetually novel start.
Historically, the challenge to this thinking has come from
the existence of opposing systems and paths of thought and
spirituality. It has therefore itself a history. The
Upanisads do not say, could not have said, what Gaudapada
found it possible and necessary in his time to say. Did
he falsify the intent of the Vedic utterance, importing
into its thought elements borrowed from alien sources, or
was he able in some measure to set free the unsaid,
implicit truth of those ancient thinkers, while appropriating a new language and speaking in a new age? Did
Samkara do this in respect of his predecessors, and in
which regard and with what success? And so with his
followers and with the other schools of Vedanta.

Much of Heidegger's work has been devoted to attempts
at saying, by means of a series of "phenomenological
interpretations" (as he described many of his early
seminars on the great Western philosophers), what remains
unsaid and unthought in their works. Should it not be

possible to attempt the same with these Indian thinkers,
"looking beyond the language which these philosophers
employ to what they intended to say," in the words of
Kant, or "wresting from the actual words that which these
words 'intended to say,'" as Heidegger puts it?[57] To be
able to do so, however, requires, as he goes on to point
out, that

> ...the interpretation must be animated and guided
> by an illuminative idea. Only through the power
> of this idea can an interpretation risk that
> which is always audacious, namely, entrusting
> itself to the secret elan of a work, in order by
> this elan to get through to the unsaid and to
> attempt to find an expression for it.

With which "illuminative idea" have subsequent thinkers in
the Vedanta tradition approached the earlier thinkers? Is
there such a directive idea, capable of confirming itself
by its own power of illumination, available to us today
for the task of interpreting the thinkers of this tradition?

These thinkers themselves did not conceive their task
in these terms but thought of themselves as continuators
and defenders of a tradition--ahistorically, reaching the
limits of impersonality and anonymity in their creative
work. How could they ever come upon the idea that
Samkara's thinking, for example, drew its sustenance from
its own unthought depths, that there was something he
himself could not think, but which Suresvara or Padmapada,
his immediate disciples, could bring out into the open,
but without their own thinking being totally transparent
to themselves? Every great thinker has his own explicitly
seen task, which he seeks to accomplish with the tools,
the energy and the gifts at his command. But in the midst
of what he actually manages to accomplish and sees himself
as achieving, something else also goes on within his work,
all unbeknownst to himself, to his contemporaries and
immediate successors almost always, often to the entire
tradition that springs out of his work. The continuity of
the mostly hidden operation of this unknown and unsaid is

the mittence (*Geschick*) which carries all history, giving it an inexhaustible potentiality of meaningfulness in the oncoming, endless future. Thus Vedantic thinking has a history, that continuity of hidden unrest that pushes it forward. Can we say about it, as Heidegger does about the "end" of the Western tradition of metaphysical thinking with Hegel and Nietzsche, that it reached its completion with Madhusudan Saraswati, or even with K.C. Bhatta-charyya? Perhaps not, perhaps the beginning (in the Upanisads) still hides a secret for future thinking and saying; perhaps Samkara's thinking still contains a meaning, still awaiting the work of thought to be clearly seen, from which his school itself was side-tracked, even while bringing it to *one* consummation, carrying it to dizzy heights of intellectual effort in a white heat of luminous creativity rarely paralleled anywhere. If so, Vedanta thinking, far from being a closed and completed whole, remains a task for the open future.

CONCLUSION

In the world of today, in this one world of "world-civilization," our relationship to tradition is an irreparably broken one and our thinking is determined by an unheard-of simultaneity of times and places, all equally remote, all equally close. If the bringing together of "Heidegger" and "Vedanta" is to have any sense it can only lie in enabling us to see that there is more to Vedanta—something that is its very own and yet unfulfilled—than providing those who are in revolt against the establishment (the religious, the Western metaphysical), and in flight from thinking, with a "mystical" alternative; that as a way or path of thinking, not so much as a doctrine, Vedanta may also have some relevance to that other task to which Heidegger points,

the task of planetary thinking, in an age of homelessness
and of the coming together of East and West in the
extremity of fate, in the task of overcoming this
universal misery of lost home by "staying on the path,
in genuine need, and learning, without straying from the
path, even though faltering, the craft (*Handwerk*)
of thinking."[58]

NOTES

1. *Vedanta und Platonismus im Lichte der Kantischen
Philosophie* (Berlin, 1922), 40-41. The penultimate
paragraph of this interesting study may be quoted here in
full since it states most concisely and lucidly the
approach to comparative philosophy most widely favoured
and which appears so questionable when we look at it from
the perspective of Heidegger's thinking. Deussen says,

> In allen Landern und zu allen Zeiten, in all
> Nähen und Fernen ist es eine und dieselbe Natur
> der Dinge, welcher einer und derselbe Geist
> betrachtend gegenubersteht. Wie sollte es da
> anders sein konnen, als dass der denkende Geist,
> sofern ihn nicht Traditionen und Vorurteile
> blenden, sofern er der Natur rein und unbefangen
> gegenubersteht, in seiner Erforschung derselben
> überall, in Indien wie in Griechenland, in alter
> wie in neuer Zeit zu den gleichen Ergebnissen
> gelangen musste! Wir haben die drei glänzendsten
> Erscheinungen der Philosophie, den Vedanta,
> Platon und Kant miteinander verglichen. Wir
> haben nicht an ihnen gedreht und gedeutet,
> gebogen und gerenkt, sondern wir haben jede
> Erscheinung in ihrer vollen individuellen Eigen-
> tumlichkeit bestehen lassen. Aber indem wir bei
> jeder von ihnen in die letzte Tiefe drangen, ge-
> langten wir zu dem inneren Einheitspunkte, aus
> dem die Anschauungen der indischen, griechischen
> und deutschen Denker entsprungen sind, und diese
> ihre innere übereinstimmung bei aller Verschie-
> denheit der Aussenseite ist eine nicht geringe
> Gewähr dafur, dass wir in allen dreien die Stimme
> der einen und mit sich einstimmigen Natur, dass
> in ihnen die Stimme der ewigen Wahrheit vernehmen.

2. Paul Deussen, *The System of the Vedanta* (Delhi: Motilal Banarsidass, 1972), 38-39.

3. *The Vedanta Sutras of Badarayana with the Commentary by Sankara*, translated by George Thibaut (New York: Dover, 1962), Part 1, 223.

4. Keeping in mind Heidegger's conception of world as the "Fourfold (*Geviert*)" of earth and sky, divinities and mortals, a systematic examination of the meaning of *devata* (divinity), of God and the gods, in the Upanisads (particularly in the *Brhadaranyaka*) and Samkara's interpretation of it may prove rewarding. The comparative task here would be to differentiate this Vedic and post-Vedic conception from the Greek. In his early work, *Studies in Vedantism*, K.C. Bhattacharyya gave an original interpretation of the notions of *devata* and *loka* (region) as part of his treatment of "Vedantic metaphysics," but these suggestions have never since been examined or followed up. See Krishnachandra Bhattacharyya, *Studies in Philosophy* (Calcutta: Progressive Publishers, 1956), 1:31-68.

5. A major exception is Paul Hacker. See his remarks on Suresvara's style as compared with Samkara's in *Untersuchungen uber Texte des fruhen Advaitavada, I. Die Schüler Sankaras* (Wiesbaden, 1951), 16-21, and on verses of praise in Samkara and the early Advaita writers in "Relations of Early Advaitins to Vaisnavism", *Wiener Zeitschrift fur die Kunde Sud- und Ostasiens*, 9 (1965), and "Sankara der Yogin und Sankara der Advaitin," ibid. 12-13 (1968-1969) (Frauwallner *Festschrift*).

6. For references to these quotations from Plato and Aristotle, see Heidegger, *What is Philosophy?* (New Haven: Yale University Press, n.d.).

7. See *The Birth of Tragedy*, Section 15 (*Basic Writings of Nietzsche*, edited by Walter Kaufmann, New York: Random House, 1968, 93-95). These quotations by no means represent adequately Nietzsche's complex attitude to Socrates.

8. *Christianity in World History* (New York: Scribners, 1964), 18.

9. "*Die zeit des Weltbildes*" in *Holzwege* (Frankfurt: Klostermann, 1950), 70.

10. *An Introduction to Metaphysics* (New York: Doubleday, 1961), 31.

11. *Poetry, Language, Thought* (New York: Harper and Row, 1971), 91-92.

12. Samkara's Commentary on the *Brhadaranyaka Upanisad*, I, iv. 7, beginning.

13. "*Dankansprache von Professor Martin Heidegger*" in *Ansprache zum 80. Geburtstage* (Messkirch: Stadt Messkirch, 1969), 35. This is a recurrent motif in Heidegger's post-*Being and Time* writings, in which he keeps coming back to the ideas of "home," "world destiny," and "world-civilization" from the perspective of the question of Being.

14. *An Introduction to Metaphysics*, 30.

15. *Nietzsche* (Pfullingen: Neske, 1961), 2:278.

16. On the notion of "planetary" thinking, see *The Question of Being* (New Haven: Yale Univ. Press, n.d.), 107 and Kostas Axelos, *Einfuhrung in ein kunftiges Denken--uber Marx und Heidegger* (Tubingen: Niemeyer, 1966), passim. See also this author's *The Philosophy of Martin Heidegger* (New York: Harper and Row, 1971), 244-254, for this as well as the whole general topic of this paper.

17. "*Holderlins Erde und Himmel*" in *Erlauterungen zu Holderlins Dichtung* (Frankfurt: Klostermann, vierte, erweiterte Auflage, 1971), 177.

18. "Der Spruch des Anaximander," in *Holzwege* (Frankfurt: Klostermann, 1950), 300.

19. Martin Heidegger--Eugen Fink, *Heraklit* (Frankfurt: Klostermann, 1970), 212.

20. *Allgemeine Geschichte der Philosophie* (Leipzig, 1894-1917), 1:36.

21. *Identity and Difference* (New York: Harper and Row, 1969), 37.

22. Ibid., 38.

23. *What is Philosophy?* 45.

24. Granting the metaphysical component in Sanskrit, however, it may be instructuve to investigate the correctives it has developed against this representational or objectifying element, thus exhibiting its own unique genius: a mode of utterance in which representation and the cancellation of the representative force are held in tension and balance. Perhaps the uniqueness of Indian philosophy and religion lies in the simultaneous de-objectification of the objectified, in the iconoclastic moment which is never for long absent from its iconism. If, as Heidegger admits (*Discourse on Thinking*, New York: Harper and Row, 1966, 46), thinking is of two kinds, calculative and meditative or representational and non-representational, it may yet be of significance to his concern to see how Indian thought took notice of the problem which it so explicitly recognized as crucial, the forms in which the problem presented itself as a haunting, ever-present task for thinking, and the solutions offered. Looked at from this point of view, the history of Indian philosophy may prove to be not just an antiquarian, humanistic pursuit but a treasure house of direct promise to the Heideggerian quest.

25. See the preface in Latin to the first issue of *Lexis*, a periodical on comparative linguistics edited by Lohmann; also "*Uber den paradigmatischen Charakter der griechischen Kultur,*" in *Die Gegenwart der Griechen im neueren Denken* (Gadamer Festschrift. Tübingen: Mohr, 1960).

26. See this author's "Heidegger and the Comparison of Indian and Western Philosophy," *Philosophy East and West* 20 (1970), for a methodologically oriented consideration of the problem of comparative philosophy, as well as Eliot Deutsch's "Commentary" on the article in the same number. The entire issue is devoted to the subject of "Heidegger and Eastern Thought."

27. *On Time and Being* (New York: Harper and Row, 1972), 57.

28. Ibid., 59.

29. Another, if possible even more basic and ultimate
problem, concerns the meaning and nature of truth. The
crucial, and culminating, point in Heidegger's thinking is
how truth (*Wahrheit*) itself can be understood in terms of
the profounder notion of *aletheia* or unhiddennness. In
the Upanisadic tradition truth (*satya*) and Being (*sat*) are
even more intimately connected than in the Greek. But,
beyond this, we have also the conception of the truth of
what is commonly called true. See *Brhadaranyaka Upanisad*
II.i.20 for "the truth of truth (*satyasya satyam*)" as the
secret name of the Self and Samkara's commentary on this.
How far the Advaita conception of *avidya-maya* (nescience-
illusion) as the "seed" of all presentedness of entities
is comparable to Heidegger's conception of *aletheia* as
necessarily involving the element of hiddenness is also a
question worth pursuing in this connection.

For a systematic and lucid exposition of Hedegger's
life-long concern with truth as *aletheia*, see Walter
Biemel, *Heidegger* (Hamburg: Rowohlt, 1973).
30. *Vortrage und Aufsatze* (Pfullingen: Neske, 1954), 227.
31. *Schellings Abhandlung über das Wesen der Menschlichen
Freiheit (1809)* (Tübingen: Niemeyer, 1971), 175.
32. See the entire quotation from Hamann in Martin
Heidegger, *Poetry, Language, Thought* (New York: Harper and
Row, 1971), 191.
33. *An Introduction to Metaphysics*, 99.
34. Hacker has pointed this out repeatedly in a number of
articles. See "Notes on the *Mandukyopanisad* and Sankara's
Agamasastravivarana" (in *India Maior*, edited by J. Ensink
and P. Gaeffke, Leiden: Brill, 1972), 125, 129-30, though
he seems to be arguing from a position extraneous to the
Vedanta (from the point of view of what we have called
"the Greek thought of Being," as mediated in Hacker's
interpretation through the Christian Thomist tradition)
when he finds that "the inadequacy of his argumentation
landed Sankara in that very nihilism which he made such

valiant efforts to combat," and when he concludes that
"Sankara never succeeded in facing the overwhelming fact
of existence." A statement like this, coming from the
most competent scholar of Advaita Vedanta in the West
since Deussen, brings to a focus the basic issues in the
comparative enterprise, whether in religion or in
philosophy. See also Hacker's ("*Sankara der Yogin und
Sankara der Advaitin*" in *Beitrage zur Geistesgeschichte
Indiens--Festschrift für Erich Frauwallner* (Wien: Gerold,
1968), 131 and "*Essere e Spirito nel Vedanta,*" in
Filosofia e Vita, 4 (1969), passim, where the problem of
Being in Samkara is dealt with extensively in the context
of a comparison of Samkara and Advaita generally with
Thomas Aquinas.

35. Commentary on *Katha Upanisad* II.iii.13.

36. Commentary on *Taittiriva Upanisad* II.vi.

37. Commentary on the *Bhagavadgita* XIII.12.

38. Commentary on *Chandogya Upanisad* VI.ii.1.

39. Commentary on *Brahma Sutra* III.ii.21.

40. Commentary on *Brahma Sutra* I.i.4.

41. Heidegger says this about the hidden relationship
between the thinker and the poet, quoting from Holderlin's
Patmos. See "What is Metaphysics?" in Werner Brock,
Existence and Being (London: Vision Press, 1949), 392.

42. See his articles "Phenomenology, Mysticism and the
'*Grammatica Speculativa*': A Study of Heidegger's
'*Habilitationsschrift,*'" *Journal of the British Society
for Phenomenology,* 5 (1974), and "Meister Eckhart and the
Later Heidegger: The Mystical Element in Heidegger's
Thought," forthcoming in *The Journal of the History
of Philosophy.*

43. See *Fruhe Schriften* (Frankfurt: Klostermann, 1972), 352.

44. *Nietzsche,* 2:28.

45. *Vortrage und Aufsatze,* 134.

46. *On the Way to Language* (New York: Harper and Row,
1971), 57.

47. Ibid., 66-67.

48. Ibid., 57.

49. Ibid., 73-74.

50. Rudolph Otto, *Mysticism East and West* (New York: Meridian, 1959), xvi.

51. *Identity and Difference*, 54-55.

52. *Being and Time* (New York: Harper and Row, 1962), 272.

53. Recognizing "*das Kreisen der Gedanken*" in Suresvara and in Advaita thinkers generally and also the fact that they are all concerned with what is "*ein einziger Gedanke*" (both features so readily intelligible from a Heideggerian perspective), Paul Hacker does not find any special virtue here but, operating with the category of "mysticism" judges Suresvara's *Naiskarmyasiddhi* in the following words, "*Die Naisk., is für uns eine geistesgeschichtlich hochbedeutsame Mischung von Logik und Mystik, wobei die Mystik der Logik, auf die das Zeitalter doch nicht verzichten kann, immer wieder Gewalt antut.*" (*Untersuchungen über Texte des frühen Advaitavada, I. Die Schüler Sankaras*, Wiesbaden, 1951). Would it not enable a reader of Suresvara's work to come closer to the thinking in it if he were to set aside, following Heidegger's critique, the concepts of "Logic" (which is not quite the same as the Indian *tarka*) and "Mysticism" as both suspect "in the realm of thinking?"

54. *Phänomenologie des Geistes* (Hamburg: Meiner, 1952), 65; 2nd paragraph of the "Introduction," *Phenomology of Mind*.

55. *On the Way to Language*, 54.

56. *Discourse on Thinking* (New York: Harper and Row, 1966), 55.

57. *Kant and the Problem of Metaphysics* (Bloomington: Indiana University Press, 1968), 207.

58. *Vortrage und Aufsatze*, 185.